ETHICS AND The Family

Revised First Edition

Edited by Czeslaw Karkowski
Mercy College

Bassim Hamadeh, CEO and Publisher
Kassie Graves, Director of Acquisitions
Jamie Giganti, Senior Managing Editor
Miguel Macias, Senior Graphic Designer
John Remington, Senior Field Acquisitions Editor
Monika Dziamka, Project Editor
Brian Fahey, Licensing Specialist
Rachel Singer, Associate Editor

Copyright © 2017 by Cognella, Inc. All rights reserved. No part of this publication may be reprinted, reproduced, transmitted, or utilized in any form or by any electronic, mechanical, or other means, now known or hereafter invented, including photocopying, microfilming, and recording, or in any information retrieval system without the written permission of Cognella, Inc.

Trademark Notice: Product or corporate names may be trademarks or registered trademarks, and are used only for identification and explanation without intent to infringe.

Cover image copyright © 2012 by Depositphotos / andresr.
         copyright © 2012 by Depositphotos / Wavebreakmedia.

Printed in the United States of America

ISBN: 978-1-5165-0943-0 (pbk) / 978-1-5165-0944-7 (br)

Contents

Preface   vii

UNIT I. TRADITIONAL AND MODERN FAMILY

1. Family Values in a Historical Perspective   3
   By Lawrence Stone

   Further Readings   19

UNIT II. TRANSFORMATION OF THE AMERICAN FAMILY

2. American Family   23
   By Daphne Lofquist, Terry Lugaila, Martin O'Connell, and Sarah Feliz

3. The Changing American Family   35
   By Cris Beam

4. Feminism and the Evolving Role of Men   41
   By Joseph Palermo

   Further Readings   45

UNIT III. FAMILY IN DECLINE

5. American Family Decline, 1960–1990: A Review and Appraisal   49
   By David Popenoe

6.	Good Riddance to "The Family": A Response to David Popenoe By Judith Stacey	65
7.	The Top Ten Myths of Marriage By David Popenoe	69
	Further Readings	72

UNIT IV. ETHICAL ISSUES

8.	Duties Towards the Body in Respect of Sexual Impulse By Immanuel Kant, translated by Louis Infield	75
9.	Plato About Love By Plato, translated by B. Jowett	79
10.	Ethics of Virtue and Abolition of Marriage By Plato, translated by B. Jowett	81
11.	Marriage as a Kind of Friendship By Aristotle, translated by W. D. Ross	85
	Further Readings	89

UNIT V. MODERN TRENDS IN FAMILY: DIVORCE

12.	Number, Timing, and Duration of Marriages and Divorces: 2009 By Rose M. Kreider and Renee Ellis	93
13.	The American Myth of Divorce By William C. Spohn	111
14.	Adultery or Divorce—Is There a Right Answer? By Mark D. White	113
	Further Readings	116

UNIT VI. MODERN TRENDS IN FAMILY: THE FUTURE OF MARRIAGE

15. Marriage as a Public Issue — 119
    By Steven L. Nock

    Further Readings — 129

UNIT VII. MODERN TRENDS IN FAMILY: FAMILY PLANNING

16. Abortion — 133
    By Jeffrey Balancio

17. Advocating Equal Protection for Men in Reproductive Rights and Responsibilities — 139
    By Illya D. Lichtenberg and Jack Baldwin Leclair

    Further Readings — 143

UNIT VIII. MODERN TRENDS IN FAMILY: PARENTHOOD

18. Rights of Children, Rights of Parents, and the Moral Basis of the Family — 147
    By Ferdinand Schoeman

19. Mothers but Not Wives: The Increasing Lag — 159
    By Christina Gibson-Davis

20. Balancing Work and Family Life, Outcomes — 167
    By Kim Parker and Wendy Wang

21. Balance of Work and Family Needs — 177
    By Carol Bennett-Speight

    Further Readings — 180

| 22. | Utilitarianism and Drugs: The Problem and the Solution | 181 |

By wetpig.com

Further Readings — 185

UNIT IX. MODERN TRENDS IN FAMILY: VIOLENCE

| 23. | Intimate Partner Violence: Causes and Prevention | 189 |

By Rachel Jewkes

| 24. | The Basics of Domestic Violence | 201 |

By H. Lien Bragg

| 25. | Domestic Violence: Facts Sheet | 215 |

By National Coalition Against Domestic Violence

Further Readings — 219

UNIT X. MODERN TRENDS IN FAMILY: AGING

| 26. | Family Relationships in an Aging Society | 223 |

By Martie Gillen, Terry Mills, and Jenny Jump

Further Readings — 228

Preface:
Ethics and Family

The family is man's most basic, most vital, and most influential institution. Humans have a need to belong. As far back as our knowledge takes us, humans have belonged to families. Anthropologists tell us that we know of no period when this was not so. They also tell us that we know of no people who have succeeded for long in dissolving the family and displacing it. It is the foundation of society, the molder of character and personality, and the mentor of cultural values. Although the family may be found in many forms throughout the world and although it may perform many functions, its basic responsibilities are much the same. For example, in all societies there seems to have been a recognition that a certain number of relatives make up a social group generally called family. Although there are different styles of family living, and different ways of relating the family to the larger community, the family is the unit where one finds companionship and assumes the responsibility of production and protection of offspring. It is family where we first learn to walk, talk and function as acceptable members of our cultural community. It is where we first learn the values and goals that will influence the direction of our life. It is where our social self is developed and where we acquire our self-image in order to navigate the greater society. It is the group where people care and support one another in good times and in hard times. To put it simply, family is what makes a difference between a 'house' and a 'home.'

The following pages contain a collection of philosophical, theological, sociological and social psychological writings focusing on topics relating to ethics and the family. In Greek the word _philosophy_ means 'love of wisdom.' It could be argued that wisdom is self-knowledge, which may be why Plato said that philosophers should rule the world. If science reveals the workings of the physical world then perhaps similar laws could be discovered in the social and cultural world. Thus, philosophers investigated all aspects of social life; they studied and analyzed political, religious, social, and moral institutions and subjected each to criticism.

Modern sociology arose as a consequence of a series of critical encounters beginning with the Enlightenment of the late 17th and 18th centuries which emphasized reason and individualism rather than tradition. It was also a reaction to the social, political and economic theories of Marxism and the Romantic-Conservative Reaction to the French Revolution and its intellectual antecedents. It was in this milieu of events and thinking that the theories of sociology crystalized. We believe these encounters helped to shape the sociological theory, especially relating to morality, i.e. good vs bad.

When we speak about moral philosophy and sociology we are discussing the field of ethics. Ethics involves fundamental principles of right and wrong behavior including: issues of universal truths, the will of God, the role of reason in forming judgments, defining morals and establishing standards that regulate conduct. They are not presented as stand-alone concepts but rather behaviors that involve duties and obligations to be followed along with their consequences. In short, ethics can be defined as a guiding philosophy.

The contributors to this volume span the centuries and all have demonstrated an ability to focus in on core concepts relating to ethics and the family from many different perspectives. This text is aimed at the beginning ethics student. One objective of the book is to communicate clearly, directly and interestingly through a selection of material designed to provide the undergraduate student with an overview of the ethical and social elements important in analyzing family. The importance of the thinkers considered for inclusion in this book is not whether their specific ideas were right or wrong but rather in the questions they addressed and in the penetrating concepts they devised in order to grapple with them. We respect their work and regard it because they offer ways of framing our view of family. We do not judge the correctness or inaccuracy of any of their ideas. Our purpose is to contribute to social reflection and inquiry. The ideas of many of the 'classical' thinkers presented have stood the test of time and we employ them in thinking about the family in the social world today.

In covering several divisions of philosophy and social theory this book can be used in conjunction with other texts or as a supplement to a comprehensive series of classroom lectures and discussions. This work may be viewed as a geological investigation of the shifting ground upon which we now stand every day in our contemporary families.

—*Dorothy Balancio, Ph.D., CFLE, IMCR Mediator*
Sociology Professor

Traditional and Modern Family

Chapter 1

Family Values in a Historical Perspective

By Lawrence Stone

LECTURE 1. FAMILY VALUES IN THE PAST

I. Introduction

A year ago, the newspapers, TV programs, and airwaves of America were filled with gabble about traditional "family values." Just what these values were was never clearly explained, but the argument evidently depended upon a theory of a Golden Age. According to this theory, somewhere in the American past, certain values had been held in high esteem, as a result of which the society as a whole had been peaceful, cooperative, hardworking, and virtuous, thus making America the greatest, the most prosperous, the freest, and politically the most stable republic on earth. The purpose of these two lectures is first to identify the history of these values and second to chart their rapid collapse over the last thirty years. In doing so, I want to put the American experience in its Western European context. (…)

A spokesman for the Family Values Research Institute recently observed that "our family values are a mom and dad rearing the child." The trouble is that this category comprises only a fifth of all households in America today. Nor were the figures much different centuries before, when high adult mortality created almost as many single-parent households as there are today, when a high adult mortality society has been replaced by a low adult mortality one. All that had happened to the family unit before 1950 was that divorce came to serve as the functional equivalent of death, just a different way of ending a marriage. Nor is it true that families are havens of security in a heartless world. Except in America, whose inhabitants are so busy killing each other randomly that the normal rules do not apply, more homicides take place within the family than without, while battered wives and sexually molested children have always been numerous, if ignored. Families

Lawrence Stone, "Family Values in a Historical Perspective," *The Tanner Lectures On Human Values*, vol. 15, pp. 67, 69–98, 108–110. Copyright © 1994 by University of Utah Press. Reprinted with permission.

have always been centers of conflict over property, power, and effect, but not in the simplistic way of gender solidarity of men against women, as some feminists are anxious to persuade us. Nor is it true that the family is the sole medium for the transmission of "family values." In all societies and especially America, which is and has always been the most religiously oriented society in the West, the role of the churches has been of major importance, as have been the schools, which until recently were so central to creating the great American melting pot.

If we try to define family values, they seem to fall into five major groups affecting behavior in five different areas. First come attitudes toward the relative roles of the society and the individual and the socialization of the child to fit into the group; second, attitudes toward work and the accumulation of worldly goods; third, the rules and regulations governing all aspects of sexual behavior; fourth, attitudes toward religion. And finally, attitudes to race, a subject I shall largely omit because of ignorance and lack of time.

Taken instrumentally, these family values can be seen as the values needed for members of the lower middle class to obtain self-respect and to get on in the world: namely hard work, thrift, sobriety, self-discipline, delayed gratification, reliability, a sense of responsibility to the self, the family, and the society, and a competitive desire for one's children to obtain an education and to succeed. (…)

There is no doubt that in America, ever since Watergate, the Wall Street scandals, and the disintegration of the inner city family, ethics have now suddenly become fashionable again, at any rate as a subject of conversation and speculation among intellectuals and on campuses. Centers for Ethical Studies are springing up all over. Hospitals are hiring ethical advisers on triage. Medical schools law schools are hurriedly introducing courses on ethics, if only to damp down malpractice suits. Harvard's new core curriculum includes, I am told, a category listed as "moral analysis." If the next generation is not more morally aware than the last, it will not be for lack of trying.

As a participant in this debate, I do have one thing going for me. I am among the few present-day historians always to have believed that history has a moral component to it. I have never agreed with the wholly relativist position taken by many of my colleagues. They have followed the anthropologists who have argued that any cultural practice, religious ritual, or political organization, however obscene, cruel, or murderous, whether it be the burning of wives in India, head-hunting in New Guinea, or clitoridectomy in East Africa, is as entitled to respect as any other, because it is part of native culture.

Nor am I one of those historians—all too common and influential these days—who carry the self-evident hypothetical and provisional aspects of truth to the point of claiming that there is no objective truth in history, but only a set of linguistic rhetorical constructions. Nor do I believe that any simple model of historical evolution will serve, whether it is based on class, as used to be so fashionable not so long ago, or even upon the now chic trio of race, class, and gender. History is too messy and complicated for such simple explanatory models. And the history of values is messier still.

The concept of family values is not a trivial theme for a historian to investigate. Emile Durkheim once said: "Tell me the code of domestic morality and I will tell you the social organization." Durkheim was here being boastful, but he and former vice-president Daniel Quayle share a point. They both see family values as affecting the social and political system.

II. Family Values in the Past

1. Basic Principles

In order to get a handle on the truth of this connection and put our present situation in its historical perspective, let us now go back 300 years and examine just what family values were and how effective they were in influencing behavior in the past.

The origins of the system of values go back to the Early Reformation Humanists, that is, intellectuals such as Erasmus and Vives, writing in the 1530s. They developed a program of moral control and thus set the stage for the future. They demanded the inculcation in the home, the pulpit, and the school of obedience and deference, in order to modify behavior and prevent any recurrence of destructive peasant revolts or rebellions of the poor against the rich. They demanded that the magistrates take a firm hand in crushing crime, robbery, and prostitution and above all inspire respect for the law; they threw in the need for a sense of community loyalty and cooperative behavior to provide a sense of citizenship. They proposed to help, by state-sponsored welfare, the old, the sick, and the unemployed. But they were prepared to hang criminals and to punish by incarceration at hard labor the idle homeless vagabonds. It was a program for moral control, constructed by both Protestants and Catholics, before Protestantism had taken hold in England or Germany. It was to be the blueprint of family values for the next 450 years.

Three hundred years ago, therefore, the overriding principle governing premodern societies was that of paternalism, shown by the reciprocal bonds of authority and deference. This is a very ancient doctrine, ideally suited to keep rough order in a precapitalist agrarian society. It was assumed as a given that God had created the domestic arrangements of society just as He had created that of the stars in the universe, that is, according to the principle of hierarchy, by which some were more powerful and richer than others, mostly through control of more property. This gave them a claim to unquestioning obedience and deference. Property was the key and personal patronage relations the cement.

The second principle was that all societies are authoritarian by nature, modified at the top in England and New England by the results of the prolonged seventeenth-century battle between king and Parliament for common law protections and ancient liberties.

According to this, it was the right of the rich to live at ease, but in return, it was their duty to govern justly. The poor had a duty to labor and obey, while the rich had a duty to save them from starvation, provided that their plight was not caused by their own laziness.

There was also widespread agreement on the application of moral concepts of justice to economic matters such as the fixing of prices, wages, and rents. Paternalism was thus a value system, based on concepts of justice, perfectly adapted to a precapitalist agrarian society, and yet one that proved to be flexible enough to survive until the early twentieth century. It was not till then that it began to give way in the face of the problems thrown up by rapid demographic growth, urbanization, industrialization, the rise of a new middle class and its ideology of individualism, and the decline of religion in the face of Darwinian science and of skepticism.

In the seventeenth century, everyone, on both sides of the Atlantic, followed Aristotle in believing that the family was a microcosm of society at large. As John Milton put it: "The Constitution and reformation of the commonwealth … is like a building: to begin orderly from the foundation thereof, which is marriage and the family."

Given this situation, what were the family values to which seventeenth-century thinkers were so attached?

2. Piety

Intense piety was a by-product of the breakup of Christianity at the Reformation, the success of the counter-Reformation, and the fissures among the Protestants into rival churches and denominations. In the late seventeenth century, in most family homes, there were "the daily performances of prayers and reading the scripture and repetition of sermons," all buttressed by attendance at church every Sunday and the taking of Holy Communion four times a year. Not until the eighteenth century did these practices start to decline. Raised in a Calvinist family on a Connecticut farm, Lyman Beecher, who was born in 1775, recorded that when he was young "we always had family prayers, and I heard the Bible read every morning."

Because of this stress on piety, before the mid-nineteenth century American universities were merely small colleges, each one dedicated to training clergymen and lawyers in its own particular sectarian branch of Protestantism. Innovation, experiment, and freedom of thought were the last things these institutions wished to encourage. Thus, in about 1870, the president of the Princeton Theological Seminary could remark with satisfaction: "Thank God, for fifty years not a single new idea has come out of Princeton." According to these principles, undergraduates were strongly discouraged from thinking freely for themselves for fear that they would come up with subversive thoughts. The value system was thus the exact opposite of what today we preach—and I hope practice—namely above all to encourage students to think for themselves.

3. Obedience

The second moral value inculcated incessantly in the sixteenth and seventeenth centuries, in church, in schools, and in the family, was obedience to superiors, expressed in overt acts of deference towards the father and husband and also toward all in official positions of authority.

Before insisting on the prime importance of obedience to superiors as the core of family values from the sixteenth to the early twentieth centuries, one caveat has to be made. There were at all times exceptional groups of radical religious sects, most prominent in seventeenth-century New England, England, and Germany. These radicals separated the original extremely egalitarian doctrines, as preached by Jesus Christ Himself, from the doctrine that magistrates and clergy imposed on the early church after the conversion of the Roman emperor to Christianity. This put the full backing of the state behind the imposition of a propertied, persecuting, and authoritarian church. Most of the radical sects were destroyed, but the best known of them, the Quakers, survived, although they still flatly refused to fight. Elements of these radical ideas are prominent in the American Constitution, but these were at the time exceptions to the rule.

The oppressive, prickly, almost paranoid insistence on instant obedience and overt marks of deference makes sense, given the instability and fragility of authority. It has to be remembered that Early Modern Europe was for over a century torn apart by mass peasant risings, aristocratic revolts, religious civil wars, and even a few radical social revolutions. Everyone knew that the state was weak, that society was unstable, and that nothing was more terrible than civil war, which led to horrible atrocities and physical and economic devastation on a large scale. The upper classes saw a Hobbesian world of disorder out there and had good reason to stress the doctrine of unquestioning obedience and respect, enforced by an ideology and by the ruthless use of coercion, as the only glue capable of holding the social and political system together.

The Reformation, by making the Bible freely available, positively reinforced the doctrine of family obedience. Never forget that John Calvin himself decreed the death penalty for children who were disobedient to their parents, and that all were convinced of the urgent need to crush Original Sin at the first sign of trouble. In 1520, William Tyndale, an early translator of the Bible into English, warned children: "If thou wilt not obey, as at His Commandment, then are we charged to arrest thee; yea, and if thou repent not and amend thyself, God shall slay thee by his officers and punish thee everlastingly." Autobiographies from the seventeenth century in America and England prove that in actual practice in most middle- and upper-class households, when the children came down to breakfast, the first thing they did was to kneel down to ask their parents' blessing. A New England book of etiquette published in 1715 told children always to bow as they entered the home and immediately to take off their hats; never to sit in their parents' presence unless invited to do so; and finally "Dispute not nor delay to obey thy parents' commands." Nor was this mere theory. Thus, the grown-up children of Jonathan Edwards of Yale were reported to have displayed exceptionally ostentatious acts of deference before their father. In New England in the seventeenth century it was a crime for a child over the age of sixteen to curse or strike a parent an act for which he or she could be publicly flogged.

These demands for ritual deference and unquestioning obedience did not of course come naturally and were the product of a massive use of both physical and psychological coercion. The beating of children began at an early age and did not end until departure from the university. Even undergraduates were flogged by the faculty. It would be hypocritical of me to pretend that I am sorry to have to tell you that Harvard was more backward than Oxford or Cambridge in abandoning this practice, not giving it up before the early eighteenth century. Psychological pressures were also applied. Parental blessing was withheld from the troublesome, and young children were warned of the prospects of Hell and eternal damnation if they failed in obedience and deference.

If children were brainwashed and beaten into submission, so also were the grown-ups. In Early Modern Europe, men and women were constantly obliged to register their subordination to superiors by overt marks of respect: the women curtseying, the men removing their hats. This is what hats were for. Those in power (fathers, schoolmasters, clergy, university faculty, judges, JPs, noblemen, etc.) insisted at all times on receiving these marks of respect. For example, if in the seventeenth century you saw President Neil Rudenstine advancing toward you in Harvard Yard, and you failed to snatch your hat off when he got within a range of fifty yards, then God help you! You were in trouble.

It must now be clear that the difference between the moral atmosphere of the Early Modern period and that of today could not be greater. We in America above all encourage individualism and self-esteem, whereas the former inculcated "the great principle of subordination" as Daniel Defoe called it. It is interesting to note that the identical methods of brutal upbringing, and the same hostility to any spark of individualism, are still alive and well in present-day China, where the deputy director of child development remarked recently: "Parents like best for their children to be obedient. I think parents are worried that if children are too individualistic they might face trouble later on." The Chinese to this day therefore teach children to "rely not on themselves but on an outside power, whether parents or society."

As for women, deferential patterns between husband and wife were based on the solemn promise by the wife at the marriage ceremony to "obey" her husband. Male commentators all reinforced the message. For example, in 1617, a clerical pamphleteer on ethics urged wives to admit that "mine husband is my superior, my better; he hath authority and rule over me. Nature hath given it to him, God hath given it to him." Indeed antifeminist zealots declared that "subjection and obedience to husbands is required as peremptorily as unto Christ himself." On the other hand, wives also had reciprocal rights, such as to be maintained financially and not to be beaten unmercifully, and it is astonishing how, within the boundaries set by the paternalist model, wives so often managed successfully to maneuver so as to get their own way.

Even in the choice of a spouse, the principle of obedience to parents was still preeminent before the late eighteenth century. One very popular tract, often republished, had this to say about children's need for parental permission in the choice of a spouse: "Children are so much the goods, the possessions of the parents, that they cannot, without a kind of theft, give themselves away without the allowance of those that have a right in them."

As we have seen, in the eyes of contemporaries, all this deference and obedience within the family was for centuries directly related to authoritarian deference and obedience in the state. It is therefore no accident that the American Revolution was accompanied by a collapse of paternalist family values and quickly followed by an explosion of violence on many campuses, including Princeton and Harvard. The students had read too much Tom Paine and had taken the first lines of the Declaration of Independence too seriously.

4. Lack of Ambition

The third family value instilled into all children was passive acquiescence in one's lot in this world. It was obvious that a few were born rich, with golden spoons in their mouths, while many were born penniless beggars. This was regarded as the natural order of things, as designed by God, and every institution in society, including the family, carried the same message: accept your lot in life without attempting to better your condition, or worse still taking up arms to try to seize the power and wealth that has been denied you. If it seems unfair, justice will be done to you in the next world, but not in this. Defoe defined "the general plague of mankind, whence … one half of their miseries flow" as "not being satisfied with the station wherein God and Nature has placed them."

5. The Calling

The way out of the paradox of hard work and diligence without any ambition to rise above one's station in life was solved by the doctrine of "the calling." Hard work was valued, not as a means of advancement in life, but rather as a means to avoid idleness, which was thought—probably rightly—to lead directly to sin.

6. Sexual Repression

The last family value commonly impressed upon all classes, although largely ignored by aristocratic males, concerned concepts of honor and shame as they relate to sexual repression, especially for women. To enforce this indoctrination there was wide use of humiliating punishments for transgressions, such as being forced to stand naked in a white sheet before the whole congregation on a Sunday morning, while confessing to the sin of fornication or adultery. Inhibiting practices of this emotional intensity, backed up by both legal force and moral and religious proscription, induced profound feelings of sexual guilt. Here the authoritarian family, the authoritarian church, and the authoritarian state were reciprocally reinforcing.

The regulation of sexuality was of particular concern to the New England Puritans of the seventeenth century. The family values applicable to a woman were to obey her father or husband, to be a good wife and mother, and above all to remain sexually faithful—a ban that did not apply to men.

In the eighteenth century, the American and English working class, without the benefit of advice from their betters, adopted a more permissive attitude, routinely permitting sexual relations after engagement instead of waiting till marriage. Marriage thus followed intercourse, rather than the other way round.

You may well ask why I have not included abortion as an issue at the core of family values in the seventeenth century. The simple answer is that at that time it was hardly ever discussed, although it was undoubtedly fairly widely practiced, as we shall see tomorrow.

III. The Self-Improvement Model of the Enlightenment

As we have seen, the ethical code of paternalism, inculcated by family, school, church, and state, was ideally suited to an agrarian and lightly populated society, fearful of outbreaks of physical violence from below. By 1720, the beginnings of commercial competition and the rise of a professional middle class resulted in the development of a second set of family values, more applicable to the new economic and social conditions.

It was still paternalism, but stripped of its emphasis on piety, less oppressive in demanding deference, and stressing self-improvement.

It still held up as the ideal a society based upon concepts of honor and shame, principles that Bernard Mandeville in his *The Fable of the Bees* in 1714 put as the first requirement of a civilized man and that he believed could be acquired by "early and artful instruction."

His model of family values applied only to males. It demanded a good knowledge of the classics and the avoiding of "gross vices, as irreligious whoring, gaming, drinking and [dueling]."

This is a set of moral values based not at all upon the tenets of Christianity, but rather upon the values of classical authors, especially Cicero and Cato. An example of his paradox that private vices can lead to public virtues involved those who were attempting to suppress prostitution. He called them "silly people," since in fact a plentiful supply of prostitutes was the best, and perhaps the only, protection of respectable wives from rape by lustful men.

The key to Mandeville's world was a code of individual self-improvement, based on behavior that made use of personal self-interest and passions so as to benefit society. It consisted of diligence, hard work, deferred sexual and other gratification, self-discipline, sobriety, thrift, punctuality, cleanliness, and obedience to legitimate orders, all operating to satisfy the greed of the individual, but thereby creating wealth for the society. Where the doctrine differed from that of the calling was that these values were specifically designed to enable the individual to better himself in the world.

The code was brilliantly illustrated by William Hogarth's great set of engravings *Industry and Idleness,* published in 1747 and deliberately intended to be widely available and to set an example for the Atlantic world. The idle apprentice slept on the job, recovering from some sexual and alcoholic debauch of the night before; he spent his leisure hours gambling in the churchyard during divine service; he was fired by his master, failed to find employment, took to a life of crime as a highwayman, was arrested, tried, convicted, and hanged at Tyburn. The industrious apprentice, however, attracted the attention of his master by his hard work and other good qualities, was encouraged by him to marry his only daughter, and so obtained the necessary capital to go into business. By skillful use of the capital he grew richer and richer and rose to higher and higher status, ending up as lord mayor of London.

Hogarth regarded himself as a moral prophet, whose engravings were "calculated for use and instruction of youth." Between them, Defoe, Hogarth, Mandeville, and others set up a self-improvement model that was ideally suited to the growing urban bourgeoisie of the eighteenth century, was eagerly adopted by Benjamin Franklin, and became the foundation of the American dream. The dream is that anyone, by personal exertions, can rise from a log cabin to the White House or from the assembly line to president of General Motors. Although it is no longer entirely true, of course, the myth is still alive, and America today is still remarkable by the standard of other Western countries for the ease of access up to the top, increasingly nowadays by the means of education. President Clinton is a perfect example of how the individual self-improvement model of family values is still flourishing in the late twentieth century. It is a code that ran parallel with that of paternalism right through until the late 1950s.

The family code for women was unaffected by the individualist self-improvement model, except to the extent that in the eighteenth and nineteenth centuries more and more aspiring middle-class men chose educated women who could be a social asset in their upward climb. From the eighteenth century onward, there was a slow improvement in the education of middle-class women. Inch by inch, women were slowly beginning to get a toehold up the educational ladder, even if the object was still to catch and keep a husband, rather than to prepare themselves for participation in the public sphere.

IV. Conclusions

The first major conclusion is that the most highly prized of family values in the past was not at all ours of individual self-improvement and independence of thought, but obedience. This stress on obedience in the past was based on the sheer fragility of social bonds, and the ever-present threat of a relapse into anarchy, chaos, and civil war, a collapse of law and order, the appalling consequence of which is only too visible today in Bosnia, Somalia, and Haiti.

A big problem for historians is how during the course of the eighteenth century the Americans, brought up like the English as obedient servants of a monarchy and of its agents down to the patriarchal father, and living in an hierarchical society where everyone knew their place and stayed in it, first rebelled and then turned themselves into the free citizens of a turbulent democracy. The democracy excluded women and black slaves, but that was only to be expected at that time; so, after all, did Classical Athens.

Today the ideology guiding family and social values in the West, and especially in America, is one of rugged independence, individualism, and frantic pursuit of personal happiness, and a deep faith in the American dream of upward social and economic mobility as a result of hard work and cutthroat competition.

We accept that we should ride our children with a loose rein, encouraging them to find things out for themselves, stimulating their desire for enquiry, praising their independence of thought, and developing their capacity to defend their own positions. We also insist that life is a competitive struggle to get ahead and better oneself, the battle being fought on a level playing field for both sexes, an idea that would have horrified our almost universally sexist forefathers.

Two conclusions stand out. First, there is no Golden Age somewhere out there, where all the values we most prize were both fully accepted and implemented. Second, value systems, being aspects of a culture, are constantly on the move, although only twice—or possibly three times—in the long history of the West have there been major value revolutions. The first was imposed on the barbarians and Roman West by the slow pressures of early Christianity, backed by the power of the Roman emperor. The possible second was the result of the Enlightenment and the French Revolution in the eighteenth century. And the third was the one that swept over the West, and above all America, in the 1960s.

How successful was this tremendous effort in the Early Modern period to use the family as an instrument to turn out generations of pious, God-fearing, obedient, deferential, sober, industrious, but unambitious and uncompetitive citizens? The short answer is that we are not really sure. Martin Luther himself was disappointed in Germany, and a modern scholar has concluded that after a century of efforts "Lutherans had not succeeded in making an impact on the population at large."

The American and British evidence seems to tell a different story, at any rate concerning piety, obedience, and sexuality. The historical evidence for the success of religious and moral indoctrination in inculcating family values in Early Modern Anglo-America is a strong one, but most of them are not exactly the values for which Pat Robertson and Dan Quayle are so anxiously seeking.

Tomorrow I will try to show how in the 1950s and 1960s both forms of paternalist family values current between the seventeenth and the twentieth centuries quite suddenly collapsed. As a result, we are living in an age of unprecedented cultural conflict between generations, between the old and the new, the outcome of which is still uncertain. This cultural shift is one of the most striking examples of Stephen Jay Gould's theory of "punctuated equilibrium" of which I know. Why it happened, and with what consequences, and what we can do to guide, encourage, or mitigate those consequences will be the subjects of my lecture tomorrow.

LECTURE 2. FAMILY VALUES IN 1993

I. Introduction

Yesterday I talked about the past, a subject about which I do know something. Today I want to talk about the present, and particularly the young, from whom I am distanced by a huge age gap and by having lived a sheltered life in academia for half a century. This lecture is a jeremiad by an old man, lamenting the corruption of the times, and it may well be I have got many things wrong.

There was a time, back in 1961, when a president of the United States could say, in his inaugural address: "Ask not what your country can do for you; ask what you can do for your country" and could reasonably hope to be reelected. Thirty years ago, the result was a flood of idealistic youths into the Peace Corps. Today any politician who dares to suggest sacrifice for the common good by raising taxes is certain to be punished in the polls, as happened to Governor James Florio in New Jersey. What seems to have happened is that the sense of responsibility for others, which used to go along with a strong sense of personal rights and liberties, has been severely eroded. The civil society is collapsing and the quality of life in the cities is unquestionably deteriorating. All that remains are excessive, almost antisocial, demands for total liberty for the individual to pursue the gratification of his or her own entirely selfish wishes, whether social or financial or sexual, without regard for the interests of the community as a whole or of anyone else.

Many serious observers have claimed that the American family has been dying before our eyes over the last twenty-five years and that the values rightly or wrongly associated with it have in consequence also changed sharply for the worse.

If I seem critical of recent trends in America, please don't misunderstand me. I expect many of you are critical too. I have lived in America for thirty years. I have been an American citizen for twenty-three, and I propose to retire and die here. I would not live anywhere else in the world, despite the fact that it is not the same America as the one to which I migrated in 1963.

II. The Cultural Revolution of the 1960s

1. The Facts

What has gone wrong? John Updike has recently talked of "the pain of feeling we no longer live nobly." This is a reasonable reaction as we nervously walk the filthy streets of New York, stepping over the inert bodies of the homeless. It is obvious that the way people treat one another in public has grown more callous. Good Samaritans are harder to find in the streets of big American cities these days than they used to be. And if you get mugged or stabbed in public, don't count on bystanders coming to your rescue.

Up to the 1950s, the old family values still held, as I explained yesterday. They included religious piety, obedience to parents and superiors, hard work, optimism about future upward mobility, and the deferment of gratification in coping with sexual passion. All these were still part of the inherited culture of the baby-boom generation, the largest in American history, who had been fathered by the veterans of World War II.

It was in the late fifties and very early sixties that the first signs of trouble made themselves felt, as electronic music from the Beatles burst over the airwaves, deafening and bewildering parents, preachers, and teachers; as Elvis Presley sang and strummed his guitar to throngs of hysterically screaming teenagers; as the pill was invented and marketed; as kids who had everything, thanks to the endless growth of more and more consumer goods churned out by a rapidly growing economy, now wanted more, but were prepared to give less in terms of obedience and hard work. The one, possibly traumatic, anxiety was the fear of the evil empire of Russia and its capacity to launch a nuclear war. People dug air-raid shelters and stocked them with food and drink—and also guns to protect them from their neighbors—while charlatans like Senator Joseph Mccarthy stalked the land to rout out closet Communists.

By 1964, the rebellion against the 1,000-year-old culture of inculcated obedience to superiors broke out on the Berkeley campus and then spread elsewhere. To the astonishment of parents, teachers, and bureaucrats, kids no longer obeyed orders. Dr. Benjamin Spock admonished insecure parents, anxious only to do the right thing, not to reach for the hairbrush no matter how obnoxiously their children behaved. The children of the professional class took to dressing like beggars and, at the university, to enrolling in basket-weaving instead of economics, which drove their parents wild. These trends culminated at Woodstock, where the counter-culture composed of free sex, drugs, and opposition to the Vietnam War reached its peak. By the 1970s, the many who still subscribed to traditional family values were facing severe competition.

Today not only does the idealism of the 1960s generation appear naive in the extreme, but the consequent trashing of the traditional cultural norms and the rejection of all social, religious, and sexual controls can be seen to have had devastating consequences, which may turn out to be long lasting. Soon after 1960, most of the key social indicators began to rise on the charts: divorce, venereal disease, illegitimacy, teenage pregnancy, abortion, child abuse, one-parent families, single-person households, drug abuse, high-school dropouts, teenage suicide, violent crime, and homicide all increased dramatically after 1960.[2] The quality of life in all the big cities began visibly to deteriorate, and nobody seemed to know what to do about it. And, quite suddenly, despite the fact that most Americans continued to believe in life after death, belief in the existence of Hell went away. Once it was there, and then it was gone. Nobody was afraid of it anymore. At the same time, the words "dishonor," "shame," and "sin" disappeared from the vocabulary.

Over the past thirty years, many liberals have thought—naively as it turned out—that permissiveness and "doing your own thing" would lead to social harmony and personal happiness. It has therefore been left to the conservatives to marshal the data and offer the conclusion that, as Mr. William Bennett put it recently, "the constitution of America is not good .... Modern day social pathologies ... seem to have gotten worse." He is absolutely right in seeing a serious deterioration in standards of social, sexual, and educational behavior among the young. Mr. Bennett is also right to claim that "our injury is self-inflicted," issuing partly from the shift from a world of apparently inescapable poverty into a world of unprecedented affluence, and partly from a hedonistic ethic of immediate gratification and self-fulfillment, regardless of the cost to others. Where Mr. Bennett goes wrong, however, is on two points. First, he fails to point out that all Western European countries are going through the same experiences as those now prevalent in America, although to a lesser degree. The deterioration of all the social indicators I have mentioned seems to go along with Western capitalist civilization, as the inhabitants of Eastern Europe and Russia are discovering, somewhat to their dismay. Homicide is the only area in which America stands alone.

It would be grossly unfair to leave the impression that there were no positive gains won by the generation of the 1960s in both the pursuit of individual happiness and the establishment of a more democratic and egalitarian society. Both men and women were finally released from their thousand-year-old grim Puritan straightjacket of prudery and suspicion about sexuality. Millions had been deprived of much sexual pleasure by these severe inhibitions. The coincidence of the removal of moral inhibitions with two technical breakthroughs—penicillin to cure venereal disease and the pill to block unwanted pregnancy—clearly increased the sum of human happiness, but it also had its dark side, which I will come to in a moment.

The other great achievement of the cultural revolution of the 1960s was to pose a challenge to all kinds of authority, from the father in the family to the tyrant or monarch in the state. Deference almost disappeared; there was a massive democratization of the power of all authority figures, who could no longer expect to be obeyed without question. This was a long process, which began in the mid-eighteenth century, and was observed by contemporaries like Dr. Samuel Johnson, but the great leap forward came in the 1960s. The most positive achievement of the generation—both black and white—that came of age in the 1960s was its success in liberating the Afro-Americans in the South from the web of Jim Crow laws that deprived them of political power and cultural equality and self-respect. That same generation also forced the authority structure at last to give equality of opportunity, both educational and in the marketplace, to blacks and women. Nor was the process a slow one. The drive began in the 1960s and today, in 1993, blacks and women are gaining access to some of the highest and most important positions in the land. These are major achievements in which, along with the defeat of Nazi Germany, my generation can take some pride.

Furthermore, if we take a close look at Mr. Bennett's depressing graphs of social and cultural indicators, it becomes clear that a significant number of them are showing signs of flattening out and stabilizing, admittedly at a level much lower than the norm back in the 1960s. Contrary to popular belief, the homicide rate per 100,000 peaked in 1980, fell to 1985, and then started rising again, but has not yet reached the 1980 level. The number of children on welfare has been flat at 8 million since

1980. Divorces per thousand married women have actually been falling a little since 1985, while the number of children affected by divorce has also been going down. SAT scores, although lower than they were in 1960, have been more or less the same since 1975. Although the proportion of high school dropouts, after falling sharply in the 1960s, has continued to decline, it has been at a much slower rate. The usage of all kinds of drugs has also been dropping in high schools since about 1980. The proportion of the population who own their own homes, and thus have a stake in the economy, has been flat ever since 1973, and perhaps before. Finally, charitable giving as a proportion of GNP is rather higher than it has ever been since 1960, which suggests that many still have faith in the community.

Moreover, against the narrowing of responsibility and the cult of egotism in the "me generation," one has to set the rapidly growing power of the environmental lobby, which suggests that, at a broader level, more and more Americans are now thinking in universal terms about the planet itself and the limits that need to be placed on the exploitation of natural resources for individual benefit. And, finally, there are signs, here and there, admittedly few and weak, that some citizens, prodded by charismatic women social workers or by black clergymen, are beginning to band together to recreate community units and to take back the streets from the gangs, the thugs, and the drug-pushers. It is not much, but it is astonishing that it is happening at all in view of the grave personal danger such work involves and the near-helplessness of the police, some of whom in some cities are on the payroll of the drug-pushers.

There are therefore, here and there, some faint signs of stabilization, although at a very low level. But today over a quarter of all children—that is, 17 million—live in single-parent homes, a proportion that has doubled in the last twenty years. Moreover, the proportion of pregnant unmarried teenagers has already reached the 10 percent level and is still rising.

2. The Causes

There are many reasons why the cultural revolution occurred when it did in the 1960s. There was the coming to maturity of the pampered baby-boomers, who had lived through the longest economic growth period in American history; the concomitant explosion of the universities thanks to generous government subsidies; the steady empowerment of women; the entry of married women on a large scale into the work force; the sexual revolution, driven by new technology and an ideology of personal pleasure without responsibility; the sudden availability of drugs; and the profound distrust of all authority engendered by the disaster of the Vietnam War, followed by the scandals of Watergate, Irangate, and so forth. These revelations of government incompetence, corruption, and abuse of power have deeply disillusioned the American public, and especially the young. The Gallup poll shows that even as late as 1970, 70 percent still had "a great deal of" or "a fair" trust in their government. By 1992, the proportion had slipped to a dismal 42 percent?

It was fourteen years ago that Christopher Lasch first castigated American culture for its moral failure—caused by carrying "the pursuit of happiness" embodied in the Declaration of Independence "to the dead end of narcissistic preoccupation with the self."

He blamed excessive individualism for the growth of selfishness, permissiveness, lack of civility, and other signs of what he perceived as a civilization in decay. Lasch saw not only a decay of public life, but also a concurrent decay of private life. This caused personal bonding to become so fragile that it broke under the slightest strain, an observation proven by the astonishing explosion of the divorce rate between 1970 and 1985. But the key mental shift was that the young no longer accepted responsibility for their own actions—a position increasingly also taken by juries in criminal cases. Lasch's recommended solution was of course a return to all the aspects of the traditional family values—the Puritan ethic of hard work, discipline, and obligation to the civil society. But how this was to be achieved he never made clear.

James Hunter, in his interesting recent book *Culture Wars*, sees a comprehensive battle in progress between conservatives and progressives, extending over the family, education, the arts, the law, and electoral politics. I do not accept this unified vision of cultural conflict, and he himself constantly admits that there is a huge group in the middle who are not being heard. The key unifying factor common to all these cultural wars is a clash of generations.

Of course, these middle-class cultural revolutions are not responsible for the plight of the inner cities and the inability of the underclass—mostly Afro-Americans—to escape from it. For them the major factor has been economic—namely the very high level of male unemployment and the debilitating experience of prolonged dependency on welfare. In the inner city ghettoes, black unemployment of male youth today approaches 100 percent. It is almost impossible to imagine the state of misery and despair induced by a situation in which the only male jobs available are the dangerous and evil ones of violent crime and drug pushing. In some ghettoes, the street gang has become the substitute for parents, school, and church, as the sole purveyor of values. A whole generation of young blacks is in danger of ending up in prison or dead.

To make matters worse, in the last decade the distribution of wealth has been shifted by government action: the very rich have gotten much richer and the poor poorer. Meanwhile, our economy ceased to grow after 1973 and so has the real income of the middle classes.

I want now to discuss what I regard as the most serious and deep-rooted crisis in our society, that of violence in the streets, itself a product of a collapse of parental control. Then I will deal with problems arising from the sexual revolution, for some of which I believe that solutions may be in sight.

III . The Symptoms of Pathology

1. Violence in the Streets

In terms of violent crime, it is impossible to deny that everything is getting worse. (…)

At that age they are flooded with hormones that provoke aggressive behavior, but in the past this was normally worked off by hard physical labor to earn a living or by service in the military. But although Europe shares the growing violence in the streets, the level of such violence in America is in a class entirely by itself. By 1980, the violent crime rate in the United States had reached a level that is many times higher than in any other society in the West today, and probably higher than at any time since the Middle Ages, to judge from statistics of homicide. Eight out of ten Americans will be a victim of one or more violent crimes during their lifetime. What makes the situation so alarming is that it is growing worse far more rapidly than the size of the juvenile age cohort. Over the past forty years, violent crime and homicide have multiplied sevenfold in America and after a fall in the early 1980s are rising again. Half of all 16-year-olds admit to having committed at least one violent crime, but teenagers are also the victims, and over a million of them have experienced rape, robbery, or assault.

At the same time, despite the public demand for punitive action, the length of time actually spent in prison by violent criminals is only half what it used to be, because of the grotesque overcrowding of courts and prisons. The courts are so choked with cases that they can only cope by the use of arbitrary plea-bargaining, while the prisons are so short of beds that dangerous criminals have to be paroled to make space for others. Willie Horton was just one example among thousands. We already have nearly twenty times as many people in jail, relative to the population, as does Britain. The numbers have increased fourfold in the last twenty years, with no visible effect at all on crime. We also already have a larger proportion of our black population in prison than did South Africa under apartheid.

We have a good idea of the main causes of the explosion of street violence. The first cause is parental negligence, when both husband and wife have exhausting full-time jobs or there is only a single working parent. This situation is exacerbated by the failure of schools to adapt their hours to the new social reality of two working parents or a single working parent. They still close at the traditional hour of 3:00 P.M., and as a result today 80 percent of all schoolchildren return to an empty home. They are easy prey for the mass psychology of the street gang, which becomes a substitute for the family and is geared to collective acts of violence. The second cause is that this void is filled with watching TV, which is closely associated with the display of more and more, and more and more brutal, acts of violence (…) Television alone has to be primarily responsible for kids as young as eleven starting to kill one another. It has been estimated that by the age of twenty-one the average American child will have witnessed no fewer than 8,000 murders on television.

The third cause of violence is the ubiquity of handguns. America today is a society armed to the teeth and therefore accustomed to a level of homicide quite unknown in any other industrialized society, or indeed in the West since the sixteenth century. The family has to be deeply implicated in this situation, since so much of the killing is perpetrated by youths. (…) In at least one in three American households there is today a gun in working order, along with ammunition, so in case of family quarrels a spouse no longer throws a plate at the other. He shoots her, or she shoots him. The fixation of Americans upon guns is for foreigners the most amazing, inexplicable, and horrific aspect of late twentieth century United States culture. (…)

2. The Sexual Revolution

The most visible sign of a sexual revolution is the end of modesty. The other day I saw an otherwise respectable-looking young woman walking along a city street, wearing a mini-skirt that barely covered her buttocks and a T-shirt with the logo "Just do it." What is odd about this is that her appearance did not raise so much as an eyebrow, much less provide incitement to a rape. This is, I believe, a unique situation, unique in the sense that such a scene could never have happened before in the West, except perhaps at the height of the French Revolution.

The most serious consequence of the sexual revolution is structural, that is, the rise of the single-parent family. We have known for decades now that single-parent families consisting of a mother alone are more prone than those with mother and father together to fail to train the child to fit into the society. The majority of these single parents are poor, female, and also black, the leftovers of decades of successive generations of teenage pregnancies, unmarried mothers, and multiple divorces. The percentage of children living in single-parent homes has trebled since 1960, to reach nearly a third of all families with children. The consequence of this development was pointed out nearly thirty years ago by Senator Daniel Moynihan, and since then has only gotten worse. Mr. Bennett is right to argue that these deep-seated factors making for disintegration of both the family and the school, together with the decline of the influence of the church, have created a situation that seems to be remarkably resistant to social engineering, whether by government or by private agencies.

When the combined effects of the pill and penicillin first arrived in the 1960s, they made a major impact on sexual behavior by removing both of the two adverse effects of sex, pregnancy and venereal disease, thus opening the way for what has been called a culture of sexual license.

If one wanted to place this sexual revolution in the worst possible light, one would point out that it has resulted in a rise to historically unprecedented levels in the proportion of illegitimate children born. Before the twentieth century, the percentage was everywhere below 10 percent, but today in America it has risen to 30 percent, with projections of a rise to 40 percent by the year 2000. It has also led to one and a half million fetuses being aborted each year; to the spread of a new, lethal, and so far incurable venereal disease, AIDS; and to the collapse of family stability, because of the increase of divorce to a point that today, if the statistics remain steady, half of all marriages in America will end in the divorce court. Serial polygamy is becoming the model of the American family. (…)

V. Conclusion: The Breakdown of Civil Society

What has broken down in recent years is not only the family, but also the civil society, what Alexis de Tocqueville called "private societies, held together by similar conditions, habits, mores." No solution to the present desperate situation will work without family, church, school, and community involvement in order to change destructive mental processes and physical habits. (…)

The traditional family of mother, father, and children is certainly shrinking as a proportion of the whole, comprising now only one household in five. The proportion of singles living alone and of single-parent households with children have both undoubtedly grown enormously as a proportion of all households. More and more couples are cohabiting without marriage, and the proportion of illegitimate children is far higher than ever in our history. It is thus undeniable that marriage as we have known it is a declining institution. This is a moral disaster, not just an expansion of multicultural options. Furthermore, our civic culture and our courtesy, in both the public and private sphere, are both dissolving, and in our passion for guns we are killing each other on a scale wholly unknown in any other civilized country.

Equally serious is the possibility that our economy will never again produce enough jobs to put the whole adult population, now both male *and* female, to work again. If this is so, the 10 percent to 15 percent of the population who today constitute the underclass may never escape from the poverty trap in the inner city ghettoes of the North and the forgotten rural villages of the South.

It is also clear that because of the conflict between the sexual revolution and the threat of an AIDS epidemic, our sexual behavior is in need of a major overhaul. Unprotected promiscuity is no longer a safe option. By far the highest divorce rate in the Western world (50 percent) does not seem to have done much to increase the sum of human happiness, and it has certainly resulted in many children being seriously damaged and neglected. (…)

And do not forget one thing. Every ill that is responsible for the decay of family values in America—except the unique salience of murder by gunfire—is visible, if to a lesser degree, in all major cities in the industrialized West. Moreover, things were nearly as bad in the past among the urban poor. Victorian London, as Charles Dickens described it, was a place of filth, cruelty, prostitution, and crime, and in Elizabethan England the homicide rate was close to that of America today. We have been living in a century of very unusual domestic peace, which is now over. What is needed to turn our society around is a politics based on hope, not fear; a moral code based on the acceptance of personal responsibility for one's actions; and greater family and community cooperation, rather than the selfish pursuit of the mirage of individual happiness, regardless of its effect on others. When Thomas Jefferson asserted that the function of the new Republic was to protect life, liberty, and the pursuit of happiness, the last thing he had in mind was an egocentric dash for consumer goods and sexual pleasure, both of them acquired, if necessary, by violence.

FURTHER READINGS

Carbone, June. *From Partners to Parents: The Second Revolution in Family Law.* New York: Columbia University Press, 2000.

Fukuyama, Francis. *Trust: The Social Virtues and the Creation of Prosperity.* New York: Free Press, 1995.

Hunter, James. D. *Culture Wars: The Struggle to Define America.* New York: Basic Books, 1991.

Stone, Lawrence. *The Family, Sex and Marriage in England, 1500–1800.* London: Penguin, 1991.

UNIT II

Transformation of the American Family

Chapter 2

American Family

By Daphne Lofquist, Terry Lugaila, Martin O'Connell, and Sarah Feliz

INTRODUCTION

The 2010 Census enumerated 308.7 million people in the United States, a 9.7 percent increase from 281.4 million in Census 2000. Of the total population in 2010, 300.8 million lived in 116.7 million households for an average of 2.58 people per household. This was down from an average of 2.59 in 2000 when 273.6 million people lived in 105.5 million households. The remaining 8.0 million people in 2010 lived in group-quarters arrangements such as school dormitories, nursing homes, or military barracks. This report presents information on the number and types of living arrangements of American households in 2010 derived from the relationship question on the 2010 Census.

Source: U.S. Census Bureau, 2010 Census questionnaire.

Figure 2.1. Reproduction of the Question on Relationship to Householder From the 2010 Census

HOUSEHOLD RELATIONSHIP QUESTION

The relationship item (Figure 2.1), a version of which has been on the census since 1880, asks the relationship of each member of the household to the householder or the person designated as the individual who owns or rents the housing unit.[1] This question provides information about

---

[1] In a case of joint ownership, one individual is chosen as the householder. If this choice cannot be made, the first person 15 years and over listed on the form is chosen as the householder.

Daphne Lofquist, Terry Lugaila, Martin O'Connell, and Sarah Feliz, from *Households and Families*: 2010, pp. 1–10. Copyright in the Public Domain.

individuals as well as the composition of families and households. Three separate categories describe the sons and daughters of the householder in 2010: biological, adopted, or stepchild. Relatives identified in the questionnaire are spouses, brothers, sisters, and parents of the householder, as well as grandchildren, parents-in-law, and sons/daughters-in-law.

Those who live in households but who were not related to the householder were identified as housemates/roommates, roomers or boarders, and unmarried partners of the householder. This latter group includes people who initially identified themselves as being same-sex spouses of the householder. The tables with same-sex couples show these groups in two ways. One estimate shows households as originally reported on the census forms. The second presents improved and preferred estimates of the same-sex household population, accounting for marking errors that inadvertently overestimated that population's size.[2] This report uses this set of estimates in the text, as it represents the best set of numbers from the 2010 Census.

People Related to the Householder

Despite the diversity of households in the United States, three relationship categories made up the majority of people in 2010. The householder, his or her spouse, and his or her sons and daughters comprised 262.0 million people or 87 percent of the population (Table 2.1). Of the 88.8 million children of householders, 93 percent were biological children. There were approximately twice as many stepchildren (4.2 million) as adopted children (2.1 million).

As expected, most of the children living with their parents were under 18 years old. These three child types exhibit different age distributions. About 73 percent of either biological or adopted children were under 18, compared with 67 percent of stepchildren. Stepchildren were more likely to be young adults ages 18 to 29 years (26 percent) than either biological or adopted children (19 percent each). Stepchildren were older in general as they reflect the blending of two different families where the spouse already has older children from a prior marriage.

In the same generation as the children of the householder are the sons-in-law and daughters-in-law of the householder. They numbered 1.2 million in 2010, and almost half of them were young adults who depended on their in-laws for housing assistance. Given their age, most were probably recently married. About one-third of all brothers and sisters of the householder (3.4 million) were 18-to-29 years old.

Another 1.1 million young adults were grandchildren of the householder. This age group made up 16 percent of the 7.1 million grandchildren living with their grandparents—the majority of these grandchildren were under 18 (82 percent). At the other end of the generational continuum were the parents and parents-in-law of the householder, comprising about 3.0 million and 926,000 relatives, respectively. Unlike people in any other relationship category, the majority of these were 65 years and over—57 percent of parents and 69 percent of parents-in-law were this age.

Although not specified by detailed type in the 2010 Census, another 4.7 million were "other relatives" who lived in households. About one-third of them were under 18 and were often nephews and nieces of the householder.[3]

---

2 See Martin O'Connell and Sarah Feliz, "Same-sex Couple Household Statistics From the 2010 Census," S EHSD Working Paper Number 2011-26, September 27, 2011, www.census.gov/hhes/samesex/data/decennial.html.

3 There were 845,000 nephews and nieces of the householder under 18 in Census 2000. See Terry Lugaila and Julia verturf, "Children and the Households They Live In: 2000," Census 2000 Special Reports, CENSR-14 (March 2004), Table 1.

Table 2.1. Relationship to Householder by Age: 2010 (For information on confidentiality protection, nonsampling errors, and definitions, see www.census.gov/prod/cen2010/doc/sf1.pdf)

Relationship type	Total	NUMBER				
		Under 18 years	18 to 29 years	30 to 44 years	45 to 64 years	65 years and over
Total household population.	300,758,215	73,920,881	47,903,506	59,766,531	80,357,019	38,810,278
Householder.	116,716,292	28,297	13,862,048	30,758,709	46,247,402	25,819,836
Spouse.	56,510,377	8,793	4,863,702	17,524,307	24,935,103	9,178,472
Biological son or daughter.	82,582,058	60,466,596	16,007,784	3,941,728	2,093,818	72,132
Adopted son or daughter.	2,072,312	1,527,020	403,558	99,376	41,282	1,076
Stepson or stepdaughter.	4,165,886	2,784,531	1,100,511	217,220	61,226	2,398
Brother or sister.	3,433,951	298,242	1,125,419	848,247	922,338	239,705
Father or mother.	3,033,003	(X)	(X)	128,343	1,187,041	1,717,619
Grandchild.	7,139,601	5,825,229	1,117,324	180,096	16,926	26
Parent-in-law.	925,713	(X)	(X)	10,178	281,266	634,269
Son-in-law or daughter-in-law.	1,216,299	25,063	593,674	428,186	158,997	10,379
Other relative.	4,662,672	1,631,262	1,268,787	774,403	648,580	339,640
Roomer or boarder.	1,526,210	142,899	559,814	376,180	363,573	83,744
Housemate or roommate.	5,223,365	42,515	3,163,824	1,084,638	769,490	162,898
Unmarried partner.	7,744,711	11,651	2,622,772	2,724,034	2,020,431	365,823
Other nonrelative.	3,805,765	1,128,783	1,214,289	670,886	609,546	182,261

(X) Not applicable
Source: U.S. Census Bureau, *2010 Census Summary File 1*.

Nonrelatives of the Householder

People who were not related to the householder numbered 18.3 million in 2010 (6.1 percent of the household population), up from 14.6 million in 2000 (5.2 percent of the household population). In fact, 1 out of every 8 homes in 2010 contained one or more people not related to the householder.[4] Roomers or boarders comprised 1.5 million individuals who represented a wide array of people such as students, migrants to an area waiting for better accommodations, or people who could not afford to rent their own home.[5] About 143,000 (9.4 percent) of roomers and boarders were less than 18 years old, suggesting they might be children of displaced families living in boarding homes. Another 61.3 percent (936,000) were in the prime working ages of 18 to 44 years, compared with 35.8 percent for the household population as a whole.

---

5 A historical perspective and the growth and characteristics of roomers and boarders is presented in Melissa Scopilliti and Martin O'Connell, "Roomers and Boarders: 1880–2005," paper presented at the Annual Meetings of the Population Association of America, New Orleans, LA, April 17–19, 2008, <www.census.gov/population /www/documentation/paa2008/Scopilliti-OConnell-PAA-2008.ppt>.

> ## Unmarried Partner Households
>
> An "unmarried partner household" consists of a householder and a person living in the household who reports that he or she is (1) an unmarried partner of the householder and of the opposite sex; (2) an unmarried partner of the householder and of the same sex; or (3) a spouse of the householder and of the same sex. Procedures for the 2010 Census edited same-sex spouse households as unmarried partner households, and these households appear as such in published Summary File 1 tabulations. During the review of the data, counts of same-sex spouses appeared inflated due to mismarking errors in the gender item on the census forms. Up to 28 percent of the total number of same-sex unmarried partner households may actually be opposite-sex households: 62 percent of reported same-sex spouses were probably marked in error compared with 7 percent of reported same-sex unmarried partners. This report presents data both for same-sex households as shown in Summary File 1 tabulations and for a set of "preferred estimates" that attempts to remove statistically same-sex households that are likely opposite-sex households.

Housemates or roommates who were coequals with the householder and who shared maintenance of the housing unit had more economic equality with the householder. Looking at the age structure of these 5.2 million people, 61 percent were young adults ages 18 to 29 who might be sharing living expenses. The percentage declined sharply for the next older age group, 30 to 44 years old (21 percent).

Overall, the unmarried partner population numbered 7.7 million in 2010 and grew 41 percent between 2000 and 2010, four times as fast as the overall household population (10 percent). Unmarried partners were generally older than housemates: 2.6 million (34 percent) were 18 to 29 years old, while 2.7 million (35 percent) were 30 to 44 years old. In addition, 26 percent of unmarried partners were 45-to-64 year olds, compared with 15 percent of housemates. This difference in age profiles reflects the transitions occurring first when a young person shares expenses as a housemate or roommate after leaving the parent's home and later when that person develops a more permanent and personal relationship with an unmarried partner.

HOUSEHOLDS

All of these various relationship types contribute to the formation of households, both family and nonfamily households. Who lives in a household has important consequences for economic resources available to housing units and for access to everyday social support systems such as care for young children or older parents. The following sections show the different types of households in 2010 and their growth over the decade.

The Number of Households Grew by Over 11 Million Since 2000.

The number of households in the United States increased 11 percent, from 105.5 million in 2000 to 116.7 million in 2010. While family households increased 8 percent, from 71.8 million in 2000

> ## Household Definitions
>
> A "household" includes all of the people who occupy a housing unit. One person in each household is designated as the "householder." In most cases, this is the person, or one of the people, in whose name the home is owned, being bought, or rented. If there is no such person in the household, any household member 15 years old and over can be designated as the householder.
>
> A family consists of a householder and one or more other people living in the same household who are related to the householder by birth, marriage, or adoption. Biological, adopted, and stepchildren of the householder who are under 18 are the "own children" of the householder. Own children do not include other children present in the household, regardless of the presence or absence of the other children's parents.
>
> A family household may also contain people not related to the householder. A family in which the householder and his or her spouse of the opposite sex are enumerated as members of the same household is a husband-wife household. In this report, husband-wife households only refer to opposite-sex spouses and do not include households that were originally reported as same-sex spouse households. Same-sex spousal households are included in the category, "same-sex unmarried partner households" but may be either a family or nonfamily household depending on the presence of another person who is related to the householder. The remaining types of family households not maintained by a husband-wife couple are designated by the sex of the householder.
>
> A nonfamily household consists of a householder living alone or with nonrelatives only, for example, with roommates or an unmarried partner.

to 77.5 million in 2010, nonfamily households increased faster, 16 percent, from 33.6 million in 2000 to 39.2 million in 2010. As a proportion of all households, family households declined from 68 percent in 2000 to 66 percent in 2010, while the proportion of nonfamily households increased from 32 percent to 34 percent, respectively.

Table 2.2 shows that husband-wife households numbered 56.5 million in 2010 and made up 73 percent of all family households in 2010 (households containing at least one person related to the householder by birth, marriage, or adoption). Family households maintained by a female householder with no spouse present numbered 15.3 million, more than twice the number maintained by a male householder with no spouse present (5.8 million). Among nonfamily households, one-person households predominated (31.2 million) and were more than three times as common as nonfamily households with two or more people (8.0 million). More women than men lived alone (17.2 million and 13.9 million, respectively). A geographic look at one-person households follows later in this report.

Despite increases in both the number of households and of people in the United States since 2000, the average household size decreased over the decade, from 2.59 to 2.58, but average family size stayed the same, 3.14.[6] These indicators show a slowing of the downward trends that have existed

---

[6] Average family size is the number of family members in the household (persons related to the householder including the householder) per family household. This computation excludes persons not related to the householder.

Table 2.2 Households by Type: 2000 and 2010 (For information on confidentiality protection, nonsampling errors, and definitions, see www.census.gov/prod/cen2010/doc/sf1.pdf)

Household type	2000		2010		Change, 2000 to 2010	
	Number	Percent	Number	Percent	Number	Percent
Total households................	**105,480,101**	**100.0**	**116,716,292**	**100.0**	**11,236,191**	**10.7**
Family household......................	71,787,347	68.1	77,538,296	66.4	5,750,949	8.0
Husband-wife households........	54,493,232	51.7	56,510,377	48.4	2,017,145	3.7
With own children...............	24,835,505	23.5	23,588,268	20.2	−1,247,237	−5.0
Without own children..........	29,657,727	28.1	32,922,109	28.2	3,264,382	11.0
Female householder, no spouse present.................................	12,900,103	12.2	15,250,349	13.1	2,350,246	18.2
With own children...............	7,561,874	7.2	8,365,912	7.2	804,038	10.6
Without own children..........	5,338,229	5.1	6,884,437	5.9	1,546,208	29.0
Male householder, no spouse present.................................	4,394,012	4.2	5,777,570	5.0	1,383,558	31.5
With own children...............	2,190,989	2.1	2,789,424	2.4	598,435	27.3
Without own children..........	2,203,023	2.1	2,988,146	2.6	785,123	35.6
Nonfamily households.................	33,692,754	31.9	39,177,996	33.6	5,485,242	16.3
Male householder.....................	15,556,103	14.7	18,459,253	15.8	2,903,150	18.7
Living alone.........................	11,779,106	11.2	13,906,294	11.9	2,127,188	18.1
Not living alone...................	3,776,997	3.6	4,552,959	3.9	775,962	20.5
Female householder................	18,136,651	17.2	20,718,743	17.8	2,582,092	14.2
Living alone.........................	15,450,969	14.6	17,298,615	14.8	1,847,646	12.0
Not living alone...................	2,685,682	2.5	3,420,128	2.9	734,446	27.3
Unmarried couple households[1].....	5,475,768	5.2	7,744,711	6.6	2,268,943	41.4
Opposite-sex partners...............	4,881,377	4.6	6,842,714	5.9	1,961,337	40.2
Same-sex partners[2]						
Summary File 1 counts.........	594,391	0.6	901,997	0.8	307,606	51.8
Preferred estimates................	358,390	0.3	646,464	0.6	288,074	80.4
Average household size.................	2.59	(X)	2.58	(X)	−0.01	(X)
Average family size.......................	3.14	(X)	3.14	(X)	0.00	(X)

(X) Not applicable.
1 Unmarried couple households can be family or nonfamily households depending on the relationship of others in the household to the householder. In this table, it is the sum of opposite-sex partners and same-sex partners from Summary File 1 counts.
2 Summary File 1 counts in this table are consistent with Summary File 1 counts shown in American FactFinder.
Sources: U.S. Census Bureau, *Census 2000 Summary File 1* and *2010 Census Summary File 1.*

since the end of the Baby Boom in the 1960s. In 1960, the average household size was 3.29 people per household, and the average family size was 3.65 people per family.[7]

The number of households within each category type increased in the last 10 years, including husband-wife households, which increased by 2.0 million. Figure 2.2 shows that, despite this increase, in 2010 less than half of all households (48 percent) were husband-wife households, down from 52 percent

---

7 Average household size for 1960 may be found in Frank Hobbs and Nicole Stoops, "Demographic Trends in the 20th Century," *Census 2000 Special Reports*, CENSR-4 (November 2002), Figure 5–3. Average family size for 1960 may be around in U.S. Census Bureau, 1960 Census of Population, Supplementary Reports, PC(S1)-38, *Families in the United States*: 1960, Table 280.

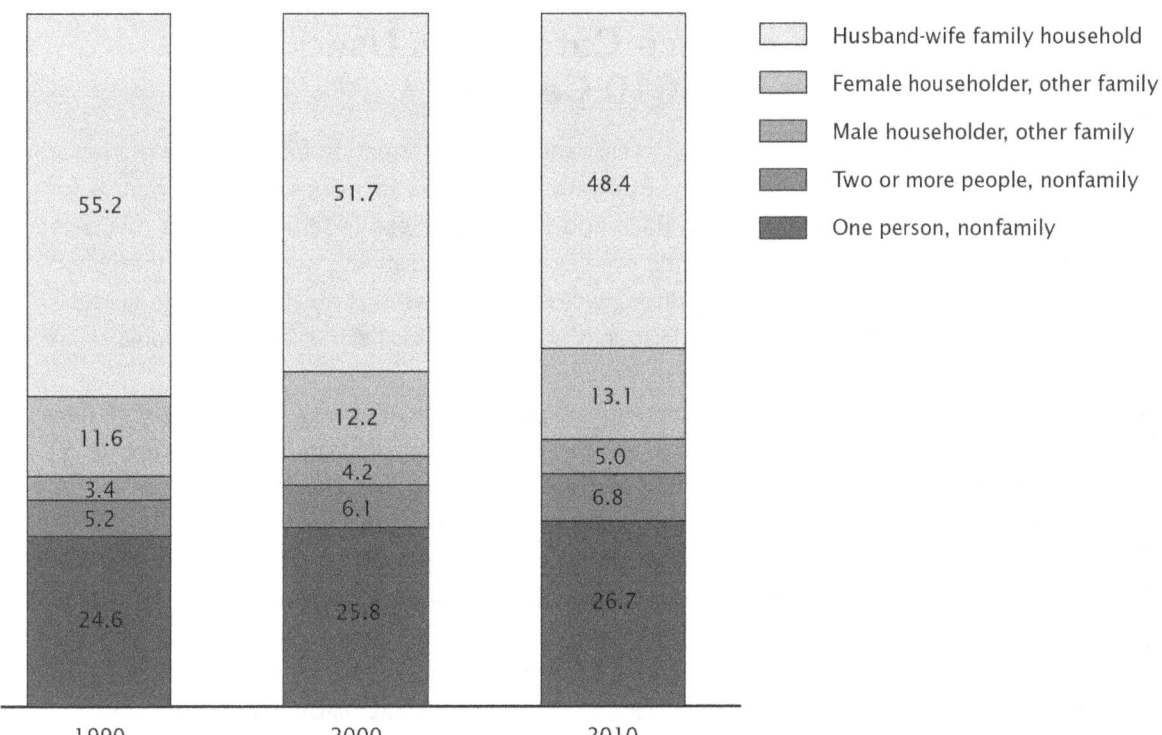

Sources: U.S. Census Bureau, *Census 2010 Summary File 1; Census 2000 Summary File 1; 1990 Census of Population, Summary Population and Housing Characteristics, United States (1990 CPH-1-1)*.

Figure 2.2 Households by Type: 1990, 2000, and 2010
(Percent distribution. For information on confidentiality protection, nonsampling error, and definitions, see *www.census.gov/prod/cen2010/doc/sf1.pdf*)

in 2000 and 55 percent in 1990. This is the first time that husband-wife families fell below 50 percent of all households in the United States since data on families were first tabulated in 1940.[8] For each of the other types of households shown in Figure 2.2, the percentage share has increased since 1990.

Opposite-sex unmarried partner households increased by 40 percent since 2000, almost four times the national average. For same-sex households, the preferred estimates for 2000 and 2010 showed an 80 percent increase. However, same-sex partner households made up less than 1 percent of all households in both 2000 and 2010.

Household Types Varied by Race of Householder in 2010.

Two-thirds of all households in the United States were family households (Table 2.3). This proportion varied considerably by race: 64 percent of non-Hispanic White alone households were family households, compared with 78 percent of Hispanic or Latino households. Households containing husband-wife families varied as well: 29 percent of all Black or African American alone households were husband-wife households, while 60 percent of Asian alone households were husband-wife families.

---

8 See the Census Bureau's Families and Living Arrangements Web page, Historical Table HH-1, www.census.gov/population/socdemo/hh-fam/hh1.xls.

> ## Definition of Race Categories Used in the 2010 Census
>
> The U.S. Census Bureau collects race and Hispanic origin information following the guidance of the U.S. Office of Management and Budget's (OMB) 1997 Revisions to the Standards for the Classification of Federal Data on Race and Ethnicity. These federal standards mandate that race and Hispanic origin (ethnicity) are separate and distinct concepts and that when collecting these data via self-identification, two different questions must be used. Individuals who responded to the question on Hispanic origin are classified as either Hispanic or as non-Hispanic.
>
> Individuals who responded to the question on race by indicating only one race are referred to as the race-alone population or the group that reported only one race category (e.g., White alone, Black or African American alone, American Indian and Alaska Native alone, Asian alone, Native Hawaiian and Other Pacific Islander alone, and Some Other Race alone). Individuals who chose more than one of the six race categories are referred to as the Two or More Races population in this report. All respondents who indicated multiple races (more than one race) or races in combination with each other can be collapsed into the Two or More Races population category, which, combined with the six race-alone categories, yields seven mutually exclusive and exhaustive categories. Thus, the six race-alone categories and the Two or More Races category sum to the total population.
>
> As a matter of policy, the Census Bureau does not advocate the use of the alone population over the alone-or-in-combination population or vice versa. The use of the alone population in sections of this report does not imply that it is a preferred method of presenting or analyzing data. The same is true for household and family tables presented in Summary Files 1 or 2 that show the alone-or-incombination population. Data on race from the 2010 Census can be presented and discussed in a variety of ways.

Three in 10 Black or African American alone households were female householder, no spouse present families, three times as high as White alone households (9.9 percent) and Asian alone households (9.5 percent). The majority of female family house-holds with no spouse present contained own children of the householder, except for Asian alone households. Male family households with no spouse present represented 5 percent of all households. Almost one-half of all of these households contained own children of the householder.

Households containing unmarried couples can be family or nonfamily households, depending on the presence of relatives of the house-holder. Nationally, 6.6 percent of all households were unmarried partner households. American Indian and Alaska Native alone households reported the largest percentage of unmarried partner households (10.9 percent). Asian alone house-holds had the lowest proportion of unmarried couple households, 3.6 percent. The majority of all unmarried partner households were opposite-sex partner households.

Also shown in Table 2.3 are the preferred estimates for same-sex partner households by race and Hispanic or Latino origin. The preferred estimates removed the households that were likely to have

Table 2.3. Household Type by Race and Hispanic Origin: 2010 (For information on confidentiality protection, nonsampling errors, and definitions, see www.census.gov/prod/cen2010/doc/sf1.pdf)

Household type	Total	White alone	Non-Hispanic White alone	Black or African American alone	American Indian and Alaska Native alone	Asian alone	Native Hawaiian and Pacific Islander alone	Some Other Race alone	Two or more races	Hispanic or Latino of any race
Total households (number)	116,716,292	89,754,352	82,333,080	14,129,983	939,707	4,632,164	143,932	4,916,427	2,199,727	13,461,366
Total households (percent)	100.0	100.0	100.0	100.0	100.0	100.0	100.0	100.0	100.0	100.0
Family households	66.4	65.4	64.3	64.9	70.4	73.9	77.0	80.8	67.6	78.4
Husband-wife households	48.4	51.2	51.1	28.5	40.1	59.7	51.3	49.6	41.0	50.1
With own children	20.2	19.9	19.0	12.8	19.4	31.8	29.0	34.2	23.0	31.3
Under 6 years only	4.6	4.5	4.4	2.3	3.6	8.9	6.1	6.9	5.7	6.4
Under 6 years and 6 to 17 years	4.4	4.1	3.7	3.0	5.1	6.3	8.2	10.8	6.0	9.4
6 to 17 years only	11.3	11.3	10.9	7.5	10.7	16.6	14.7	16.5	11.3	15.5
Without own children	28.2	31.2	32.1	15.7	20.7	27.9	22.2	15.4	18.0	18.8
Female householder, no spouse present	13.1	9.9	9.2	30.1	21.4	9.5	17.0	20.2	19.2	19.2
With own children	7.2	5.2	4.7	17.4	12.3	4.1	9.8	13.6	12.3	12.1
Under 6 years only	1.5	1.1	1.0	3.6	2.6	0.7	2.2	2.6	3.0	2.4
Under 6 years and 6 to 17 years	1.3	0.8	0.7	3.7	2.8	0.5	2.3	3.4	2.6	2.9
6 to 17 years only	4.4	3.3	3.1	10.1	6.8	2.8	5.3	7.6	6.8	6.9
Without own children	5.9	4.7	4.5	12.7	9.2	5.5	7.2	6.6	6.9	7.1
Male householder, no spouse present	5.0	4.3	4.0	6.3	8.9	4.7	8.7	10.9	7.3	9.1
With own children	2.4	2.1	2.0	2.9	4.6	1.4	4.3	5.7	3.8	4.7
Under 6 years only	0.7	0.6	0.5	0.8	1.3	0.4	1.3	1.8	1.2	1.5
Under 6 years and 6 to 17 years	0.4	.03	0.2	0.5	0.9	0.2	0.9	1.4	0.7	1.1
6 to 17 years only	1.4	1.3	1.2	1.6	2.3	0.9	2.0	2.5	1.8	2.1
Without own children	2.6	2.2	2.0	3.4	4.3	3.2	4.4	5.3	3.5	4.4
Nonfamily households	33.6	34.6	35.7	35.1	29.6	26.1	23.0	19.2	32.4	21.6
One person	26.7	27.6	28.6	29.7	22.6	19.0	15.7	12.6	23.4	15.2
Two or more people	6.8	7.0	7.1	5.4	7.0	7.2	7.3	6.6	9.0	6.4
Unmarried couple households[1]	6.6	6.4	6.2	7.0	10.9	3.6	9.3	10.2	9.8	9.4
Opposite-sex partner	5.9	5.6	5.4	6.4	10.0	3.1	8.2	9.4	8.8	8.6
With own children	2.3	1.9	1.7	3.3	5.4	1.0	4.3	6.1	4.3	5.2
Without own children	3.6	3.7	3.7	3.1	4.6	2.1	3.9	3.2	4.5	3.3
Same-sex partner—										
Summary File 1 counts[2]	0.8	0.8	0.8	0.6	0.9	0.5	1.1	0.8	1.0	0.8
With own children	0.2	0.2	0.1	0.2	0.3	0.2	0.4	0.4	0.3	0.3
Without own children	0.6	0.7	0.7	0.4	0.6	0.4	0.7	0.4	0.7	0.5
Same-sex partner—										
Preferred estimates[3]	0.6	0.6	0.6	0.4	0.6	0.4	0.9	0.5	0.8	0.5
With own children	0.1	0.1	0.1	0.1	0.2	0.1	0.3	0.2	0.2	0.2
Without own children	0.5	0.5	0.5	0.3	0.5	0.3	0.6	0.3	0.6	0.4

1 Unmarried couple households can be family or nonfamily households depending on the relationship of others in the household to the householder. In this table it is the sum of opposite-sex partners and same-sex partners from Summary File 1 counts.
2 Summary File 1 counts in this table are consistent with Summary File 1 counts shown in American FactFinder.
3 Preferred estimates remove likely numbers of opposite-sex couples included in same-sex tabulations.
Source: U.S. Census Bureau, *2010 Census Summary File 1*.

31

been opposite-sex house-holds as judged by inconsistencies between their first names and their responses to the gender item.[9] This resulted in a reduction of same-sex households as a percentage of all households from 0.8 percent to 0.6 percent. About 0.1 percent of all households in the United States in 2010 were estimated to be same-sex partner households with own children of the householder present, the highest being 0.3 percent for Native Hawaiian and Pacific Islander alone households.

Thirty-one Percent of All Households were in Four States

Table 2.4 shows that four states contained 31 percent of all households enumerated in 2010: California (12.6 million), Texas (8.9 million), Florida (7.4 million), and New York (7.3 million).[10] These states also had the most households in 2000, although Florida, which had the fourth-highest number of house-holds in 2000, was the third highest in 2010, topping New York. Sixteen states had less than 1.0 million households, with Wyoming having the fewest (227,000). Nevada, which had 751,000 house- holds in 2000, had slightly over 1.0 million households in 2010. No state experienced a decline in the number of households in 2010. On a regional basis, more house-holds were located in the South (43.6 million) than any other region in the country.[11]

The average number of people per household in 2010 ranged from a low of 2.30 in North Dakota to a high of 3.10 in Utah, the only state in 2010 that averaged more than 3 people per household. The District of Columbia averaged only 2.11 people per household, a decline from 2.16 in 2000. Regionally, the West had the highest average number of people per household (2.74), while the lowest average was in the Midwest (2.49).

Utah had the highest average number of people per family (3.56), followed by California (3.45) and Hawaii (3.42). Ten states averaged less than 3 people per family in 2010: Maine, New Hampshire, and Vermont in the Northeast; West Virginia and Kentucky in the South; Iowa, North Dakota, and Wisconsin in the Midwest; and Montana and Wyoming in the West.

---

9 See O'Connell and Feliz, op. cit., for a detailed discussion of this statistical procedure.

10 These four states (California, Texas, Florida, and New York) also were the states with the largest populations.

11 There were four regions (Northeast, Midwest, South, and West). The Northeast region includes Connecticut, Maine, Massachusetts, New Hampshire, New Jersey, New York, Pennsylvania, Rhode Island, and Vermont. The Midwest region includes Illinois, Indiana, Iowa, Kansas, Michigan, Minnesota, Missouri, Nebraska, North Dakota, Ohio, South Dakota, and Wisconsin. The South region includes Alabama, Arkansas, Delaware, the District of Columbia, Florida, Georgia, Kentucky, Louisiana, Maryland, Mississippi, North Carolina, Oklahoma, South Carolina, Tennessee, Texas, Virginia, and West Virginia. The West region includes Alaska, Arizona, California, Colorado, Hawaii, Idaho, Montana, Nevada, New Mexico, Oregon, Utah, Washington, and Wyoming.

Table 2.4. Households and Families for the United States, Regions, States, and for Puerto Rico: 2000 and 2010
(For information on confidentiality protection, nonsampling errors, and definitions, see www.census.gov/prod/cen2010/doc/sf1.pdf)

Area	All households		Percent of households in 2010									Average number of people in 2010	
			Family households						Nonfamily households				
			Husband-wife households		Female family		Male family households[1]		One person				
	April 1, 2000	April 1, 2010	Total	With own children under 18 years	Total	With own children under 18 years	Total	With own children under 18 years	Total	With householder 65 years and over	Two or more people	Per houshold	Per family
United States	105,480,101	116,716,292	48.4	20.2	13.1	7.2	5.0	2.4	26.7	9.4	6.8	2.58	3.14
REGION													
Northeast	20,285,622	21,215,415	46.9	19.5	13.3	6.9	4.7	2.1	28.1	10.7	7.0	2.53	3.12
Midwest	24,734,532	26,215,951	48.8	19.7	11.9	6.9	4.6	2.4	28.1	10.1	6.5	2.49	3.06
South	38,015,214	43,609,929	48.3	19.7	14.2	7.8	4.9	2.3	26.4	9.0	6.3	2.56	3.10
West	22,444,733	25,674,997	49.5	22.1	12.2	6.6	5.6	2.8	24.8	8.4	8.0	2.74	3.30
STATE													
Alabama	1,737,080	1,883,791	47.9	18.5	15.3	8.1	4.6	2.0	27.4	9.8	4.8	2.48	3.02
Alaska	221,600	258,058	49.4	22.7	10.7	6.8	6.0	3.5	25.6	5.4	8.2	2.65	3.21
Arizona	1,901,327	2,380,990	48.1	19.5	12.4	7.1	5.6	3.0	26.1	9.1	7.7	2.63	3.19
Arkansas	1,042,696	1,147,084	49.5	18.9	13.4	7.7	4.7	2.4	27.1	10.1	5.3	2.47	3.00
California	11,502,870	12,577,498	49.4	23.4	13.3	6.8	6.0	2.8	23.3	8.1	8.0	2.90	3.45
Colorado	1,658,238	1,972,868	49.2	21.4	10.1	6.0	4.6	2.5	27.9	7.8	8.1	2.49	3.08
Connecticut	1,301,670	1,371,087	49.0	20.9	12.9	7.1	4.4	1.9	27.3	10.6	6.5	2.52	3.08
Delaware	298,736	342,297	48.3	18.3	14.2	7.6	5.0	2.4	25.6	9.7	7.0	2.55	3.06
District of Columbia	248,338	266,707	22.0	7.9	16.4	7.9	3.9	1.3	44.0	9.7	13.7	2.11	3.01
Florida	6,337,929	7,420,802	46.6	16.6	13.5	7.1	5.0	2.3	27.2	11.1	7.6	2.48	3.01
Georgia	3,006,369	3,585,584	47.8	21.1	15.8	8.9	4.9	2.2	25.4	7.5	6.1	2.63	3.17
Hawaii	403,240	455,338	50.5	20.1	12.6	5.2	5.8	2.4	23.3	8.1	7.7	2.89	3.42
Idaho	469,645	579,408	55.3	24.0	9.6	5.9	4.7	2.8	23.8	8.8	6.6	2.66	3.16
Illinois	4,591,779	4,836,972	48.2	21.0	12.9	6.9	4.7	2.2	27.8	9.7	6.4	2.59	3.20
Indiana	2,336,306	2,502,154	49.6	19.9	12.4	7.3	4.9	2.6	26.9	9.5	6.2	2.52	3.05
Iowa	1,149,276	1,221,576	51.2	20.0	9.3	5.9	4.2	2.5	28.4	11.1	6.9	2.41	2.97
Kansas	1,037,891	1,112,096	51.1	21.3	10.4	6.5	4.5	2.6	27.8	9.9	6.2	2.49	3.06
Kentucky	1,590,647	1,719,965	49.3	19.1	12.7	7.1	4.8	2.4	27.5	9.8	5.6	2.45	2.98
Louisiana	1,656,053	1,728,360	44.4	17.6	17.2	9.3	5.5	2.6	26.9	8.9	6.0	2.55	3.10
Maine	518,200	557,219	48.5	16.7	10.0	6.0	4.5	2.7	28.6	11.3	8.4	2.32	2.83
Maryland	1,980,859	2,156,411	47.6	20.4	14.6	7.6	4.8	2.2	26.1	8.7	6.8	2.61	3.15
Massachusetts	2,443,580	2,547,075	46.3	19.7	12.5	6.8	4.2	1.8	28.7	10.6	8.3	2.48	3.08
Michigan	3,785,661	3,872,508	48.0	18.9	13.2	7.3	4.8	2.4	27.9	10.2	6.2	2.49	3.05
Minnesota	1,895,127	2,087,227	50.8	21.2	9.5	5.9	4.3	2.3	28.0	9.7	7.4	2.48	3.05
Mississippi	1,046,434	1,115,768	45.4	17.8	18.5	10.0	5.2	2.4	26.3	9.5	4.6	2.58	3.11
Missouri	2,194,594	2,375,611	48.4	18.9	12.3	7.1	4.6	2.5	28.3	10.1	6.4	2.45	3.00
Montana	358,667	409,607	49.2	17.8	9.0	5.4	4.5	2.6	29.7	10.7	7.5	2.35	2.91
Nebraska	666,184	721,130	50.8	21.2	9.8	6.2	4.2	2.3	28.7	10.4	6.5	2.46	3.04
Nevada	751,165	1,006,250	46.0	19.6	12.7	7.0	6.6	3.3	25.7	7.9	9.1	2.65	3.20
New Hampshire	474,606	518,973	52.1	20.4	9.7	5.7	4.5	2.5	25.6	9.2	8.0	2.46	2.96
New Jersey	3,064,645	3,214,360	51.1	23.3	13.3	6.6	4.8	2.0	25.2	10.1	5.5	2.68	3.22
New Mexico	677,971	791,395	45.3	17.9	14.0	7.8	6.2	3.4	28.0	9.3	6.5	2.55	3.13
New York	7,056,860	7,317,755	43.6	18.7	14.9	7.5	5.0	2.1	29.1	10.5	7.3	2.57	3.20
North Carolina	3,132,013	3,745,155	48.4	19.6	13.7	7.8	4.6	2.3	27.0	9.1	6.3	2.48	3.01
North Dakota	257,152	281,192	48.6	18.6	8.2	5.2	4.1	2.2	31.5	11.0	7.7	2.30	2.91
Ohio	4,445,773	4,603,435	47.2	18.2	13.1	7.5	4.7	2.4	28.9	10.4	6.2	2.44	3.01
Oklahoma	1,342,293	1,460,450	49.5	19.7	12.3	7.0	5.0	2.7	27.5	9.9	5.8	2.49	3.04
Oregon	1,333,723	1,518,938	48.3	18.7	10.5	6.1	4.7	2.5	27.4	9.7	9.1	2.47	3.00
Pennsylvania	4,777,003	5,018,904	48.2	18.3	12.2	6.5	4.6	2.2	28.6	11.4	6.5	2.45	3.02
Rhode Island	408,424	413,600	44.5	17.6	13.5	7.7	4.8	2.2	29.6	11.3	7.6	2.44	3.04
South Carolina	1,533,854	1,801,181	47.2	17.7	15.6	8.4	4.7	2.2	26.5	9.2	5.9	2.49	3.01
South Dakota	290,245	322,282	50.1	19.7	9.7	6.2	4.4	2.6	29.4	10.9	6.4	2.42	3.00
Tennessee	2,232,905	2,493,552	48.7	18.7	13.9	7.5	4.8	2.3	26.9	9.4	5.7	2.48	3.01
Texas	7,393,354	8,922,933	50.6	23.7	14.1	8.0	5.2	2.5	24.2	7.2	5.9	2.75	3.31
Utah	701,281	877,692	61.0	31.7	9.7	5.5	4.4	2.2	18.7	6.4	6.1	3.10	3.56
Vermont	240,634	256,442	48.5	17.6	9.6	6.0	4.4	2.6	28.2	10.3	9.3	2.34	2.85
Virginia	2,699,173	3,056,058	50.2	21.1	12.4	6.7	4.4	2.0	26.0	8.5	7.0	2.54	3.06
Washington	2,271,398	2,620,076	49.2	20.4	10.5	6.2	4.7	2.5	27.2	8.7	8.4	2.51	3.06
West Virginia	736,481	763,831	49.8	17.0	11.2	5.7	4.8	2.3	28.4	11.6	5.8	2.36	2.88
Wisconsin	2,084,544	2,279,768	49.6	19.4	10.3	6.4	4.5	2.5	28.2	10.2	7.4	2.43	2.99
Wyoming	193,608	226,879	50.9	19.6	8.9	5.6	4.8	2.8	28.0	8.8	7.4	2.42	2.96
Puerto Rico	1,261,325	1,376,531	45.0	18.2	22.6	10.9	5.5	2.2	23.8	9.5	3.1	2.68	3.17

1 No spouse present in household.
Sources: U.S. Census Bureau, Census 2000 Summary File 1 and 2010 Census Summary File 1.

Chapter 3

The Changing American Family

By Cris Beam

If all you did was watch television commercials for minivans, you might think that the traditional all-American family was still intact—Mom, Dad, dog, and the 2.5 kids buckle up and drive off every day on TV. But ads (depending on your perspective) are either selling aspirations or guilt: This is the family you're supposed to have, supposed to want.

In real life, in big cities and in smaller towns, families are single moms, they're stepfamilies, they're boyfriends and girlfriends not getting married at the moment, they're foster parents, they're two dads or two moms, they're a village. In real life, in 2005, families are richly diverse.

AND ARE ONLY GETTING MORE SO

In fact, the very definition of "family" is changing dramatically. The year 2000 marked the first time that less than a quarter (23.5 percent) of American households were made up of a married man and woman and one or more of their children—a drop from 45 percent in 1960. This number is expected to fall to 20 percent by 2010.

Why the Changes?

The change in the makeup of the American family is the result of two primary factors, says Martin O'Connell, chief of fertility and family statistics at the U.S. Census Bureau, which collects such figures every 10 years. First, more babies (about a third) are now born out of wedlock, and second, divorce rates continue to climb so that nearly half of all marriage contracts are broken.

The overall attitude toward relationships and commitment has shifted. More than half of female high school seniors say that having a child outside of marriage is acceptable, according to

Cris Beam, "The Changing American Family," *American Baby Magazine*. Copyright © 2005 by Cris Beam. Reprinted with permission.

a recent poll from the University of Michigan Survey Research Center. And census data shows that 26 percent of all households are made up of a single person, living alone (as opposed to 13 percent back in 1960).

While a good portion of these singles are likely senior citizens, others are younger career folks who don't feel yesteryear's societal pressure to rush into partnerships.

"In 2002, the median age for a woman's first marriage was 27," says O'Connell. That's five years older than it was even in 1980. Sometimes young singles establish their individual identities so solidly that they never marry, even if they have children. These couples may partner up—but without the papers.

Adoption, no marriage: Such was the case with Steve Wilson and Erin Mayes, a couple in their mid-30s living in Austin, Texas. They've been together for 10 years, own a home together, and though they've talked about it, have decided it isn't necessary to get married. Still, they wanted a family and, last June, adopted a baby boy.

Wedding after baby: Another example is Jared and Lori Goldman, of San Mateo, California. Their relationship was relatively new when Lori got pregnant in 2000. They agreed to raise the child together but didn't get engaged. But not long after their daughter was born, Jared proposed. "Reverse order worked better for us," he says. Lori agrees: "Our wedding felt more meaningful happening on its own time instead of on the traditional schedule. What girl wants a shotgun wedding?"

Single moms on the rise: Of course, because currently one-third of all babies are born out of wedlock, it's no surprise that many mothers remain single. When she got pregnant, Pam Hansell says her boyfriend initially seemed supportive. Then he began dodging her phone calls and e-mails, and eventually cut contact. Deeply hurt but determined to give her child a good life, Hansell moved in with her parents, outside of Philadelphia, and gave birth to a daughter in March. "When I realized I couldn't count on the father, it was devastating. I'm so thankful that family and friends have stepped in," Hansell says.

Two dads: Finally, Dean Larkin and Paul Park are living out another common-in-today's-world scenario. They live together in Los Angeles, and Larkin has a 21-year-old daughter from a previous marriage. Now he and Park are planning a second child, via a surrogate mother. They'd like to marry, but gay marriage is not legal nationally.

Reactions from the Trenches

Perhaps no one has a better ringside seat to all these untraditional family setups than those involved in the childbirth industry. "I've seen unmarried couples come in, lesbian couples, mothers who have been here with one father and then come in with a new father—the family dynamics and structures have changed a lot over the past 25 years," says Barbara Hotelling, president of Lamaze International and a long-time childbirth instructor.

Based in Rochester Hills, Michigan, Hotelling probably sees a good cross section of American families and, while she doesn't ask the marital status of her students, estimates that around 20 percent are unmarried, compared with maybe 5 percent when she first began her career.

Hotelling has shifted her language with the times. She says she used to call her students moms and dads, but now, "I say 'moms and partners' and hope nobody screams."

According to 1999 figures from the Population Resource Center, families in which the mother is the head of the household are, by and large, living on less. Because of the wage gap, female-headed households earn, on average, $26,164 a year; male-headed households earn $41,138 per year; and married households earn $56,827 per year.

Then, there are the more than 1,100 federal benefits that married households can take advantage of during a lifetime. Under the Family and Medical Leave Act, married partners can take leave from work when their spouse gets sick; unmarried partners cannot. Federal Medicaid laws permit only married couples to keep their homes when one partner needs nursing home care; an unmarried partner can lose the house. When a married person dies, the spouse inherits Social Security benefits; an unmarried partner gets nothing.

All told, according to the Los Angeles-based American Association for Single People and cited in an October 2003 Business Week article, with health benefits, retirement, and so on, married families can "earn" 25 percent more than unmarried ones.

Marriage Penalties

How does this stack up with the so-called "marriage penalty" that people complain about at tax time? Two of the major tax penalties were eliminated in 2003, says Fred Grant, a senior tax analyst at Turbo Tax, a corporation that produces electronic tax preparation programs.

Used to be, married couples filing jointly had a lower standard deduction than two singles living together, and married couples (in the lowest two income brackets) got bumped into a higher tax bracket on a combined income, thus paying more taxes overall. Now, only the richest three tiers pay more as marrieds than as cohabiters.

There are a few other penalties married couples face (for example, they need a lower combined income to qualify for a $1,000 per-child tax credit), but, Grant warns, taxes are such a complex soup incorporating home ownership, itemizations, and more, it's almost impossible to state assertively which type of family comes out ahead tax-wise.

Money, Marriage—and Children

What is safe to say is that the kids of untraditional families can wind up penalized. Of course, there are many possible scenarios. In the best cases, kids living with, for instance, only their mother also receive financial support from a father. But as many single moms will tell you, not all fathers pay their full share of childcare costs.

Statistics also show that there are many kids lacking basic health insurance—at last count, about 8.4 million, according to the U.S. Census. All told, there are 11 million children (16 percent) living at or below the poverty line, and while that's not broken down into the number of kids with married or unmarried parents, it's a sure bet that many impoverished kids are in untraditional families.

Though a growing number of couples are fine with never getting married, the vast majority of cohabiting relationships change into either marriage or separation after an average of 18 months, says Susan Brown, PhD, associate professor of sociology at Bowling Green State University's Center for Family and Demographic Research and a contributor to the 2002 collection of essays and studies *Just Living Together*. She says that according to some research, there may be a psychological cost to raising a family without the mental safety net of marriage.

"I've found that cohabiters are more depressed than married people, and it seems to be because of relationship instability," Brown says. That means most unmarried parents who live together get married eventually—or break up and seek other potential spouses.

The Growth of Gay Families

According to the Urban Institute, 2 in 5 gay or lesbian couples live in a house with children under age 18. But because the U.S. Census Bureau doesn't figure same-sex relationships into their data, it's hard to pinpoint exactly how many children are living with gay or lesbian parents.

The American Academy of Pediatrics (AAP) places its bet between one and nine million children, which means somewhere between 1.4 percent and 12.5 percent of all kids. While the AAP issued a statement saying that children of same-sex couples deserve two legally recognized parents, no state can grant federal marriage benefits to these couples, and only these states—California, Connecticut, Massachusetts, New Jersey, and Vermont—allows state rights, such as the guarantee that unmarried parents can visit a child in the hospital.

Two moms, one donor: One couple, Sue Hamilton and Christy Sumner, used a sperm bank when they decided to have a baby. While the couple isn't able to marry in their home state of California, Hamilton recently adopted their daughter, which is legal there. Negotiating state laws puts extra stress on gay and lesbian families, but Hamilton and Sumner have encountered a few sympathizers. "One of the hospital workers fell in love with our family," Hamilton says.

"She thought it was nutty that birth certificates have to read 'mother' and 'father,' and typed up a mock certificate that just has our names on it."

Can Your Employer Help You?

Some large employers are scrambling to catch up to how families are changing. Traditionally, companies required workers to be married if they wanted benefits for household members. But now, "in order to attract and retain quality employees, the benefits need to be more flexible," says Kevin Marrs of the American Society of Employers, an organization that tracks information for firms in the Detroit area. He concedes, however, that because domestic partner benefits can cost a company more money, many small independent businesses don't yet offer them.

Few laws protect untraditional families. In fact, at this point federal laws don't prohibit discrimination based on marital status, so unmarried families can and do face discrimination in these key areas:

- housing
- employment
- adoption
- insurance
- child custody
- hospital visitation
- the ability to make a decision for a partner or child in an emergency

Wilson and Mayes are lucky—their decision to not get married is made easier by the fact that their state, Texas, permits common-law marriage status. Declaring that lets them enjoy joint health coverage through Mayes's employer, and it smoothed the adoption process. If all states had such laws, a great many people would benefit. But only 16 states recognize common-law marriage—and three of those require couples to prove they've been living together since the '90s, according to Nolo Press, which publishes plain-English legal information.

Why Aren't Laws Catching Up to How We're Living?

To many politicians, pushing for marriage is easier than changing laws. President Bush proposed spending $1.5 billion over five years on a Healthy Marriage Initiative to encourage couples (especially in poor communities) to marry. The money hasn't been approved, but the Department of Health and Human Services is running the program.

"Bush [advocates] marriage among low-income populations as a way to ameliorate poverty. But I'm not sure that's the answer," Brown says.

Daniel Lichter, a sociology professor at Ohio State University, goes even further. In his 2003 study, "Is Marriage a Panacea?" he shows that poverty rates for disadvantaged women who marry and then divorce are actually higher than for women who never marry in the first place. (One thought is that the loss of financial stability as a direct result of divorce—which costs money in itself—may set women back.) So getting married doesn't always ease the financial burden of raising kids, and it certainly doesn't help open the rigid boundaries of what "counts" as a family.

The answer probably lies in making sure all families—whether Mom and Dad drive the minivan to soccer practice or Mom piles her stepkids onto the city bus—receive the same kinds of rights, benefits, and treatment. Access to affordable childcare and living wages are also more direct solutions.

Discrimination against unmarried families is still real. But those families also have the love and courage it takes to press for change. Says Hamilton, "It really doesn't matter what kind of relationship the parents are in—what matters is the love they have for their child. That is what makes a family."

Chapter 4

Feminism and the Evolving Role of Men

By Joseph Palermo, M.A.

As our social institutions and networks are redefined and evolving to include women as equal partners, let us pause, and consider men as unemployed framers of society. This has become transparent and of ethical importance to both of the sexes and society. The role of women in society today, spearheaded by university and media leadership has secured its place in the cultural psyche of our modern workplace and family. This role as a voice is channeled through education and television programming and has evolved into a resounding accusation of man as patriarch and the chief reason for social inequality between men and women in careers, roles and salaries.

With the patriarchal foundation shaken and uprooted so as to strip a man of his royal status we are replanting the Garden of Eden and Adam again bites to Eve's apple. Man has played many a role since the beginning of time and today his social presence has him quiet and watching as we transform male and female gender roles to a type unprecedented in American history. The presence of mother, sister, lover, wife and daughter as friend, foe and ally in cahoots or in defense or offense of this status quo is an essential part of our new dilemma.

ROLE DIFFUSION

Present mans' historical "self" is disoriented to a degree of self-loathing and an insecure sense of identity; his foundation shattered. It is not a surprise that images, metaphors and archetypes of men range from super-heroes to predators of women and children. Today's social male is experiencing the psychic and ethical dilemma of role diffusion. When we explore the history and the present in context of male and female relationships as social constructs, we can come together as one. As equals, let us examine this socio-historical revolution of gender stereotyping. Let us begin with the family and conclude with media as the breeding ground for gender role, place and socialization.

The family now has a new structure and way of fending for itself and man is not its chief provider, bread winner and inseminator. His presence is profoundly compromised by the social evolution of feminism, technology and women's new role in the family and at the work place. Men (with women) as inventors and engineers have minimized men's omnipotence. For example, the invention and approval of birth control pills, abortion and IVF redefine the function of family, the roles of men and women, child bearing and child rearing.

Family was traditionally the domain where man as protector and provider was a king "home from the hunt." This social fact does necessitate a separation of the sexes. The male bands of secret societies need not serve as an impetus to female secret societies. Together as one, we can lift the veil of secrecy and an oppressive patriarchal system into a shared society of male and female orientations and evolve as equal players at work and home.

A Time of Role Transformation

Like the age of enlightenment: "political correctness" and "gender equality" in social settings (from home and the workplace to the military and sports arena), this movement offer us a new way of seeing men and women relationships. Clearly, both men and women, as co-creators and domestic engineers changed the status of man as protector and provider; beliefs in male superiority, virility, lineage and heirs to the throne have been redefined by social evolution—technology, globalization and civil rights. This technology is not just a device but sanctioned and promoted by political agendas, media and law. Today's man in power, in court and the media is not the man of 'yore; he is viewed as the guilty party, primo genitor, a corporate raider, a seducer, a chauvinist, a manipulator, a pervert, immature, boob or abuser of women who covets his power and possessions in fear or in retaliation or control of the feminist movement.

Granted, the entire history of modern man in America, in both our courts and churches, gives substantial proof of male domination. Issues of male oppression abound: the abuse and neglect of women at home and at work, in schools, in sports, in military, in every institution where the equality clause has established its rightful presence, man is at fault and guilty of patriarchal ideology and influence.

However, the conflicting message of man as an ogre leaves man like an itinerant sociopath (as described in a TV show) and derelict; as the cultural mores and norms of a society that "he" created on paper are being rewritten and language redefined, he is a genetic male sexual species in part illiterate, anomic and disoriented. As these charges bear substance, the walls of that patriarchal social contract and secure psyche of male fortitude formerly defined by male principles of power and provider of the family have shifted their weight and position. Man, hypothetically dethroned and emasculated remains concerned, confused and on the fence as to his new role. He settles in and holds on to his remote control for some sense of reprieve and entertainment.

Men of the Past

We must visit the past to put the present in perspective. Historical "Man" as an entity and an ascribed status, as everything powerful and strong in a physical context, fortified his ego with high self-esteem and narcissistic virtue. A social system documented and reinforced by laws and literature as to man as king to the throne was an empowering and stable personification of the alpha male, like a God. Imagine the experience of being blessed and sanctioned legal heir to the environment around you justified by law, competition and brute strength. No doubt that a "man" in such a social milieu was required by society to act as such and the outside world surrounding his psyche supportive of such delusions of grandeur and megalomania were bound to keep him strong and omniscient. But this is no longer the state of man, if ever it was a fact.

Man, who published the initial letters and bylaws as an enterprise. Man of the bible; men of the Supreme Court, Generals, CEOs and Governors. Man who enforced male dominance by law and force is now speechless and lost for words both in his "castle" and in the workplace. In fact, his psyche is torn as the history of building empires and corporations is feminized by equality clauses and fairness across the board. In the political sphere of it all, man's female partner, an oftentimes silent partner, provides the nurturance and feminine perspective all the while raising children and managing the home.

Men and Women

The presence of women since day one is just as relevant to our patriarchal society and its historical foundation. If the past defines today, women were the object of mans' affection and vice versa; man, guilty of misogyny and sexism by default man was only a player in the much larger game of economy, politics, business and the family. Social history is shared by both sexes. This new social modification redefines the cliché "behind every successful man there is a woman."

We can recall the past male image of cowboy, knight and farmer and remember the wives, daughters, mothers and sisters in the forefront and the background. The 'damsel in distress:," the dating manuals encouraging man to be debonair and romantic; the days of courting, engagement and marriage involved "two to tango." Man alone is not guilty for our patriarchy and if so, he is today a part of the solution to gaining equality for both sexes.

Men and women together reinforce "macho" stereotypes. Today we can redefine the rules of engagement, of netiquette, sexual relations and the political correctness of communication and cultural sensitivity training. Together we can transcend the dichotomous thinking that stifles communication. Yesterday's man of having to "man up" or be the "macho man" is unnecessary in this fair and just demand for equality.

These stereotypes of man as men and brute forces of nature and testosterone laden bullies, are labels that lead to role-confusion, malice and large populations of men incarcerated, addicted, mentally ill and impotent; ostracized in the community. Their partners left to fend for themselves, their children and place in society. The Male included in the neo-feminist rhetoric, as an equal partner at home and work provides a genuine opportunity to heal and restore family and relationships for both sexes.

Let's skip this language of reverse discrimination while the issues of what defines man and woman are being exploited and redirected. As "we" sign women on to governmental, corporate, military and sports contracts let us revisit the inclusion clause and be mindful of the new generation of men, evolved and tempered by the feminist mystique as defined by men (nurturing, calculating and shrewd). Let us together help the new generations of men and women alike make sense of their new roles in life planning, parenting, sharing of the chores and a changing of the guard; from wall street to the farm, from the white house to town hall.

The real challenge to a liberated and fair clause society is the structure of men's secure fraternal social ties to the good ole boy network, e-spirit de corps of masculinity and male camaraderie in agencies that were built on strength, competition, power and control. These male tendencies, by nature, are being transformed by the feminine mystique and inclusion clauses. If the sorority sisters and feminist representatives are to reach their goals without distancing from male politics at a new level, men must be invited into the conversation as a co-conspirator and equal partner.

CONCLUSION

Man as hunter awaits the change as he has always waited for the next move in war, at play and in life. Man's competitive nature is never exempt from social upheaval; he fights or takes flight and today is on a quiet platform listening and observing while our institutional blueprints change their colors.

May the oxytocin prevalent in women's innate need to tend and appease meet our testosterone driven nature halfway to the finish line. Perhaps cooperate competitively or compete cooperatively, as fair share decides what is best to attain a mutual benefit of trust and respect for both sexes. Let the remnants of man transform as equal in the forum of discourse that is shaping this new world order of gender politics, trans-gender goals and gender role reassignments. Today we are on a new horizon in relationship building and communication. The vision, the dream, the script and the playbook of its future have to be created in a unified perspective—male and female.

FURTHER READINGS

Aulette, Judith R. *Changing American Families*. 3rd ed. Upper Saddle River, NJ: Pearson, 2009.

Coontz, Stephanie. *The Way We Never Were*. New York: Basic Books, 2000.

Coontz, Stephanie. *Marriage: A History*. New York: Penguin, 2006.

Rubin, Lillian. *Families on the Fault Line: America's Working Class Speaks About the Family, the Economy, Race, and Ethnicity*. New York: HarperCollins, 1994.

Family in Decline

Chapter 5

American Family Decline, 1960–1990: A Review and Appraisal

By David Popenoe

Family decline in America continues to be a debatable issue, especially in academia. Several scholars have recently written widely-distributed trade books reinforcing what has become the establishment position of many family researchers-that family decline is a "myth," and that "the family is not declining, it is just changing". Many academic books (and dozens of articles) have echoed the same theme, including one outspokenly entitled The Myth of Family Decline.

(…) My view is just the opposite. Like the majority of Americans, I see the family as an institution in decline and believe that this should be a cause for alarm—especially as regards the consequences for children. In some sense, of course, the family has been declining since the beginning of recorded history—yet we've survived. But often over-looked in the current debate is the fact that recent family decline is unlike historical family change. It is something unique, and much more serious. The argument for this position, and the evidence to support it, are provided below.

OVERVIEW

At the beginning of this century there was a widespread belief that the child rearing functions of the family, coming to full fruition, would stamp the character of our era. In this century's first decade, for instance, the famous Swedish feminist Ellen Key (1909) wrote a book called "The Century of the Child". Translated into several languages, it quickly became a European best seller. Key maintained that the twentieth century would be focused on the expansion of children's rights, most importantly the right of the child to have a happy, stable home with devoted parents. The American historian Arthur W. Calhoun (1945) reiterated this theme in the first major history of the American family, published in 1917–1919: "On the whole it cannot be doubted that America

David Popenoe, "American Family Decline, 1960–1990: A Review and Appraisal," *Journal of Marriage and Family*, vol. 55, no. 3, pp. 527–542. Copyright © 1993 by John Wiley & Sons, Inc. Reprinted with permission.

has entered upon 'the century of the child' .... As befits a civilization with a broadening future, the child is becoming the center of life" (p. 131).

By midcentury a higher proportion of American children were growing up in stable, two-parent families than at any other time in American history. To this degree these early commentators were prescient. Whatever else it may have been, the decade of the 50s was certainly an era of high birthrates, high marriage rates, low divorce rates, and general family" togetherness" and stability. Children were highly valued by their parents and by their culture. It was also, of course, the heyday of the so-called "traditional nuclear family," the family consisting of a heterosexual, monogamous, life-long marriage in which there is a sharp division of labor, with the female as full-time housewife and the male as primary provider and ultimate authority.

But since the 1950s the situation for children, far from being the focus of national concern, has in many ways grown progressively worse. In the past 30 years, with remarkable speed, we have moved ever further from the position of a family, and a culture, that places children at the center of life. As we approach the end of the twentieth century, it appears that early prognosticators of a child-centered society were well wide of the mark.

The abrupt and rapid change in the situation of families and children that began in the 1960s caught most family scholars by surprise. At first there was great reluctance to admit that a dramatic change was underway. But, although they may differ about its meaning and social consequences, scholars of all ideological persuasions now view the change as momentous and profound. The liberal authors of a recent history of the American family put it this way: "What Americans have witnessed since 1960 are fundamental challenges to the forms, ideals, and role expectations that have defined the family for the last century and a half" (Mintz & Kellogg, 1988, p. 204). A conservative family scholar similarly opined: "The social assumptions that had guided human conduct in this nation for centuries were tossed aside with a casualness and speed that were astonishing" (Carlson, 1987, p. 1).

In what ways has the family in America actually changed over the past 30 years? Below, I sketch out the answer to this question with the help of the latest statistics (from the U.S. Census, unless otherwise indicated) and recent social science findings. Data are presented contrasting the American family situation in the late 1980s and early 1990s with that in the late 1950s and early 1960s, a period just prior to the time when the massive family changes began to occur. The data support the thesis, I shall argue, that this period has witnessed an unprecedented decline of the family as a social institution. Families have lost functions, social power, and authority over their members. They have grown smaller in size, less stable, and shorter in life span. People have become less willing to invest time, money, and energy in family life, turning instead to investments in themselves.

Moreover, there has been a weakening of child-centeredness in American society and culture. Familism as a cultural value has diminished. The past few decades have witnessed, for the first time in America history, the rise of adult-only communities, the massive voting down of local funds for education, and a growth in the attitude of "no children allowed." Both in the political process and in the market place, children's issues have been ignored.

WHAT IS A "FAMILY"?

What, exactly, is the institutional entity that is declining? Answering such a question may seem a spectacularly unexciting way to begin, but the term family has been used in so many ambiguous ways in recent years that the explanation of its use has special importance. Indeed, the term has even become controversial over how it should be defined, as is now well known, helped to prematurely end the 1980 White House The struggle Conference on Families. Some participants wanted the term to refer to the traditional family; others wanted it to include, for example, a homosexual couple living together. How the term is defined for legislative purposes, of course, makes a significant difference. A unit defined as a family may be in line to receive such special benefits as housing, health care, and sick leave. The controversy over defining the family is very much alive today in classrooms, conferences, and legislatures across the nation.

Family is a "nice" term, one with which we all want to be associated in some way, and therein lies a problem. The term has become a sponge concept, with multiple meanings that can include two friends who live together, the people who work in an office, a local unit of the Mafia, and the family of man. I wish to restrict the term to its most common meaning of a domestic group—a group in which people typically live together in a household and function as a cooperative unit, particularly through the sharing of economic resources, in the pursuit of domestic activities. Within this meaning of a domestic group, I do not use the term family to refer exclusively to parents and their children, as some traditionalists would have it. But neither do I include any two or more people who happen to live together, such as roommates or even adults who merely have an intimate relationship of some kind. I define the family as a relatively small domestic group of kin (or people in a kin-like relationship) consisting of at least one adult and one dependent person. This definition is meant to refer particularly to an intergenerational unit that includes (or once included) children, but handicapped and infirm adults, the elderly, and other dependents also qualify. And it is meant to include single-parent families, stepfamilies, non-married and homosexual couples, and all other family types in which dependents are involved.

This definition is not all-purpose, and will not please everyone. Many will doubtless wish that I had included a married couple with no dependents. But it is important to distinguish a mere intimate relationship between adults, no matter how permanent, from the group that results when children or other dependents are present; this is the important point missed by scholars who want us to redefine the family as a sexually bonded or sexually based primary relationship.

Conservatives ill bemoan the fact that the traditional nuclear family is not the focus. Others will object that the definition focuses on a discrete domestic group, arguing that parents need not be living together (as in the case of divorce). And there will be concern that the definition is not broad enough to include many family forms prominent in other cultures, such as that consisting of several kin groups living in a single, complex household. If the definition were more inclusive, however, it would be less meaningful. The domestic group of kin with dependents is its focus; this lies at the heart of most people's meaning of family.

Turning from the question of what a family is to what a family does, the domestic kin groups should be thought of as carrying out certain functions (or meeting certain needs) for society. These functions or needs, as spelled out in almost every textbook of marriage and the family, have traditionally included the following: procreation (reproduction) and the socialization of children; the provision to its members of care, affection, and companionship; economic cooperation (the sharing of economic resources, especially shelter, food, and clothing); and sexual regulation (so that sexual activity in a society is not completely permissive and people are made responsible for the consequences of their sexuality.)

Saying that the institution of the family is declining is to say that the domestic kin groups are weakening in carrying out these functions or meeting these societal needs. In other words, for whatever reasons, families are not as successfully meeting the needs of society as they once were (this generalization, of course, does not mean all families). There are many possible reasons for such weakening. It may be that societies are asking less of family members because functions the family has traditionally carried out are no longer as important as they once were, because family members are less motivated to carry out family functions, because other institutions have taken over some of these functions, and so on. These are all matters that must be explored.

AMERICAN FAMILY CHANGE, 1960–1990

To put the following family trends in perspective, it is important to keep in mind two points. The first is that many of these trends, such as rising divorce and decreasing fertility, had their inception well before 1960; indeed, some have been evident in industrializing nations for centuries. What happened, beginning in the 1960s, is that they either suddenly accelerated, as in the case of divorce, or suddenly reversed direction, as in the case of fertility. The divorce rate had been going up for 100 years, for example, before it rose so precipitously in the sixties.

The second point to consider is that the decade of the 1950s was an unusual period, and should be used as a baseline for comparative purposes only with caution. It is a period that requires as much explanation as the period that followed it. The fertility rate, for example, which had been decreasing for more than 100 years, dramatically reversed its direction in the late 1940s, only to dramatically return again, beginning in the 1960s, to the very low fertility levels of the 1930s.

The Number of Children

Although far from being the most important dimension of family decline, the decline in the number of children in the typical family, and in our society as a whole, is assuredly one of the most carefully studied. Of course a family (and a society) that has fewer children can be just as child-centered, and value children just as much, as a family with more children. The issue of quantity versus quality is real and important. One feature of the traditional nuclear family that a rose with industrialization and urbanization was that it had fewer children than prior family types precisely because it valued, and wanted to do more for each child. At some point, however, quantity does become an issue. A society needs a certain number of children just to continue from generation to generation.

Since the late 1950s, childbearing among American women, both as an ideal and a practice, has rapidly lost popularity. As a practice, there has been a sharp drop in the total fertility rate. In the late 1950s, the average American woman had 3.7 children over the course of her life. Thirty years later this rate had been cut by nearly one-half. In 1990, the average woman had only 1.9 children, below the figure of 2.1 necessary for population replacement and below the relatively low fertility levels found in the first half of the century. (Following the small and probably temporary baby boom of the last few years, the 1992 total fertility rate stood slightly higher, at 2.0).

In the early 1960s, when the trend of lower fertility of the last 3 decades first became evident, the favored interpretation of demographers was that women's desired family size had dropped; also, mainly because women started having their first child later in life, fewer women ever reached their desired family size. In other words, it was not that fewer women were having children but that women were having fewer children. Because child postponement has become so extensive, however, some demographers have predicted that between 20% and 25% of the most recent cohorts will remain completely childless, and that nearly 50% will either be childless or have only one child. A far higher percentage of women than this say they want to have children-in fact two children-but the prevailing theory is that they are waiting so long to have them that the desires of many will never be fulfilled. Although the childless estimate of 20% to 25% has recently been lowered to around 15% to 20%, it is clear that a substantial portion of young women today will reach the end of their child-bearing years never having given birth.

This change is connected with a dramatic, and probably historically unprecedented, decrease in positive feelings toward parenthood and motherhood. Between 1957 and 1976, the percentage of adults who felt positive about parenthood-that is, who viewed parenthood as a role that could fulfill their major values—dropped from 58 to 44. It has probably dropped still lower today. And between 1970 and 1983, the percentage of women who gave the answer "being a mother, raising a family" to the question, "What do you think are the two or three most enjoyable things about being a woman today?" dropped from 53 to 26 (New York Times Poll, 1983). These attitudinal changes are associated with a remarkable decrease in the stigma associated with childlessness. In less than 2 decades, from 1962 to 1980, the proportion of American mothers who stated that "all couples should have children" declined by nearly half, from 84% to 43%.

For all these reasons, children today make up a much smaller proportion of the American population than ever before (a situation that is accentuated by increased longevity). Whereas, in 1960, children under 18 constituted more than one-third of the population, their proportion has now dropped to only a little over one-quarter. This need not be a cause for concern about the imminent depopulation of America; much of our population growth today comes from immigration, and new immigrants tend to have a higher fertility rate than the native population. Also, in environmental terms, if not economically, it can plausibly be argued that we have become an overpopulated society. Nevertheless, the continuing decline in the number of children has significant ramifications for the priority our society gives to children, and for the cultural attitudes we hold concerning the importance of children in the overall scheme of life.

Marital Roles

Apart from their declining number, a large percentage of children who are born today grow up in a remarkably different family setting than did their forebears of 30 years ago. Major elements of the traditional nuclear family have almost become a thing of the past. First, and in some ways foremost, the marital roles associated with the traditional nuclear family have altered. As a cultural ideal, the doctrine of separate spheres, in which adult women were expected to be full-time house-wife-mothers while their husbands were the breadwinners, has virtually ended. In 1960, 42% of all families had a sole male breadwinner; by 1988, this figure had dropped to 15%. A recent survey found that some 79% of adult Americans agreed that "it takes two paychecks to support a family today." And only 27% favored a return to "at least one parent raising children full-time" (Mass Mutual American Family Values Study, 1989).

Today, mothers are in the labor market to al-most the same extent as non mothers, with the fastest increases occurring for mothers of young children. In 1960, only 19% of married women (husband present) with children under 6 years of age were in the labor force full- or part-time or were looking for work. By 1990, that figure had climbed to 59%. For married women with children 6 to 17 years of age, the change has been equally spectacular. In all, 57% of women were in the labor force in 1990, up from 38% in 1960. (It should be noted that this entry of married women into the labor force has been accompanied by a decline in male labor force participation, especially among older males; between 1960 and 1988, the percentage of males aged 65 and over in the civilian labor force declined from 33 to 16; for males aged 55 to 64, the decline was from 87% to 67%;.)

Family Structure and Marital Dissolution

At the same time that our society has disclaimed the role of wives in the traditional nuclear family, it has also heavily discarded the basic structure of that family type—two natural parents who stay together for life. Put another way, we have not only rejected the traditional nuclear family but are in the process of rejecting the nuclear family it-self-a sort of throwing out of the baby with the bath water. Although the two trends are not necessarily causally related, they have at least been closely associated temporally. In 1960, 88% of children lived with two parents; by 1989, only 73% did so. Even more telling, in 1960, 73% of all children lived with two natural parents both married only once. This figure was projected to drop to 56% by 1990.

One family type that has replaced the intact family of biological parents, and currently is the focus of much social research and public discussion, is the stepparent family. But the fastest growing new family type in recent years has been the single-parent family (almost 90% of which are headed by women). In 1960, only 9% of all children under 18 lived with a lone parent. This was about the same percentage as lived with a lone parent in 1900; at that time, however, 27% of the single-parent children lived with their father. By 1990, the proportion of single-parent children had jumped to 24%, or nearly one-quarter of all children in America (the comparable figures for black children only are 22% in 1960 and 55% in 1990.).

The above data refer to a snapshot of the population at a single point in time. More dramatic still are the altered chances that children will live in a single-parent family sometime during their lifetimes. Of children born between 1950 and 1954, only 19% of whites (48% of blacks) had spent some time living in single-parent families by the time they reached age 17. But for white children born in 1980, this figure was projected by one estimate to be 70% (94% for black children). Another way of measuring this phenomenon is the proportion of their childhood that children can be expected to live with both parents. For white children born between 1950 and 1954, that figure is 92% (78% for blacks). For children born in 1980, the figure drops to 69% (41% for blacks).

One of the main factors accounting for the increase in single-parent families is the growing incidence and acceptance of divorce, especially divorce involving children. Many different divorce rates are in use, and all show striking increases. In number of divorces per 1000 existing marriages, the United States divorce rate in 1960 was 9. That figure by 1987 had more than doubled to 21. In number of divorced persons in the population per 1000 married persons (with spouse present), the 1960 figure was 35. That figure nearly quadrupled by 1988 to 133.

Perhaps the most widely-discussed divorce rate is the probability that a marriage will end in divorce. For white females, this probability increased from about 20% in 1960 to 45% by 1980, leading to the often heard statement that nearly one out of two marriages contracted today will end in divorce. With under-reporting taken into account, and including marital separation along with divorce, other scholars have placed the probability of dissolution of a first marriage contracted today at about 60%.

It is true that divorce has replaced death as a dissolver of marriages. In times past, the early death of one spouse often ended a union in which children were involved, although single-parent families were never so common as they are today. In 1900, for example, only 2% of single-parent children lived with a divorced parent, and 3.4% with a never-married parent. A landmark of sorts was passed in 1974, when for the first year in American history more marriages ended in divorce than in death. According to data for the mid-1980s, death now causes only 78% as many marital dissolutions as divorce.

The causes of the rising divorce rate in modem societies are, of course, multiple. They include growing affluence that weakens the family's traditional economic bond, higher psychological expectations for marriage today, secularization, and the stress of changing gender roles. To some extent, divorce feeds upon itself. With more divorce occurring, the more normal it becomes, with fewer negative sanctions to oppose it and more potential partners available. One of the significant changes of recent years is the rising acceptance of divorce, especially when children are involved. Divorces in which children are involved used to be in the category of the unthinkable. Today, children are only a minor inhibitor of divorce, although more so when the children are male than female. As one measure of the acceptance of divorce involving children, the proportion of persons who disagreed with the statement, "when there are children in the family, parents should stay together even if they don't get along," jumped from 51% to 82% between 1962 and 1985. In other words, less than one-fifth of those asked believe that the presence of children should deter parents from breaking up. (…)

Another reason for the increase in single-parent families is that many more of today's families start out with just one parent; the children are born out-of-wedlock and the father is absent. In 1960, only 5% of all births (22% of black births) occurred to unmarried mothers. By 1990, the number had climbed to 24%, or nearly a quarter of all children born (62% of black births). This is the highest national rate of out-of-wedlock births ever recorded in the United States; it is related to what has been referred to as "a disappearing act by fathers". Clearly, then, family instability has come to be a dominant characteristic of our time. If childhood experiences and adult risks of marital disruption are taken into account, only a minority of children born today are likely to grow up in an in-tact, two-parent family, and also, as adults, to form and maintain such a family. And because the children of broken homes, compared to the children of intact families, have a much higher chance as adults of having unstable marriages of their own, the future in this regard does not look bright.

Marriage

A widespread retreat from marriage is another of the major family changes of our time. In the sense of being postponed, the institution of marriage itself has been in steep decline in recent years. With a median age at first marriage of 24.1 years, young women in 1991 were marrying nearly 4 years later than their mothers (the median age at first marriage was 20.3 in 1960). Thus, between 1960 and 1990, the proportion of women aged 20 to 24 who had never married more than doubled, from 28.4% to 62.8%; for women aged 25 to 29, the increase was even greater from 10.5% to 31.1%.

The proportion ever marrying has also dropped, but not as substantially. For females born in the period from 1938 to 1942, and thus reaching the marital age around 1960, a remark-able 97% (of those surviving until age 16) could be expected to marry at some time during their lives. For females born in 1983, however, the chances of ever marrying are calculated to be slightly less than 90%. For certain segments of the population, the proportion expected eventually to marry is even lower: only about 80% for women with a college education, for example, and 75% for black women.

It is important to point out that both the median age of marriage and the proportion ever marrying have returned to about where they stood at the end of the last century. The 1950s were, therefore, an anomaly in this respect. Also, the older one's age at marriage, the lower the chances of eventual divorce, at least until about age 30. In this sense, marriage at older ages is beneficial for children and for society. It does not follow, however, that societies with older average ages at marriage have a lower divorce rate. The nation with the oldest average age of marriage today is Sweden, but it also has one of the highest divorce rates.

The marriage rate is expected to drop further in the future. One reason is that attitudes toward the unmarried adult have changed dramatically in recent decades. In 1957, 80% of the population agreed with the statement, "for a woman to remain unmarried she must be sick, neurotic or immoral;" by 1978, the proportion agreeing had dropped to 25%. Still, the proportion of the population that expects to marry remains very high at 90%, and has shown almost no decline since 1960.

The psychological character of the marital relationship has changed substantially over the years. Traditionally, marriage has been understood as a social obligation –an institution designed mainly for economic security and procreation. Today, marriage is understood mainly as a path toward self-fulfillment. One's own self-development is seen to require a significant other, and marital partners are picked primarily to be personal companions. Put another way, marriage is becoming deinstitutionalized. No longer comprising a set of norms and social obligations that are widely enforced, marriage today is a voluntary relationship that individuals can make and break at will. As one indicator of this shift, laws regulating marriage and divorce have become increasingly more lax.

Apart from the high rate of marital dissolution, there is growing evidence that the quality of married life in America has taken a turn for the worse. There has always been a strong relationship between being married and being relatively happy in life. But an analysis of survey data over the years between 1972 and 1989 indicates that this relationship is weakening. There is an increasing proportion of reportedly happy never-married men and younger never-married women, and a decreasing proportion of reportedly happy married women. Thus to be happy, men may not need marriage as much as they once did, and fewer women are finding happiness through marriage.

Nonfamily Living

(…) Along with the high divorce rate and the residential independence of the elderly, early home-leaving is a major factor that lies behind the tremendous increase in nonfamily households and nonfamily living. Nonfamily households (defined by the U.S. Census as a household maintained by a person living alone or with one or more persons to whom he or she is not related) amounted to 29% of all households in 1990, compared to just 15% in 1960. About 85% of nonfamily house-holds consist of just one person. The rapid 20- year upward trend of nonfamily households came to a temporary halt in the period from 1986 to 1987 (Waldrop, 1988).

Also on the rise has been non-marital cohabitation, or unmarried couples of the opposite sex living together. In part, the declining marriage rate has been offset by the increasing cohabitation rate. While non-marital couples still make up only a small proportion of all households (3.1% in 1990), their numbers are growing. The 1990 figure of 2,856,000 unmarried couple households is more than 6 times the 1960 figure of 439,000. More importantly, the proportion of first marriages preceded by cohabitation increased from only 8% for marriages in the late 1960s to about 50% for marriages today. There is evidence that life for young adults in a nonfamily household may become a self-fulfilling prophecy; not only does it reflect a flight from family life but it may actually promote such a flight. Especially for young women, it has been found that living away from home prior to marriage changes attitudes and plans away from family and toward individual concerns. Also, living independently may make it more difficult, when marriage finally does take place, to shift from purely individual concerns to a concern for the needs and desires of other family members, especially children. As for non-marital cohabitation, it has been shown that levels of certainty about the relationship are substantially lower than for marriage.

There is also a growing body of evidence that premarital cohabitation is associated with proneness for divorce, although the effect may be declining with time. Cohabitation does not seem to serve very well the function of a trial marriage, or of a system that leads to stronger marriages through weeding out those who find that, after living together, they are unsuitable for each other. More likely, a lack of commitment at the beginning may signal a lack of commitment at the end.

Up until the past 30 years, partly due to steadily increasing longevity, Americans had actually spent more years in marriage and as parents with each passing year. But between 1960 and 1980, mainly due to markedly lower fertility and higher divorce rates, the absolute number of years spent in these family statuses declined for the first time in American history. The proportion of adult lives spent as a spouse, a parent, or a member of a conjugal family unit declined even more, reaching the lowest point in history. As early as 1800, the proportion of one's life spent with spouse and children was an estimated 56%; it rose to a high of 62% in 1960, and reached an all-time low of 43% in 1980. It has been estimated that white women in the period from 1940 to 1945 spent nearly 50% of their lives in a marriage (including both first marriages and remarriages); by the period from 1975 to 1980, this figure had dropped to just 43%.

FAMILY CHANGE AS FAMILY DECLINE

(…) The problem is not only that the family as an institution has declined, but also that a specific family form-the traditional nuclear family-has declined. And therein lies the basis for much ideological conflict. The 1950s hegemony of the traditional nuclear family helped to fuel the modem women's movement. Reacting strongly to the lingering male dominance of this family form, as well as to its separate-sphere removal of women from the labor market, the women's movement came to view the traditional nuclear family in very negative terms. Today, those who believe in less male dominance and greater equality for women-and that includes most academics and other intellectuals, including myself—share the views of the women's movement in favoring an egalitarian family form, with substantial economic independence for wives. From this perspective, the movement away from the traditional nuclear family is regarded as progress, not decline.

Speaking of family decline under these ideological circumstances, therefore, is seen to be implicitly favoring a discredited family form, one that oppresses women. Indeed, the term decline has been used most forcefully by those conservatives who tend to view all recent family change as negative, and who have issued a clarion call for a return to the traditional nuclear family. But properly used, the term decline should not carry such ideological baggage. To conclude empirically that the family as an institution is declining shouldn't automatically link one to a particular ideology of family forms or gender equality. The two facets of decline-the weakening of the traditional form of the family and the weakening of the family as an institution-must be disaggregated. It is possible after all, at least theoretically, for the family to have become a stronger institution in its shift to a more egalitarian form.

For me, the term "decline" is important because it provides a "best fit" for many of the changes that have taken place. These changes, in my view, clearly indicate that the family as an institution has weakened. A main cause of this weakening may or may not be the shift of the family away from its traditional nuclear form; that is some-thing requiring further investigation. Those who believe that the family has not declined, on the other hand, must logically hold one of two positions—either that the family has strengthened, or that its institutional power within society has remained unchanged. I believe that one is very hard put, indeed, to find supporting evidence for either of these two positions.

Let us review the evidence supporting the idea of family decline, or weakening. The evidence can be amassed in three broad areas - demographic, institutional, and cultural. In the course of this review I hope that the reader will suspend, for the moment, the automatic reaction of associating decline only with that which is negative. Some of the following aspects of family decline, as discussed below, certainly can be considered beneficial, or positive.

Demographic

Family groups have declined as a demographic reality. They have decreased in size and become a smaller percentage of all households; they survive as groups for a shorter period of time and they incorporate a smaller percentage of the average person's life course. Family groups are being replaced in people's lives by nonfamily groups-people living alone, without children, with an unrelated individual, in an institution, and so forth.

This trend, of course, is not proof that the family institution is declining. Religion does not necessarily decline with a smaller number of churches and synagogues; education does not necessarily decline with fewer schools. But smaller numbers surely, by the same token, do not help to bolster the belief that the family is strengthening.

Institutional

There are three key dimensions to the strength of an institution: the institution's cohesion or the hold which it has over its members, how well it performs its functions, and the power it has in society relative to other institutions. The evidence suggests that the family as an institution has weakened in each of these respects.

First, individual family members have become more autonomous and less bound by the group; the group as a whole, therefore, has become less cohesive. A group or organization is strong (sometimes the phrase used is highly institutionalized) when it maintains close coordination over the internal relationships of members and directs their activities toward collective goals. In a strong group, the members are closely bound to the group and largely follow the group's norms and values. Families have clearly become weaker (less institutionalized) in this sense.

With more women in the labor market, for example, the economic interdependence between husbands and wives has been declining. Wives are less dependent on husbands for economics support; more are able, if they so desire, to go it alone. This means that wives are less likely to stay in bad marriages for economic reasons. And, indeed, some scholars have found a positive correlation between wives' income and the propensity to divorce—that is, the higher the wife's income, the greater the likelihood of divorce. By the same token, if a wife has economic independence (for example, through state welfare support), it is easier for a husband to abandon her if he so chooses. However one looks at it, and unfortunate though it may be, the decline of economic interdependence between husband and wife (primarily the economic dependence of the wife) appears to have led, in the aggregate, to weaker marital units as measured by higher rates of divorce and separation.

As the marital tie has weakened in many families, so also has the tie between parents and children. A large part of the history of childhood and adolescence in the twentieth century is the decline of parental influence and authority, and the growth in importance of both the peer group and the mass media. Typically, the influence of the mass media is conducted through the peer group. There are few parents today who will deny that parental influence over children is on the wane. Similarly, there is much less influence today of the elderly over their own children. For example, the proportion of the elderly seeing a child at least once a week declined by 25% between 1962 and 1984

The second dimension of family institutional decline is that the family is less able-and/or less willing-to carry out its traditional social functions. This is, in part, because it has become a less cohesive unit. The main family functions in re-cent times have been the procreation and socialization of children, the provision to its members of affection and companionship, sexual regulation, and economic cooperation. With a birthrate that is below the replacement level, it is demonstrably the case that the family has weakened in carrying out the function of procreation. A strong case can also be made that the family has weakened in conducting the function of child socialization. "Since 1960 the conjugal family has begun to divest itself of care for children in much the same way that it did earlier for the elderly". Quantitative measures of such divestiture are the absenteeism rate of fathers, the decline in the amount of time that parents spend with their children, and the growing proportion of a child's life that is spent alone, with peers, in day care, or in school.

A decline in the provision of affection and companionship among adult family members is more difficult to measure, although some data mentioned above seem to suggest that such a decline has taken place. It is difficult to deny, however, that, in sheer number, social ties to nonrelated friends have gained, while social ties to family members have dropped. Measures of this are late marriage, increased single living, high divorce, and fewer family households.

By almost everyone's reckoning, marriage today is a more fragile institution than ever before precisely because it is based mainly on the provision of affection and companionship. When these attributes are not provided, the marriage often dissolves. The chances of that happening today are near a record high.

A decline of the family regulation of sexual behavior is one of the hallmarks of the past 30 years. Against most parents' wishes, young people have increasingly engaged in premarital sex, at ever younger ages. And against virtually all spousal wishes, the amount of sexual infidelity among married couples has seemingly increased. (Solid empirical support for this proposition is difficult to find, but it is certainly the belief of most Americans).

Finally, the function of the family in economic cooperation has diminished substantially, as noted above. The family is less a pooled bundle of economic resources, and more a business partnership between two adults (and one which, in most states, can unilaterally be broken at any time.) Witness, for example, the decline of joint checking accounts and the rise of prenuptial agreements.

With reference to children, it once was the case that the great majority of households in the nation were family households including children. This meant that most income to households was shared in such a way that children were beneficiaries. Today, households with children make up only 35% of the total, a decline from 49% in 1960. Income to the great majority of households is not shared with children, and therein lies one of the reasons why children are economically falling behind others, and why 40% of the poor in America today are children.

The third dimension of family institutional decline is the loss of power to other institutional groups. In recent centuries, with the decline of agriculture and the rise of industry, the family has lost power to the workplace and, with the rise of mandatory formal education, it has lost power to the school. The largest beneficiary of the transfer of power out of the family in recent years has been the state. State agencies increasingly have the family under surveillance, seeking compliance for increasingly restrictive state laws covering such issues as child abuse and neglect, wife abuse, tax payments, and property maintenance. The fact that many of these laws are designed to foster the egalitarian treatment of family members, the protection of children, and the advancement of public welfare, should not detract from their denial of power to the family unit.

Cultural

Family decline has also occurred in the sense that familism as a cultural value has weakened in favor of such values as self-fulfillment and egalitarianism. In other words, the value placed on the family in our culture, compared to competing values, has diminished. Familism refers to the belief in a strong sense of family identification and loyalty, mutual assistance among family members, a concern for the perpetuation of the family unit, and the subordination of the interests and personality of individual family members to the interests and welfare of the family group.

It is true that most Americans still loudly proclaim family values, and there is no reason to question their sincerity about this. The family ideal is still out there. Yet apart from the ideal, the value of family has steadily been chipped away. The percentage of Americans who believe that "the family should stay together for the sake of the children" has declined precipitously. And fewer Americans believe that it is important to have children, to be married if you do, or even to be married, period.

REFERENCES

Aquilino, W. S. (1991). Family structure and home-leaving: A further specification of the relationship. *Journal of Marriage and the Family, 53*, 999–1010.

Bane, M. J. (1976). *Here to stay: American families in the twentieth century*. New York: Basic Books.

Bane, M. J., & Jargowsky, P. A. (1988). The links between government policy and family structure: What matters and what doesn't. In A. Cherlin (Ed.). *The changing American family and public policy* (pp. 219–255). Washington, DC: Urban Institute Press.

Bellah, R. N., Madsen, R., Sullivan, W. M., Swidler, A., & Tipton, S. M. (1985). *Habits of the heart: Individualism and commitment in American life*. Berkeley: University of California Press.

Bianchi, S. M. (1990). America's children: Mixed prospects. *Population Bulletin, 45*, 1–43.

Bloom, D. E., & Trussell, J. (1984). What are the determinants of delayed childbearing and permanent childlessness in the United States? *Demography, 21*, 591–611.

Booth, A., & Johnson, D. (1988). Premarital cohabitation and marital success. *Journal of Family Issues, 9*, 255–272.

Bumpass, L. L. (1990). What's happening to the family? Interactions between demographic and institutional change. *Demography, 27*, 483–498.

Bumpass, L. L., & Sweet, J. A. (1989). National estimates of cohabitation: Cohort levels and union stability. *Demography, 26*, 615–625.

Bumpass, L. L., Sweet, J. A., & Cherlin, A. (1991). The role of cohabitation in declining marriage rates. *Journal of Marriage and the Family, 53*, 913–927.

Calhoun, A. W. (1945). *A Social History of the American Family* (Vol. 3). New York: Barnes & Noble. (Original work published 1917–1919).

Carlson, A. C. (1987). Treason of the professions: The case of home economics. *The Family in America, 1*, 6.

Cherlin, A. J. (1981). *Marriage, divorce, remarriage*. Cambridge: Harvard University Press.

Cherlin, A. J. (1992). *Marriage, divorce, remarriage* (rev. ed). Cambridge: Harvard University Press.

Cherlin, A., & Furstenberg, F. F., Jr. (1988). The changing European family: Lessons for the American reader. *Journal of Family Issues, 9*, 291–297.

Coontz, S. (1992). *The way we never were*. New York: Basic Books.

Davis, K. (Ed.). (1985). *Contemporary marriage: Comparative perspectives on a changing institution*. New York: Russell Sage Foundation.

D'Emilio, J., & Freedman, E. B. (1988). *Intimate matters: A history of sexuality in America*. New York: Harper & Row.

DeMaris, A. J., & Rao, K. V. (1992). Premarital cohabitation and subsequent marital stability in the United States: A reassessment. *Journal of Marriage and the Family, 54*, 178–190.

Dobson, J., & Bauer, G. L. (1990). *Children at risk*. Dallas: Word Publishing.

Dornbusch, S. M., & Strober, M. H. (Eds.). (1988). Feminism, children and the new families. New York: Guilford Press.

Espenshade, T. J. (1985a). Marriage trends in America: Estimates, implications, and underlying causes. *Population and Development Review, 11*, 193–245.

Espenshade, T. J. (1985b). The recent decline of American marriage. In K. Davis, (Ed.), *Contemporary marriage: Comparative perspectives on a changing institution* (pp. 53–90). New York: Russell Sage Foundation.

Friedan, B. (1963). *The feminine mystique*. New York: W. W. Norton.

Fuchs, V. R., & Reklis, D. M. (1992). America's children: Economic perspectives and policy options. *Science, 255*, 41–46.

Furstenberg, F. F., Jr. (1990). Divorce and the American family. *Annual Review of Sociology, 16*, 379–403.

Glendon, M. A. (1989). *The transformation of family law*. Chicago: University of Chicago Press.

Glenn, N. (Ed.). (1987). The state of the American family. [Special issue]. *Journal of Family Issues, 8* (4).

Glenn, N. (1991). The recent trend in marital success in the United States. *Journal of Marriage and the Family, 53*, 261–270.

Glenn, N. D., & Weaver, C. N. (1988). The changing relationship of marital status to reported happiness. *Journal of Marriage and the Family, 50*, 317–324.

Glick, P. C. (1984). Marriage, divorce, and living arrangements: Prospective changes. *Journal of Family Issues, 5*, 7–26.

Glick, P. C. (1988). Fifty years of family demography: A record of social change. *Journal of Marriage and the Family, 50*, 861–873.

Goldscheider, C., & Goldscheider, F. K. (1987). Moving out and marriage: What do young adults expect? *American Sociological Review, 52*, 278–285.

Goldscheider, F. K., & Waite, L. J. (1991). *New families, no families? The transformation of the American home.* Berkeley, CA: University of California Press.

Goode, W. J. (1984). Individual investments in family relationships over the coming decades. *The Tocqueville Review, 6,* 51–83.

Gordon, L., & McLanahan, S. (1991). Single parenthood in 1900. *Journal of Family History, 16,* 97–116.

Greeley, A. M. (1991). *Faithful attraction: Discovering intimacy, love, and fidelity in American marriage.* New York: Tor.

Greenstein, T. N. (1990). Marital disruption and the employment of married women. *Journal of Marriage and the Family, 52,* 657–676.

Gubrium, J. F., & Holstein, J. A. (1990). *What is Family?* Mountain View, CA: Mayfield.

Hawes, J. M., & Hliner, N. R. (Eds.). (1985). *American Childhood.* Westport, CT: Greenwood Press.

Heaton, T. B. (1990). Marital stability throughout the child-rearing years. *Demography, 27,* 55–63.

Hernandez, D. J. (1988). Demographic trends and the living arrangements of children. In E. M. Hetherington & J. D. Arasteh (Eds.), *Impact of divorce, single parenting, and stepparenting on children* (pp. 3–22). Hillsdale, NJ: Lawrence Erlbaum.

Hewlett, S. A. (1991). *When the bough breaks: The cost of neglecting our children.* New York: Basic Books.

Hofferth, S. L. (1985). Updating children's life course. *Journal of Marriage and the Family, 47,* 93–115.

Inkeles, A. (1984). The responsiveness of family patterns to economic change in the United States. *The Tocqueville Review, 6,* 5–50.

Jacob, H. (1988). *Silent revolution: The transformation of divorce law in the United States.* Chicago: University of Chicago Press.

Kain, E. L. (1990). *The myth of family decline.* Lexington, MA: D. C. Heath.

Kertzer, D. I. (1991). Household history and sociological theory. *Annual Review of Sociology, 17,* 155–179.

Key, E. (1909). *The century of the child.* New York: G. P. Putnam's Sons.

Kitson, G. C., Babri, K. B., & Roach, M. J. (1985). Who divorces and why: A review. *Journal of Family Issues, 6,* 255–293.

Lasch, C. (1977). *Haven in a heartless world: The family besieged.* New York: Basic Books.

Lasch, C. (1978). *The culture of narcissism.* New York: W. W. Norton

Lee, G. R., Seccombe, K., & Shehan, C. L. (1991). Marital status and personal happiness: An analysis of trend data. *Journal of Marriage and the Family, 53,* 839–844.

Lenski, G., & Lenski, J. (1987). *Human societies.* New York: McGraw Hill.

Levitan, S. A., & Belous, R. S. (1981). *What's happening to the American family?* Baltimore: Johns Hopkins University Press.

Levitan, S. A., Belous, R. S., & Gallo, F. (1988). *What's happening to the American family?* (rev. ed.). Baltimore: Johns Hopkins University Press.

Levy, F., & Michel, R. C. (1991). *The economic future of American families.* Washington, DC: Urban Institute Press.

Louv, R. (1990). *Childhood's future.* Boston: Houghton Mifflin.

Martin, T. C., & Bumpass, L. L. (1989). Recent trends in marital disruption. *Demography, 26,* 37–51.

Mass Mutual American Family Values Study. (1989). Washington, DC: Mellman & Lazarus.

McFalls, J. A., Jr. (1990). The risks of reproductive impairment in the later years of childbearing. *Annual Review of Sociology, 16,* 491–519.

McLanahan, S., & Bumpass, L. (1988). Intergenerational consequences of family disruption. *American Journal of Sociology, 94,* 130–152.

Mintz, S., & Kellogg, S. (1988). *Domestic revolutions: A social history of American family life*. New York: Free Press.

Mitterauer, M., & Sieder, R. (1982). *The European family*. Chicago: University of Chicago Press.

Modell, J. (1989). *Into one's own: From youth to adulthood in the United States. 1920–1975*. Berkeley, CA: University of California Press.

Modell, J., Furstenberg, F. F., Jr., & Strong, D. (1978). The timing of marriage in the transition to adulthood: Continuity and change, 1860–1975. *American Journal of Sociology, 84*, S120-S150.

Morgan, S. P., Lye, D., & Condran, G. (1988). Sons, daughters, and the risk of marital disruption. *American Journal of Sociology, 94*, 110–129.

National Commission on Children. (1991). *Beyond rhetoric: A new American agenda for children and families*. Washington, DC: Author.

New York Times poll. (1983, December 4). *The New York Times*, p. A-1.

Peden, J. R., & Glahe, F. R. (Eds.). (1986). *The American family and the state*. San Francisco: Pacific Research Institute for Public Policy.

Phillips, R. (1988). *Putting asunder: A history of divorce in western society*. New York: Cambridge University Press.

Popenoe, D. (1987). Beyond the nuclear family: A statistical portrait of the changing family in Sweden. *Journal of Marriage and the Family, 49*, 173–183.

Popenoe, D. (1988). *Disturbing the nest: Family change and decline in modern societies*. New York: Aldine de Gruyter.

Preston, S. H. (1984). Children and the elderly: Divergent paths for America's dependents. *Demography, 21*, 435–457.

Preston, S. H. (1986). Changing values and falling birth rates. *Population and Development Review, 12* (Supplement), 176–195.

Rossi, A. S. (1980). Life span theories and women's lives. Signs: *Journal of Women in Culture and Society, 6*, 4–32.

Ryder, N. B. (1990). What is going to happen to American fertility? *Population and Development Review, 16*, 433–454.

Scanzoni, J., Polonko, K., Teachman, J., & Thompson, L. (1989). *The sexual bond. Rethinking families and close relationships*. Newbury Park, CA: Sage.

Schoen, R. (1987). The continuing retreat from marriage: Figures from the 1983 U.S. marital status life tables. *Social Science Research, 71*, 108–9.

Schoen, R. (1992). First unions and the stability of first marriages. *Journal of Marriage and the Family, 54*, 281–284.

Schoen, R., Urton, W., Woodrow, K., & Baj, J. (1985). Marriage and divorce in twentieth century American cohorts. *Demography, 22*, 101–114.

Select Committee on Children, Youth, and Families. (1989). *U.S. children and their families: Current conditions and recent trends*. Washington, DC: U.S. Government Printing Office.

Skolnick, A. (1991). *Embattled paradise: The American family in an age of uncertainty*. New York: Basic Books.

Stacey, J. (1990). *Brave new families*. New York: Basic Books.

Sugarman, S. D., & Kay, H. H. (Eds.). (1990). *Divorce reform at the crossroads*. New Haven: Yale University Press.

Sweet, J. A., & Bumpass, L. L. (1987). *American families and households*. New York: Russell Sage Foundation.

Thomson, E., & Colella, U. (1992). Cohabitation and marital stability. *Journal of Marriage and the Family, 54*, 259–267.

Thornton, A. (1989). Changing attitudes toward family issues in the United States. *Journal of Marriage and the Family, 51*, 873–893.

Thornton, A., & Freedman, D. (1982). Changing attitudes toward marriage and single life. *Family Planning Perspectives, 14*, 297–303.

van den Berghe, P. L. (1990). *Human family systems: An evolutionary view.* Prospect Heights, IL: Waveland Press. (Original work published 1979)

Veroff, J., Douvan, E., & Kulka, R. A. (1981). *The inner American: A self-portrait from 1957 to 1976.* New York: Basic Books.

Waite, L. J., Goldscheider, F. K., & Witsberger, C. (1986). Nonfamily living and the erosion of traditional family orientations among young adults. *American Sociological Review, 51*, 541–554.

Waite, L., & Lillard, L. A. (1991). Children and marital disruption. *American Journal of Sociology, 96*, 930–953.

Waldrop, J. (1988, March). The fashionable family. *American Demographics*, pp. 23–26.

Watkins, S. C., Menken, J. A., & Bongaarts, J. (1987). Demographic foundations of family change. *American Sociological Review, 52*, 346–358.

Westoff, C. F. (1986). Perspective on nuptiality and fertility. *Population and Development Review, 12* (Supplement), 155–170.

White, L. K. (1990). Determinants of divorce: A review of research in the eighties. *Journal of Marriage and the Family, 52*, 904–912.

Wilkie, J. R. (1991). The decline in men's labor force participation and income and the changing structure of family economic support. *Journal of Marriage and the Family, 53*, 111–122.

Yankelovich, D. (1981). *New rules: Searching for self-fulfillment in a world turned upside down.* New York: Random House.

Zelizer, V. A. (1985). *Pricing the priceless child: The changing social value of children.* New York: Basic Books.

Chapter 6

Good Riddance to "The Family": A Response to David Popenoe

By Judith Stacey

What "American Family Decline" makes clear is that Popenoe and I agree that "the family" is in decline, but we conceptualize "the family" in fundamentally incompatible ways. For Popenoe, the family is a positivist, empirical institution, amenable to a structural-functional definition. Popenoe struggles, with little consistency or success, to expand the conventional structural-functional definition of the nuclear family to accommodate critiques made by feminists and gay liberationists of the gender and sexual oppression in that family form. Thus, in order to encompass single-parent families, stepfamilies, cohabitants and homosexuals, he defines the family as "a relatively small domestic group of kin (or people in a kin-like relationship) consisting of at least one adult and one dependent person"(p. 529).

In contrast, I believe that no positivist definition of the family, however revisionist, is viable. Anthropological and historical studies convince me that the family is not an institution, but an ideological, symbolic construct that has a history and a politics. In the United States, as Popenoe con-cedes, this concept has been employed primarily to signify a heterosexual, conjugal, nuclear, domestic unit, ideally one with a male primary breadwinner, a female primary homemaker, and their dependent offspring. This unitary, normative definition of legitimate domestic arrangements is what my book identifies as ephemeral, and with little regret, because of the race, class, gender, and sexual diversity it has occluded and the in-equities it has exacerbated.

Family values rhetoric, in my view, serves as a sanitized decoy for these less reputable prejudices. Thus, I read Dan Quayle's now infamous attack on Murphy Brown as an ill-fated attempt to play the Willie Horton card in white face. Without resorting to overt racist rhetoric, the image conjured up frightening hordes of African American welfare mothers rearing infant fodder for sex, drugs, and videotaped rebellions, such as had just erupted in Los Angeles. Likewise, when in January of 1993, Republicans attempted to scuttle passage of the Family Leave Act, the new President Clinton's own first family values offering, they did so through appeals to homophobia.

Judith Stacey, "Good Riddance to The Family: A Response to David Popenoe," *Journal of Marriage and Family*, vol. 55, no. 3, pp. 545–547. Copyright © 1993 by John Wiley & Sons, Inc. Reprinted with permission.

To his credit, Popenoe attempts to distinguish his version of family values rhetoric from these reactionary ones, but the weaknesses in his effort demonstrate the inherently flawed, and conservative, character of a structural-functionalist approach to family sociology.

Three systematic errors in Popenoe's analysis of family decline suggest the weaknesses of such an approach. First, Popenoe's latter-day coda of the tired "loss of family functions" lament rests upon a flawed history and anthropology of kinship. It is simply anthropologically incorrect to claim that the family was "once the only social institution in existence"(p. 538). When and where was this ever so? Certainly never in the recorded history of the U.S., nor in that of the many cultures from which our ethnically and racially diverse population derives. If Popenoe means, by this, that kinship organization was the dominant form of social organization in the distant anthropological past, then he is using "the family" in a tautological, and ahistorical sense, with little relevance for his argument about family decline since 1960.

Secondly, Popenoe's more proximate historical framework is equally flawed. Although he concedes that the 1950s were a demographically and culturally anomalous decade in U.S. family history, nonetheless, he proceeds to use it as his baseline for assessing subsequent decline. The most serious consequence of this decision is not that it exaggerates recent "family decline," but that it distorts crucial historical sources of the past few decades of domestic upheaval. Thus, Popenoe fails to analyze the postindustrial economic transformations that have eroded occupations that once paid a family wage to male bread-winners at the same time that opportunities and necessities for female employment have expanded. Feminist critiques of the nuclear family, as I have argued, were as much responses to, and scapegoats for, such developments as they were catalysts to further family change.

Finally, Popenoe offers an incomplete assessment of the alternatives to his view that "the family as an institution" has declined. Illogically, he claims that those who dissent "must logically hold one of two positions—either that the family has strengthened, or that its institutional power within society has remained unchanged"(p. 536). But this is only true if one accepts, as I do not, his institutional definition of the family. I fully agree with Popenoe that, since the 1950s, the Ozzie and Harriet form of family structure and ideology has suffered irremediable defeats, accompanied by the collapse of cultural and statistical consensus on a normative family ideology. That is why I call the present situation of domestic diversity and politicized family contest the postmodern family condition.

Furthermore, I agree with Popenoe that women's capacity to survive outside marriage, however meagerly, has been a central factor in the escalating rates of divorce and single motherhood of recent decades, and that marriage has be-come increasingly fragile as it has become less obligatory, particularly for women. In my view, however, these developments expose the inequity and coercion that always lay at the vortex of the supposedly voluntary companionate marriage of the "traditional nuclear family." It strikes me as a sad, revealing commentary on the benefits to women of the traditional nuclear family that, even in a period when women retain primary responsibility for maintaining children and other kin, when most women continue to earn substantially less than men with equivalent cultural capital, and when women and their children suffer substantial economic decline after divorce, so many regard divorce as the lesser of evils.

Although I interpret the sources and meaning of contemporary processes of family reconstitution quite differently from Popenoe, I share his concern about the grim prospects confronting most of our nation's children. Not even a wild-eyed antifamily extremist, of the sort Popenoe's made me out to be, could deny that far too many children today suffer serious deprivations or that most children (and their relatives) could benefit from massive infusions of the loving attention, economic and social security, and innocence and optimism that Ozzie and Harriet families have come to symbolize. However, I believe that Popenoe, and especially the more reactionary representatives of the family values crowd, consistently confuse symbol with reality and misdiagnose the social sources of contemporary family distress. The nostalgia for the family that they peddle is singularly unhelpful to children or to a social policy arena that has been criminally slow to respond to profound family transformations.

Moreover, Popenoe's well-intentioned attempt to distinguish his stance from that of Falwell, Buchanan, and Quayle by expanding the definition of the traditional nuclear family to accommodate a tepid norm of gender equality strikes me as myopic and ill-fated. It fails to confront a disturbing contradiction at the heart of a fully volitional marriage system. Certainly under present conditions of political, economic, social, and sexual in-equality, truly egalitarian marriage is not possible for the majority. One can only conjecture whether a fully egalitarian marriage system would be compatible with lifelong commitments to dyadic intimacy under utopian conditions of gender, sexual, racial, and economic justice. If, as many feminists have begun to suspect, a stable marriage system depends upon systemic forms of inequality, it will take more than thought reform or moralistic jeremiads about family decline to stanch our contemporary marital hemorrhage. Recent proposals by "communitarians "like Popenoe, to re-strict access to divorce implicitly recognize, but fail to address, this unpleasant contradiction, one which poses a serious dilemma for a democracy.

This bleaker view of the roots of contemporary marital fragility has profound implications for child-rearing which must be faced more honestly than they yet have been in the political arena. Without coercion, divorce and single motherhood rates will remain high. Certainly the consequences of divorce for children are not trivial, but divorce, in and of itself, does not harm the young nearly so much as Popenoe and others have claimed. Most of the studies upon which alarmist views rely conflate the negative economic, geographic, and social consequences that children now unjustly suffer after many divorces with the psychological effects of marital rupture. Yet the most careful studies suggest that it is not the loss of a parent, but a hostile emotional environment preceding this loss that causes most of the emotional damage to children.

Short of exhorting or coercing people to enter or remain in unequal, hostile marriages, family decline critics offer few social proposals to address children's pressing needs. Further stigmatizing the increasing numbers who live in "nontraditional" families is surely no help. Rather, family sociologists should be directing public attention to legal, economic, and social policy reforms that could mitigate the unnecessarily injurious effects of divorce and single parenthood on the fourth of our nation's children who now suffer these. Restructuring work schedules and benefit policies to accommodate familial responsibilities, redistributing work opportunities to reduce unemployment rates that destroy spirits and families, enacting comparable worth standards of pay equity to enable women as well as men to earn a family wage, providing universal health, prenatal, and child care, and sex education and reproductive rights to make it possible to choose to parent with responsibility, revitalizing public education, passing and enforcing strict gun control laws, and rectifying the economic inequities of present divorce property and income dispositions are among the many genuinely child-friendly pro-family measures we should be advocating.

The election of a President who was reared, as was George Washington, by a single parent provides an excellent opportunity to end the scapegoating of unconventional families and to begin rebuilding public responsibility for all of our children, and for their kin. Solvent, secure, publicly respected families provide better hope for a democratic future than do impoverished, distraught, stigmatized ones. Family sociologists should take the lead in burying the ideology of "the family" and in rebuilding a social environment in which diverse family forms can sustain themselves with dignity and mutual respect.

REFERENCES

Allison, P. D., & Furstenberg, F. F. (1989). How marital dissolution affects children: Variations by age and sex. *Developmental Psychology*, 25, 540–549.

Cherlin, A. J. (1991, June 7). Longitudinal studies of effects of divorce on children in Great Britain and the United States. *Science*, pp. 1386–1389.

Kline, M., Johnston, J. R., & Tschann, J. M. (1991). The long shadow of martial conflict: A model of children's postdivorce adjustment. *Journal of Marriage and the Family*, 53, 297–309.

Popenoe, D. (1988). *Disturbing the nest: Family change and decline in modern societies*. New York: Aldine de Gruyter.

Popenoe, D. (1992, December 26). The controversial truth: Two-parent families are better. *The New York Times*, p. 13.

Stacey, J. (1990). *Brave new families: Stories of domestic upheaval in late 20th century America*. New York: Basic Books.

Chapter 7

The Top Ten Myths of Marriage

By David Popenoe

A DISCUSSION OF THE MOST COMMON MISINFORMATION ABOUT MARRIAGE

1. Marriage benefits men much more than women.
Contrary to earlier and widely publicized reports, recent research finds *men and women to benefit about equally from marriage*, although in different ways. Both men and women live longer, happier, healthier and wealthier lives when they are married. Husbands typically gain greater health benefits while wives gain greater financial advantages.[1]

2. Having children typically brings a married couple closer together and increases marital happiness.
Many studies have shown that *the arrival of the first baby commonly has the effect of pushing the mother and father farther apart*, and bringing stress to the marriage. However, couples with children have a slightly lower rate of divorce than childless couples.[2]

3. The keys to long-term marital success are good luck and romantic love.
Rather than luck and love, *the most common reasons couples give for their long-term marital success are commitment and companionship*. They define their marriage as a creation that has taken hard work,

---

[1] The research on this topic is reviewed in Linda J. Waite and Maggie Gallagher, *The Case for Marriage* (New York: Doubleday, 2000): Ch. 12

[2] Carolyn Pape Cowan and Philip A. Cowan, *When Partners Become Parents: The Big Life Change for Couples* (New York: Basic Books, 1992); Jay Belsky and John Kelly, *The Transition to Parenthood* (New York: Dell, 1994); Tim B. Heaton, "Marital Stability Throughout the Child-rearing Years" *Demography* 27 (1990):55–63; Linda Waite and Lee A. Lillard, "Children and Marital Disruption" *American Journal of Sociology* 96 (1991):930–953

David Popenoe, "The Top Ten Myths of Marriage." Copyright © 2002 by David Popenoe. Reprinted with permission.

dedication and commitment (to each other and to the institution of marriage). The happiest couples are friends who share lives and are compatible in interests and values.[3]

4. The more educated a woman becomes, the lower are her chances of getting married.
A recent study based on marriage rates in the mid-1990s concluded that *today's women college graduates are more likely to marry* than their non-college peers, despite their older age at first marriage. This is a change from the past, when women with more education were less likely to marry.[4]

5. Couples who live together before marriage, and are thus able to test how well suited they are for each other, have more satisfying and longer-lasting marriages than couples who do not.
Many studies have found that *those who live together before marriage have less satisfying marriages* and a considerably higher chance of eventually breaking up. One reason is that people who cohabit may be more skittish of commitment and more likely to call it quits when problems arise. But in addition, the very act of living together may lead to attitudes that make happy marriages more difficult. The findings of one recent study, for example, suggest "there may be less motivation for cohabiting partners to develop their conflict resolution and support skills." (One important exception: cohabiting couples who are already planning to marry each other in the near future have just as good a chance at staying together as couples who don't live together before marriage).[5]

6. People can't be expected to stay in a marriage for a lifetime as they did in the past because we live so much longer today.
Unless our comparison goes back a hundred years, there is no basis for this belief. The enormous increase in longevity is due mainly to a steep reduction in infant mortality. And while adults today can expect to live a little longer than their grandparents, they also marry at a later age. The life span of a typical, divorce-free marriage, therefore, has not changed much in the past fifty years. Also, many couples call it quits long before they get to a significant anniversary: half of all divorces take place by the seventh year of a marriage.[6]

7. Marrying puts a woman at greater risk of domestic violence than if she remains single.
Contrary to the proposition that for men "a marriage license is a hitting license," a large body of research shows that *being unmarried—and especially living with a man outside of marriage—is associated with a considerably higher risk of domestic violence for women*. One reason for this finding is that married

---

3 Finnegan Alford-Cooper, *For Keeps: Marriages that Last a Lifetime* (Armonk, NY: M. E. Sharpe, 1998); Judith Wallerstein and Sandra Blakeslee. *The Good Marriage* (Boston: Houghton Mifflin, 1995); Robert Lauer and Jeanette Lauer, "Factors in Long-Term Marriage" *Journal of Family Issues* 7:4 (1986): 382–390

4 Joshua R. Goldstein and Catherine T. Kenney, "Marriage Delayed or Marriage Forgone? New Cohort Forecasts of First Marriage for U. S. Women" *American Sociological Review* 66 (2001):506–519

5 Alfred DeMaris and K. Vaninadha Rao, "Premarital Cohabitation and Marital Instability in the United States: A Reassessment" *Journal of Marriage and the Family* 54 (1992):178–190; Pamela J. Smock, "Cohabitation in the United States" *Annual Review of Sociology* 26 (2000); William G. Axinn and Jennifer S. Barber, "Living Arrangements and Family Formation Attitudes in Early Adulthood" *Journal of Marriage and the Family* 59 (1997):595–611; Susan L. Brown, "The Effect of Union Type on Psychological Well-Being: Depression Among Cohabitors Versus Marrieds" *Journal of Health and Social Behavior* 41 (2000):241–55; Catherine L. Cohan and Stacey Kleinbaum, "Toward a Greater Understanding of the Cohabitation Effect: Premarital Cohabitation and Marital Communication" *Journal of Marriage and the Family* 64 (2002): 180–192

6 Norval D. Glenn, "A Critique of Twenty Family and Marriage and Family Textbooks" *Family Relations* 46–3 (1997):197–208

women may significantly underreport domestic violence. Further, women are less likely to marry and more likely to divorce a man who is violent. Yet it is probably also the case that married men are less likely to commit domestic violence because they are more invested in their wives' wellbeing, and more integrated into the extended family and community. These social forces seem to help check men's violent behavior.[7]

8. Married people have less satisfying sex lives, and less sex, than single people.
According to a large-scale national study, *married people have both more and better sex than do their unmarried counterparts*. Not only do they have sex more often but they enjoy it more, both physically and emotionally.[8]

9. Cohabitation is just like marriage, but without "the piece of paper."
Cohabitation *typically does not bring the benefits—in physical health, wealth, and emotional wellbeing—that marriage does*. In terms of these benefits cohabitants in the United States more closely resemble singles than married couples. This is due, in part, to the fact that cohabitants tend not to be as committed as married couples, and they are more oriented toward their own personal autonomy and less to the wellbeing of their partner.[9]

10. Because of the high divorce rate, which weeds out the unhappy marriages, people who stay married have happier marriages than people did in the past when everyone stuck it out, no matter how bad the marriage.
According to what people have reported in several large national surveys, *the general level of happiness in marriages has not increased and probably has declined slightly*. Some studies have found in recent marriages, compared to those of twenty or thirty years ago, significantly more work-related stress, more marital conflict and less marital interaction.[10]

---

7 Jan E. Stets, "Cohabiting and Marital Aggression: The Role of Social Isolation" *Journal of Marriage and the Family* 53 (1991):669–680; Richard J. Gelles, Intimate Violence in Families, 3rd ed. (Thousand Oaks, CA: 1997); Linda J. Waite and Maggie Gallagher, *The Case for Marriage* (New York: Doubleday, 2000): Ch. 11

8 Linda J. Waite and Kara Joyner, "Emotional and Physical Satisfaction with Sex in Married, Cohabiting, and Dating Sexual Unions: Do Men and Women Differ?" Pp. 239–269 in E. O. Laumann and R. T. Michael, eds., *Sex, Love, and Health in America* (Chicago, IL: University of Chicago Press, 2001); Edward O. Laumann, J. H. Gagnon, R. T. Michael and S. Michaels, *The Social Organization of Sexuality: Sexual Practices in the United States* (Chicago, IL: University of Chicago Press, 1994)

9 Stephen L. Nock, "A Comparison of Marriages and Cohabiting Relationships" *Journal of Family Issues* 16–1 (1995): 53–76; Amy Mehraban Pienta, et. al., "Health Consequences of Marriage for the Retirement Years" *Journal of Family Issues* 21–5 (2000):559-586; Susan L. Brown, "The Effect of Union Type on Psychological Well-Being: Depression Among Cohabitors versus Marrieds" *Journal of Health and Social Behavior* 41(2000):241-255; Susan L. Brown and Alan Booth, "Cohabitation Versus Marriage: A Comparison of Relationship Quality" *Journal of Marriage and the Family* 58 (1996):668-678.

10 Norval D. Glenn, "Values, Attitudes, and the State of American Marriage" Pp. 15–33 in David Popenoe, D. Blankenhorn and J. B. Elshtain (eds.) *Promises to Keep: Decline and Renewal of Marriage in America* (Lanham, MD: Rowman and Littlefield, 1996); Stacy J. Rogers and Paul R. Amato, "Is Marital Quality Declining: The Evidence from Two Generations" *Social Forces* 75 (1997); Stacy J. Rogers and Paul R. Amato, "Have Changes in Gender Relations Affected Marital Quality?" *Social Forces* 79 (2000):731-753; General Social Survey, National Opinion Research Center, University of Chicago.

FURTHER READINGS

Bumpass, Larry L. *The Declining Significance of Marriage: Changing Family Life in the United States.* Center for Demography and Ecology, University of Wisconsin-Madison, NSFH Working Paper No. 66, 1994.

Lamanna, Mary Ann, and Agnes Riedmann. *Marriages, Families and Relationships: Making Choices in a Diverse Society.* Belmont, CA: Wadsworth, 2011.

Pew Research Center. "Decline of Marriage and Rise of New Families." http://www.pewsocialtrends.org/2010/11/18/the-decline-of-marriage-and-rise-of-new-families/2/.

Ethical Issues

Chapter 8

Duties Towards the Body in Respect of Sexual Impulse

By Immanuel Kant, translated by Louis Infield

Amongst our inclinations there is one which is directed towards other human beings. They themselves, and not their work and services, are its Objects of enjoyment. It is true that man has no inclination to enjoy the flesh of another—except, perhaps, in the vengeance of war, and then it is hardly a desire—but none the less there does exist an inclination which we may call an appetite for enjoying another human being. We refer to sexual impulse. Man can, of course, use another human being as an instrument for his service; he can use his hands, his feet, and even all his powers; he can use him for his own purposes with the other's consent. But there is no way in which a human being can be made an Object of indulgence for another except through sexual impulse. This is in the nature of a sense, which we can call the sixth sense; it is an appetite for another human being. We say that a man loves someone when he has an inclination towards another person. If by this love we mean true human love, then it admits of no distinction between types of persons, or between young and old. But a love that springs merely from sexual impulse cannot be love at all, but only appetite. Human love is good-will, affection, promoting the happiness of others and finding joy in their happiness. But it is clear that, when a person loves another purely from sexual desire, none of these factors enter into the love. Far from there being any concern for the happiness of the loved one, the lover, in order to satisfy his desire and still his appetite, may even plunge the loved one into the depths of misery. Sexual love makes of the loved person an Object of appetite; as soon as that appetite has been stilled, the person is cast aside as one casts away a lemon which has been sucked dry. Sexual love can, of course, be combined with human love and so carry with it the characteristics of the latter, but taken by itself and for itself, it is nothing more than appetite. Taken by itself it is a degradation of human nature: for as soon as a person becomes an Object of appetite for another, all motives of moral relationship cease to function, because as an Object of appetite for another a person becomes a thing and can be treated and used as such by everyone. This is the only case

Immanuel Kant, "Duties Towards the Body in Respect of Sexual Impulse," *Lectures on Ethics*, trans. Louis Infield, pp. 162-171. Copyright © 1980 by Hackett Publishing Company, Inc. Reprinted with permission.

in which a human being is designed by nature as the Object of another's enjoyment. Sexual desire is at the root of it; and that is why we are ashamed of it, and why all strict moralists, and those who had pretensions to be regarded as saints, sought to suppress and extirpate it. It is true that without it a man would be incomplete; he would rightly believe that he lacked the necessary organs, and this would make him imperfect as a human being; none the less men made presence on this question and sought to suppress these inclinations because they degraded mankind.

Because sexuality is not an inclination which one human being has for another as such, but is an inclination for the sex of another, it is a principle of the degradation of human nature, in that it gives rise to the preference of one sex to the other, and to the dishonoring of that sex through the satisfaction of desire. The desire which a man has for a woman is not directed towards her because she is a human being, but because she is a woman; that she is a human being is of no concern to the man; only her sex is the object of his desires. Human nature is thus subordinated. Hence it comes that all men and women do their best to make not their human nature but their sex more alluring and direct their activities and lusts entirely towards sex. Human nature is thereby sacrificed to sex. If then a man wishes to satisfy his desire, and a woman hers, they stimulate each other's desire; their inclinations meet, but their object is not human nature but sex, and each of them dishonours the human nature of the other. They make of humanity an instrument for the satisfaction of their lusts and inclinations, and dishonour it by placing it on a level with animal nature. Sexuality, therefore, exposes mankind to the danger of equality with the beasts. But as man has this desire from nature, the question arises how far he can properly make use of it without injury to his manhood. How far may persons allow one of the opposite sex to satisfy his or her desire upon them? Can they sell themselves, or let themselves out on hire, or by some other contract allow use to be made of their sexual faculties? Philosophers generally point out the harm done by this inclination and the ruin it brings to the body or to the commonwealth, and they believe that, except for the harm it does, there would be nothing contemptible in such conduct in itself. But if this were so and if giving vent to this desire was not in itself abominable and did not involve immorality then anyone who could avoid being harmed by them could make whatever use he wanted of his sexual propensities. For the prohibitions of prudence are never unconditional; and the conduct would in itself be unobjectionable, and would only be harmful under certain conditions. But in point of fact, there is in the conduct itself something which is contemptible and contrary to the dictates of morality. It follows, therefore, that there must be certain conditions under which alone the use of the "facultates sexuales" would be in keeping with morality. There must be a basis for restraining our freedom in the use we make of our inclinations so that they conform to the principles of morality. We shall endeavour to discover these conditions and this basis. Man cannot dispose over himself because he is not a thing; he is not his own property; to say that he is would be self-contradictory; for in so far as he is a person he is a Subject in whom the ownership of things can be vested, and if he were his own property, he would be a thing over which he could have ownership. But a person cannot be a property and so cannot be a thing which can be owned, for it is impossible to be a person and a thing, the proprietor and the property.

Accordingly, a man is not at his own disposal. He is not entitled to sell a limb, not even one of his teeth. But to allow one's person for profit to be used by another for the satisfaction of sexual desire, to make of oneself an Object of demand, is to dispose over oneself as over a thing and to make of oneself a thing on which another satisfies his appetite, just as he satisfies his hunger upon a steak. But since the inclination is directed towards one's sex and not towards one's humanity, it is clear that one thus partially sacrifices one's humanity and thereby runs a moral risk. Human beings are, therefore, not entitled to offer themselves, for profit, as things for the use of others in the satisfaction of their sexual propensities. In so doing they would run the risk of having their person used by all and sundry as an instrument for the satisfaction of inclination. This way of satisfying sexuality is "vaga libido", in which one satisfies the inclinations of others for gain. It is possible for either sex. To let one's person out on hire and to surrender it to another for the satisfaction of his sexual desire in return for money is the depth of infamy. The underlying moral principle is that man is not his own property and cannot do with his body what he will. The body is part of the self; in its togetherness with the self it constitutes the person; a man cannot make of his person a thing, and this is exactly what happens in vaga libido. This manner of satisfying sexual desire is, therefore, not permitted by the rules of morality. But what of the second method, namely "concubinatus". Is this also inadmissible? In this case both persons satisfy their desire mutually and there is no idea of gain, but they serve each other only for the satisfaction of sexuality. There appears to be nothing unsuitable in this arrangement, but there is nevertheless one consideration which rules it out. Concubinage consists in one person surrendering to another only for the satisfaction of their sexual desire whilst retaining freedom and rights in other personal respects affecting welfare and happiness. But the person who so surrenders is used as a thing; the desire is still directed only towards sex and not towards the person as a human being. But it is obvious that to surrender part of oneself is to surrender the whole, because a human being is a unity. It is not possible to have the disposal of a part only of a person without having at the same time a right of disposal over the whole person, for each part of a person is integrally bound up with the whole. But concubinage does not give me a right of disposal over the whole person but only over a part, namely the "organa sexualia". It presupposes a contra: This contract deals only with the enjoyment of a part of the person and not with the e circumstances of the person. Concubinage is certainly a contract, but it is one-sided: the rights of the two parties are not equal. But if in concubinage I enjoy a part of a person. I: by enjoy the whole person; yet by the ten the arrangement I have not the rights over the whole person, but only over a part; I, therefore; make the person into a thing. For that reason this method of satisfying sexual desire is also not permitted by the rules of morality. The sole condition on which we are free to make use our sexual desire depends upon the right to dispose over the person as a whole—over the welfare and happiness and generally over all the circumstances of that person. If I have the right over the whole person I have also the right over the part and so I have the right to use that person's "organa sexualia" for the satisfaction of sexual desire. But how am I to obtain these rights over the whole person? Only by giving that person the same rights over the whole of myself. This happens only in marriage. Matrimony is an agreement between two persons by which they grant each other equal reciprocal rights, each of them undertaking to surrender the whole of their person to the other with a complete right of disposal over it. We can now apprehend by reason how a "commercium sexuale" is possible without degrading humanity and breaking the moral laws. Matrimony is the only condition in which use can be made of one's sexuality. If one devotes one's person to another, one devotes not only sex but the whole person; the two cannot be separated. If, then, one yields one's person, body and soul, for good and ill and in every respect, so that the other has complete rights over it, and if the other does not similarly yield himself in return and does not extend in return the same rights and privileges, the arrangement is one-sided. But if I yield myself completely to another and obtain the person of the other in return, I win myself back: I have given myself up as the property of another, but in turn I take that other as my Property, and so win myself back again in winning the person whose property I have become.

In this way the two persons become a unity of will. Whatever good or ill, joy or sorrow befall either of them, the other will share in it. Thus sexuality leads to a union of human beings, and I that union alone its exercise is possible. This condition of the use of sexuality, which is only fulfilled in marriage, is a moral condition. But let us pursue this aspect further and examine.

The case of a man who takes two wives. In such a case each wife would have but half a man, although she would be giving herself wholly and ought in consequence to be entitled to the whole man. To sum up: "vaga libido" is ruled out moral grounds; the same applies to concubinage: there only remains matrimony, and in matrymony polygamy is ruled out also for moral reasons; we, therefore, reach the conclusion that the only feasible arrangement is that of monogamous marriage. Only under that condition can I indulge my "facultas sexualis". We cannot here pursue that subject further.

But one other question arises, that of incest. Incest consists in intercourse between the sexes in a form which, by reason of consanguinity, must be ruled out; but are there moral grounds on which incest, in all forms of sexual intercourse must be ruled out? They are grounds which apply conditionally, except in one case, in which they have absolute validity. The sole case in which the moral grounds against incest apply absolutely is that of intercourse between parents and children. Between parents and children there must be a respect which should continue throughout life, and this rules out of court any question of equality. Moreover, in sexual intercourse each person submits to the other in the highest degree, whereas between parents and their children subjection is one-sided; the children must submit to the parents only; there can, therefore, be no equal union. This is the only case in which incest is absolutely forbidden by nature. In other cases incest forbids itself, but is not incest in the order of nature. The state prohibits incest, but at the beginning there must have been intermarriage between brothers and sisters. At the same time nature has implanted in our breasts a natural opposition to incest. She intended us to combine with other races and so to prevent too great a sameness in one society. Too close a connection, too intimate an acquaintance produces sexual indifference and repugnance. But this propensity must be restrained by modesty; otherwise it becomes commonplace, reduces the object of the desire to the commonplace and results in indifference. Sexual desire is very fastidious; nature has given it strength, but it must be restrained by modesty. It is on that account that savages, who go about stark-naked, are cold towards each other; for that reason, too, a person whom we have known from youth evokes no desire within us, but a strange person attracts us much more strongly. Thus nature has herself provided restraints upon any desire between brother and sister.

Chapter 9

Plato About Love

By Plato, translated by B. Jowett

In the first place, let me treat of the nature of man and what has happened to it; for the original human nature was not like the present, but different. The sexes were not two as they are now, but originally three in number; there was man, woman, and the union of the two, having a name corresponding to this double nature, which had once a real existence, but is now lost, and the word 'Androgynous' is only preserved as a term of reproach. In the second place, the primeval man was round, his back and sides forming a circle; and he had four hands and four feet, one head with two faces, looking opposite ways, set on a round neck and precisely alike; also four ears, two privy members, and the remainder to correspond. He could walk upright as men now do, backwards or forwards as he pleased, and he could also roll over and over at a great pace, turning on his four hands and four feet, eight in all, like tumblers going over and over with their legs in the air; this was when he wanted to run fast. Now the sexes were three, and such as I have described them; because the sun, moon, and earth are three; and the man was originally the child of the sun, the woman of the earth, and the man-woman of the moon, which is made up of sun and earth, and they were all round and moved round and round like their parents. Terrible was their might and strength, and the thoughts of their hearts were great, and they made an attack upon the gods; of them is told the tale of Otys and Ephialtes who, as Homer says, dared to scale heaven, and would have laid hands upon the gods. Doubt reigned in the celestial councils. Should they kill them and annihilate the race with thunderbolts, as they had done the giants, then there would be an end of the sacrifices and worship which men offered to them; but, on the other hand, the gods could not suffer their insolence to be unrestrained. At last, after a good deal of reflection, Zeus discovered a way. He said: 'Methinks I have a plan which will humble their pride and improve their manners; men shall continue to exist, but I will cut them in two and then they will be diminished in strength and increased in numbers; this will have the advantage of making them more profitable to us. They shall walk upright on two legs. (…)

Plato, from *Symposium*, trans. Benjamin Jowett. Copyright in the Public Domain.

And when one of them meets with his other half, the actual half of himself, (…) the pair are lost in an amazement of love and friendship and intimacy, and one will not be out of the other's sight, as I may say, even for a moment: these are the people who pass their whole lives together; yet they could not explain what they desire of one another. For the intense yearning which each of them has towards the other does not appear to be the desire of lover's intercourse, but of something else which the soul of either evidently desires and cannot tell, and of which she has only a dark and doubtful presentiment.

You hear people say that lovers are seeking for their other half; but I say that they are seeking neither for the half of themselves, nor for the whole, unless the half or the whole be also a good. (…) Then love may be described generally as the love of the everlasting possession of the good? (…)

There is a certain age at which human nature is desirous of procreation— (…) and this procreation is a divine thing; for conception and generation are an immortal principle in the mortal creature, (…)

For love, is not the love of the beautiful only. What then? The love of generation and of birth in beauty. But why of generation? (…) 'Because to the mortal creature, generation is a sort of eternity and immortality,' she replied; 'and if, as has been already admitted, love is of the everlasting possession of the good, all men will necessarily desire immortality together with good: Wherefore love is of immortality.' (…)

For he who would proceed aright in this matter should begin in youth to visit beautiful forms; and first, if he be guided by his instructor aright, to love one such form only—out of that he should create fair thoughts; and soon he will of himself perceive that the beauty of one form is akin to the beauty of another; and then if beauty of form in general is his pursuit, how foolish would he be not to recognize that the beauty in every form is and the same! And when he perceives this he will abate his violent love of the one, which he will despise and deem a small thing, and will become a lover of all beautiful forms; in the next stage he will consider that the beauty of the mind is more honourable than the beauty of the outward form (…) and to understand that personal beauty is a trifle; and (…) drawing towards and contemplating the vast sea of beauty, he will create many fair and noble thoughts and notions in boundless love of wisdom; until on that shore he grows and waxes strong, and at last the vision is revealed to him of a single science, which is the science of beauty everywhere.

Chapter 10

Ethics of Virtue and Abolition of Marriage

By Plato, translated by B. Jowett

And can there be anything better for the interests of the State than that the men and women of a State should be as good as possible?

There can be nothing better. (…)

Then we have made an enactment not only possible but in the highest degree beneficial to the State?

True.

Then let the wives of our guardians strip, for their virtue will be their robe, and let them share in the toils of war and the defence of their country; only in the distribution of labours the lighter are to be assigned to the women, who are the weaker natures, but in other respects their duties are to be the same. (…)

The law, I said, which is the sequel of this and of all that has preceded, is to the following effect,—'that the wives of our guardians are to be common, and their children are to be common, and no parent is to know his own child, nor any child his parent.'

Yes, he said, that is a much greater wave than the other; and the possibility as well as the utility of such a law are far more questionable.

I do not think, I said, that there can be any dispute about the very great utility of having wives and children in common; the possibility is quite another matter, and will be very much disputed.

I think that a good many doubts may be raised about both. (…)

First, I think that if our rulers and their auxiliaries are to be worthy of the name which they bear, there must be willingness to obey in the one and the power of command in the other; the guardians must themselves obey the laws, and they must also imitate the spirit of them in any details which are entrusted to their care.

That is right, he said.

Plato, from *The Republic*, trans. Benjamin Jowett. Copyright in the Public Domain.

You, I said, who are their legislator, having selected the men, will now select the women and give them to them;—they must be as far as possible of like natures with them; and they must live in common houses and meet at common meals. None of them will have anything specially his or her own; they will be together, and will be brought up together, and will associate at gymnastic exercises. And so they will be drawn by a necessity of their natures to have intercourse with each other—necessity is not too strong a word, I think?

Yes, he said;—necessity, not geometrical, but another sort of necessity which lovers know, and which is far more convincing and constraining to the mass of mankind.

True, I said; and this, Glaucon, like all the rest, must proceed after an orderly fashion; in a city of the blessed, licentiousness is an unholy thing which the rulers will forbid.

Yes, he said, and it ought not to be permitted.

Then clearly the next thing will be to make matrimony sacred in the highest degree, and what is most beneficial will be deemed sacred?

Exactly.

And how can marriages be made most beneficial?—that is a question which I put to you, because I see in your house dogs for hunting, and of the nobler sort of birds not a few. Now, I beseech you, do tell me, have you ever attended to their pairing and breeding?

In what particulars?

Why, in the first place, although they are all of a good sort, are not some better than others?

True.

And do you breed from them all indifferently, or do you take care to breed from the best only?

From the best.

And do you take the oldest or the youngest, or only those of ripe age?

I choose only those of ripe age.

And if care was not taken in the breeding, your dogs and birds would greatly deteriorate?

Certainly.

And the same of horses and animals in general?

Undoubtedly.

Good heavens! my dear friend, I said, what consummate skill will our rulers need if the same principle holds of the human species! (...)

Our rulers will find a considerable dose of falsehood and deceit necessary for the good of their subjects: we were saying that the use of all these things regarded as medicines might be of advantage.

And we were very right.

And this lawful use of them seems likely to be often needed in the regulations of marriages and births.

How so?

Why, I said, the principle has been already laid down that the best of either sex should be united with the best as often, and the inferior with the inferior, as seldom as possible; and that they should rear the offspring of the one sort of union, but not of the other, if the flock is to be maintained in first-rate condition. Now these goings on must be a secret which the rulers only know, or there will be a further danger of our herd, as the guardians may be termed, breaking out into rebellion. (...)

(...)

The proper officers will take the offspring of the good parents to the pen or fold, and there they will deposit them with certain nurses who dwell in a separate quarter; but the offspring of the inferior, or of the better when they chance to be deformed, will be put away in some mysterious, unknown place, as they should be.

Yes, he said, that must be done if the breed of the guardians is to be kept pure.

They will provide for their nurture, and will bring the mothers to the fold when they are full of milk, taking the greatest possible care that no mother recognises her own child; and other wet-nurses may be engaged if more are required. Care will also be taken that the process of suckling shall not be protracted too long; and the mothers will have no getting up at night or other trouble, but will hand over all this sort of thing to the nurses and attendants.

You suppose the wives of our guardians to have a fine easy time of it when they are having children. Why, said I, and so they ought (…)

That also, he said, is a reasonable proposition. But how will they know who are fathers and daughters, and so on?

They will never know. The way will be this:—dating from the day of the hymeneal, the bridegroom who was then married will call all the male children who are born in the seventh and tenth month afterwards his sons, and the female children his daughters, and they will call him father, and he will call their children his grandchildren, and they will call the elder generation grandfathers and grandmothers. All who were begotten at the time when their fathers and mothers came together will be called their brothers and sisters, and these, as I was saying, will be forbidden to inter-marry. This, however, is not to be understood as an absolute prohibition of the marriage of brothers and sisters; if the lot favours them, and they receive the sanction of the Pythian oracle, the law will allow them.

Quite right, he replied.

Such is the scheme, Glaucon, according to which the guardians of our State are to have their wives and families in common.

Chapter 11

Marriage as a Kind of Friendship

By Aristotle, translated by W. D. Ross

KINDS OF FRIENDSHIP

Friendship Both Necessary and Noble: Main Questions About It

1. AFTER what we have said, a discussion of friendship would naturally follow, since it is a virtue or implies virtue, and is besides most necessary with a view to living. For without friends no one would choose to live, though he had all other goods; even rich men and those in possession of office and of dominating power are thought to need friends most of all; for what is the use of such prosperity without the opportunity of beneficence, which is exercised chiefly and in its most laudable form towards friends? Or how can prosperity be guarded and preserved without friends? The greater it is, the more exposed is it to risk. And in poverty and in other misfortunes men think friends are the only refuge. It helps the young, too, to keep from error; it aids older people by ministering to their needs and supplementing the activities that are failing from weakness; those in the prime of life it stimulates to noble actions—'two going together'1—for with friends men are more able both to think and to act. Again, parent seems by nature to feel it for offspring and offspring for parent, not only among men but among birds and among most animals; it is felt mutually by members of the same race, and especially by men, whence we praise lovers of their fellow men. (…)

Three Objects of Love: Implications of Friendship

2. The kinds of friendship may perhaps be cleared up if we first come to know the object of love. For not everything seems to be loved but only the lovable, and this is good, pleasant, or useful; but it would seem to be that by which some good or pleasure is produced that is useful, so that it is the good and the pleasant that are lovable as ends. Do men love, then, the good, or what is good

Aristotle, from *The Nichomachean Ethics, Book VIII*, trans. W. D. Ross. Copyright in the Public Domain.

for them? These sometimes clash. So too with regard to the pleasant. Now it is thought that each loves what is good for himself, and that the good is without qualification lovable, and what is good for each man is lovable for him; but each man loves not what is good for him but what seems good. This however will make no difference; we shall just have to say that this is 'that which seems lovable'. Now there are three grounds on which people love: of the love of lifeless objects we do not use the word 'friendship', for it is not mutual love, nor is there a wishing of good to the other (for it would surely be ridiculous to wish wine well; if one wishes anything for it, it is that it may keep, so that one may have it oneself); but to a friend we say we ought to wish what is good for his sake. But to those who thus wish good we ascribe only goodwill, if the wish is not reciprocated; goodwill when it is reciprocal being friendship. Or must we add 'when it is recognized'? For many people have goodwill to those whom they have not seen but judge to be good or useful; and one of these might return this feeling. These people seem to bear goodwill to each other; but how could one call them friends when they do not know their mutual feelings? To be friends, then, they must be mutually recognized as bearing goodwill and wishing well to each other for one of the aforesaid reasons.

Three Corresponding Kinds of Friendship: Superiority of Friendship Whose Motive Is Good

3. Now these reasons differ from each other in kind; so, therefore, do the corresponding forms of love and friendship. There are therefore three kinds of friendship, equal in number to the things that are lovable; for with respect to each there is a mutual and recognized love, and those who love each other wish well to each other in that respect in which they love one another. Now those who love each other for their utility do not love each other for themselves but in virtue of some good which they get from each other. So too with those who love for the sake of pleasure; it is not for their character that men love ready-witted people, but because they find them pleasant. Therefore those who love for the sake of utility love for the sake of what is good for themselves, and those who love for the sake of pleasure do so for the sake of what is pleasant to themselves, and not in so far as the other is the person loved but in so far as he is useful or pleasant. And thus these friendships are only incidental; for it is not as being the man he is that the loved person is loved, but as providing some good or pleasure. Such friendships, then, are easily dissolved, if the parties do not remain like themselves; for if the one party is no longer pleasant or useful the other ceases to love him.

Now the useful is not permanent but is always changing. Thus when the motive of the friendship is done away, the friendship is dissolved, inasmuch as it existed only for the ends in question. This kind of friendship seems to exist chiefly between old people (for at that age people pursue not the pleasant but the useful) and, of those who are in their prime or young, between those who pursue utility. And such people do not live much with each other either; for sometimes they do not even find each other pleasant; therefore they do not need such companionship unless they are useful to each other; for they are pleasant to each other only in so far as they rouse in each other hopes of something good to come. Among such friendships people also class the friendship of host and guest. On the other hand the friendship of young people seems to aim at pleasure; for they live under the guidance of emotion, and pursue above all what is pleasant to themselves and what is immediately before them; but with increasing age their pleasures become different. This is why they quickly become friends and quickly cease to be so; their friendship changes with the object that is found pleasant and such pleasure alters quickly. Young people are amorous too; for the greater part of the friendship of love depends on emotion and aims at pleasure; this is why they fall in love and quickly fall out of love, changing often within a single day. But these people do wish to spend their days and lives together; for it is thus that they attain the purpose of their friendship.

Perfect friendship is the friendship of men who are good, and alike in virtue; for these wish well alike to each other qua good, and they are good in themselves. Now those who wish well to their friends for their sake are most truly friends; for they do this by reason of their own nature and not incidentally; therefore their friendship lasts as long as they are good—and goodness is an enduring thing. And each is good without qualification and to his friend, for the good are both good without qualification and useful to each other. So too they are pleasant; for the good are pleasant both without qualification and to each other, since to each his own activities and others like them are pleasurable, and the actions of the good are the same or like. And such a friendship is as, might be expected, permanent, since there meet in it all the qualities that friends should have. For all friendship is for the sake of good or of pleasure— good or pleasure either in the abstract or such as will be enjoyed by him who has the friendly feeling—and is based on a certain resemblance ; and to a friendship of good men all the qualities we have named belong in virtue of the nature of the friends themselves; for in the case of this kind of friendship the other qualities also are alike in both friends, and that which is good without qualification is also without qualification pleasant, and these are the most lovable qualities. Love and friendship therefore are found most and in their best form between such men. (…)

RECIPROCITY OF FRIENDSHIP

In Unequal Friendships a Proportion Must Be Maintained

7. But there is another kind of friendship, viz. that which involves an inequality between the parties, e.g. that of father to son and in general of elder to younger, that of man to wife and in general that of ruler to subject. And these friendships differ also from each other; for it is not the same that exists between parents and children and between rulers and subjects, nor is even that of father to son the same as that of son to father, nor that of husband to wife the same as that of wife to husband. For the virtue and the function of each of these is different, and so are the reasons for which they love; the love and the friendship are therefore different also. Each party, then, neither gets the same from the other, nor ought to seek it; but when children render to parents what they ought to render to those who brought them into the world, and parents render what they should to their children, the friendship of such persons will be abiding and excellent. In all friendships implying inequality the love also should be proportional, i.e. the more useful, and similarly in each of the other cases; for when the love is in proportion to the merit of the parties, then in a sense arises equality, which is certainly held to be characteristic of friendship. (…)

Loving Is More of the Essence of Friendship Than Being Loved

8. Most people seem, owing to ambition, to wish to be loved rather than to love; which is why most men love flattery; for the flatterer is a friend in an inferior position, or pretends to be such and to love more than he is loved; and being loved seems to be akin to being honoured, and this is what most people aim at. But it seems to be not for its own sake that people choose honour, but incidentally. For

most people enjoy being honoured by those in positions of authority because of their hopes (for they think that if they want anything they will get it from them; and therefore they delight in honour as a token of favour to come); while those who desire honour from good men, and men who know, are aiming at confirming their own opinion of themselves ; they delight in honour, therefore, because they believe in their own goodness on the strength of the judgment of those who speak about them. In being loved, on the other hand, people delight for its own sake; whence it would seem to be better than being honoured, and friendship to be desirable in itself. But it seems to lie in loving rather than in being loved, as is indicated by the delight mothers take in loving; for some mothers hand over their children to be brought up, and so long as they know their fate they love them and do not seek to be loved in return (if they cannot have both), but seem to be satisfied if they see them prospering; and they themselves love their children even if these owing to their ignorance give them nothing of a mother's due. Now since friendship depends more on loving, and it is those who love their friends that are praised, loving seems to be the characteristic virtue of friends, so that it is only those in whom this is found in due measure that are lasting friends, and only their friendship that endures.

It is in this way more than any other that even un-equals can be friends; they can be equalized. Now equality and likeness are friendship, and especially the likeness of those who are like in virtue; for being steadfast in themselves they hold fast to each other, and neither ask nor give base services, but (one may say) even prevent them; for it is characteristic of good men neither to go wrong themselves nor to let their friends do so. But wicked men have no steadfastness (for they do not remain even like to themselves), but become friends for a short time because they delight in each other's wickedness. Friends who are useful or pleasant last longer; i.e. as long as they provide each other with enjoyments or advantages. Friendship for utility's sake seems to be that which most easily exists between contraries, e.g. between poor and rich, between ignorant and learned; for what a man actually lacks he aims at, and one gives something else in return. But under this head, too, one might bring lover and beloved, beautiful and ugly. This is why lovers sometimes seem ridiculous, when they demand to be loved as they love; if they are equally lovable their claim can perhaps be justified, but when they have nothing lovable about them it is ridiculous. Perhaps, however, contrary does not even aim at contrary by its own nature, but only incidentally, the desire being for what is intermediate; for that is what is good, e.g. it is good for the dry not to become wet but to come to the intermediate state, and similarly with the hot and in all other cases. These subjects we may dismiss; for they are indeed somewhat foreign to our inquiry. (…)

12. Between man and wife friendship seems to exist by nature; for man is naturally inclined to form couples-even more than to form cities, inasmuch as the household is earlier and more necessary than the city, and reproduction is more common to man with the animals. With the other animals the union extends only to this point, but human beings live together not only for the sake of reproduction but also for the various purposes of life; for from the start the functions are divided, and those of man and woman are different; so they help each other by throwing their peculiar gifts into the common stock. It is for these reasons that both utility and pleasure seem to be found in this kind of friendship. But this friendship may be based also on virtue, if the parties are good; for each has its own virtue and they will delight in the fact. And children seem to be a bond of union (which is the reason why childless people part more easily); for children are a good common to both and what is common holds them together.

How man and wife and in general friend and friend ought mutually to behave seems to be the same question as how it is just for them to behave; for a man does not seem to have the same duties to a friend, a stranger, a comrade, and a school fellow.

FURTHER READINGS

Blustein, Jeffrey. *Parents and Children: The Ethics of the Family*. New York: Oxford University Press, 1982 (especially "The Family in Western Philosophical Thought," pp. 17–89).

Kneller, Jane. "Kant on Sex and Marriage Right." In *The Cambridge Companion to Kant and Modern Philosophy*, edited by Paul Guyer, 447–504. New York: Oxford University Press, 2006.

Levy, Donald. "The Definition of Love in Plato's Symposium." In *Sex, Love, and Friendship: Studies of the Society for the Philosophy of Sex, 1977-1992*, edited by Alan Soble. New York: Rodoni, 1997.

McEvoy, Adrianne Leigh, ed. *Sex, Love, and Friendship: Studies of the Society for the Philosophy of Sex and Love, 1993–2003*. New York: Rodoni, 2011.

Modern Trends in Family: Divorce

Chapter 12

Number, Timing, and Duration of Marriages and Divorces: 2009

By Rose M. Kreider and Renee Ellis

INTRODUCTION

Marriage and divorce are central to the study of living arrangements and family composition. Social and economic events as well as changes in cultural attitudes shape marital behavior, which then affect family life and other interactions. The study of the evolving patterns of marriage and divorce requires basic measures of the incidence of these events.

The Survey of Income and Program Participation (SIPP) is one of few data sources that can provide a comprehensive look at both current and historical marital patterns in the United States. SIPP data contain a detailed marital history for men and women aged 15 and over, as well as extensive information about the characteristics of adults, their households, and the people with whom they live. In addition, information about both husbands and wives is available for people who are currently married.[1]

---

[1] Since 2008, the American Community Survey (ACS) has been asking adults whether they had married, divorced, separated, or been widowed in the year before the survey, as well as the number of times married and the year the latest marriage began. Estimates of indicators such as the characteristics of people who had a recent marital event, the percentage of men and women who have ever divorced, and the percentage of recent marriages in which both the bride and groom were marrying for the first time are now available in both the SIPP and the ACS. See the following paper for more information: Elliott, Diana B, Tavia Simmons, and Jamie M. Lewis, *Evaluation of the Marital Events Items on the ACS, 2010*, available at <www.census.gov/hhes/socdemo/marriage/data /acs/Evaluation_paper.pdf>. While ACS adds valuable information about recent U.S. marital patterns, especially state-level data, SIPP still contains the most detailed, comprehensive data available at the national level. A forthcoming report will showcase the new ACS marital events data.

Rose M. Kreider and Renee Ellis / U.S. Census Bureau, "Number, Timing, and Duration of Marriages and Divorces: 2009," *Number, Timing, and Duration of Marriages and Divorces: 2009*, pp. 1-6, 14-22. Copyright in the Public Domain.

The marital history data have been collected in SIPP since 1986 and reports were published starting with the 1996 data. Before that time, marital history reports used Current Population Survey data, which included a marital history from 1975 through 1995. The SIPP marital history topical module is a nationally representative survey which is fielded approximately every 5 years, with the most recent data collection prior to this survey occurring in 2004.[2] This report updates some of the tables shown in the previous reports and tables with data collected in the second interview of the SIPP 2008 Panel, collected in January through April of 2009, and adds several tables covering other topics.[3]

In 2009, marital history data were collected from men and women 15 years and over in approximately 39,000 households. In the sample, 55,497 ever-married adults were asked questions about the number of times they had been married and the month and year of marital events (including marriage, separation, divorce, and widowhood) for their first, second, and most recent marriages. Since fewer than 1 percent of adults have been married four or more times, few events are missed by using this approach.

The first section of this report examines changes in marital patterns during the period that SIPP data were collected, 1986 to 2009. Additionally, this section describes changes in the age at marriage, divorce, and remarriage across different cohorts of men and women born since 1940 to 1944. The second section provides current indicators of the percentage of the population who have married more than once, who have ever divorced, or who experienced other marital events. This section also answers questions about how long first marriages last, the median age at which people marry or divorce, and what percentage of currently married couples involve spouses who are both in their first marriage. The third section profiles the characteristics of people who experienced a marital event in the year prior to the survey.

HISTORICAL MARITAL PATTERNS

Changes From 1986 to 2009

One of the most noticeable changes in marital patterns has been the increase in the age at first marriage.[4] This is reflected in an increasing proportion of younger adults who are never married. Table 12.1 shows the percentage of women never married, by 5-year age groups, from 25 to 29 to 55 and over. While the proportion of all women who are never married at age 25 to 29 has increased substantially from 1986 to 2009 (27 percent to 47 percent), it did not differ statistically for women aged 55 and over (5 percent to 6 percent).[5]

---

2   The tables for 2004 are available on the Census Bureau Web site at <www.census.gov/hhes /socdemo/marriage/data/sipp/2004/tables.html>. The most recent report in this series was written using SIPP 2001 Panel data and is available at <www.census.gov/prod/2005pubs/p70-97.pdf>. The earlier 1996 report is also available at <www.census.gov/prod/2002pubs/p70-80.pdf>.

3   The population represented in this report (the population universe) is the civilian noninstitutionalized adult (15 years and over) population living in the United States. The items asked in the marital history topical module are available at <www.census.gov/sipp/core_content/2008/quests/wave2/2008w2core.pdf>.

4   See "Estimated Median Age at First Marriage, by Sex: 1890 to the Present," Table MS-2 at <www.census.gov/population /socdemo/hh-fam/ms2.xls>.

5   The estimates in this report are based on responses from a sample of the population. As with all surveys, estimates may vary from the actual values because of sampling variation and other factors. All comparisons made in this report have undergone statistical testing and are significant at the 90 percent confidence level unless otherwise noted.

> ## Case Study
>
> **Marital status.** The marital status classification refers to the status at the time of interview. "Married, spouse present" applies to husband and wife if both were living in the same household, even though one may be temporarily absent, for example, on business, vacation, a visit, or in a hospital. "Married, spouse absent" relates to people who are living apart for reasons other than marital problems, for example, spouses living apart because one or the other was employed elsewhere, on duty with the Armed Forces, or incarcerated. "Separated" refers to couples who are living apart due to marital problems. "Divorced" indicates people who report that they have received a legal divorce decree and have not remarried. "Widowed" indicates that a person's last marriage ended in the death of their spouse. The term "never married" applies to those who have never been legally married, as well as to those whose marriages were annulled.
>
> **Marital history.** A marital history was collected from each person in the household aged 15 and over. There were 55,497 people in the sample from approximately 39,000 households. Respondents answered questions about when they had been married, separated, divorced, and widowed, if they had experienced these events. Dates for the beginning and end of up to three marriages were regardless of whether this was the third or later marriage. Since very few people marry more than three times, few events are missed by using this approach to data collection. Although questions were asked only of people aged 15 and over, some people reported marital events as occurring before age 15.
>
> **Marital event.** Refers to a change in marital status—getting married, getting divorced, or being widowed.
>
> **Birth or marriage cohort.** A cohort signifies a group of people born or married in a specified time period—for example, people born from 1945 through 1949.
>
> **Current age.** Age at reference month, which is the month preceding the interview.
>
> **Median.** The median is the value which divides a distribution into two equal parts; half of the cases fall below this value and half exceed it.

This pattern varied by race and ethnicity, with a higher percentage of Black women than non-Hispanic White women never married in each age group in 2009 (Table 12.1, Figures 12.1 and 12.2).[6] For example, 71 percent of Black women aged 25 to 29 had never married, compared with 43 percent of non-Hispanic White women in 2009. Corresponding percentages for never-married women aged 55 and over in 2009 were 5 percent for non-Hispanic White women and 13 percent for Black women. Similar to 2009, a higher proportion of Black women had never married than non-Hispanic White women at all age groups in 1986 except the proportion never married for those aged 55 and over.

While the percentage of Black women who had never married was considerably higher than for non-Hispanic White women in many age groups, the magnitude of the increase between 1986 and

---

6 Because Hispanics may be any race, data in this report for Hispanics overlap with data for the White, Black, Asian, and all remaining races and combinations populations. Based on the population 15 years and over in SIPP 2008 Wave 2, 16 percent of the White population, 6 percent of the Black population, 2 percent of the Asian population, and 16 percent of all remaining races and combinations were of Hispanic origin.

Table 12.1. Percent Never Married for Women by Age, Race, and Hispanic Origin,[1] for Selected Years: 1986 to 2009

Year	25 to 29 years	30 to 34 years	35 to 39 years	40 to 44 years	45 to 49 years	50 to 54 years	55 and over
TOTAL							
1986	26.9	14.0	10.0	5.3	4.9	3.5	4.8
1996	35.3	18.7	14.1	9.8	7.3	5.5	4.1
2001	37.3	21.7	15.6	12.1	8.9	7.3	4.0
2004	41.3	22.3	16.2	13.0	10.8	8.5	5.1
2009	46.8	26.7	17.3	14.1	12.0	10.1	5.8
WHITE							
1986	23.8	11.2	8.2	4.3	4.1	3.0	4.9
1996	30.8	14.8	11.2	7.7	6.0	4.6	3.8
2001	33.1	16.6	12.7	9.1	6.9	6.3	3.4
2004	36.7	18.2	12.5	10.4	8.3	7.3	4.5
2009	41.6	22.6	13.8	11.2	9.7	8.2	5.0
WHITE, NON-HISPANIC							
1986	24.0	11.3	8.2	3.8	4.2	2.6	4.8
1996	31.1	14.3	10.9	7.7	5.9	4.6	3.6
2001	34.1	17.1	12.3	9.0	7.1	5.9	3.1
2004	38.3	18.6	12.3	9.9	8.4	7.4	4.4
2009	43.3	22.0	13.5	10.3	9.4	7.8	4.7
BLACK							
1986	44.3	34.8	23.9	13.3	12.7	6.3	3.5
1996	57.7	39.4	33.6	25.0	15.9	11.7	6.6
2001	59.4	49.5	34.0	31.3	23.9	16.3	9.4
2004	66.3	47.0	39.0	30.3	28.5	18.0	10.9
2009	70.5	53.6	39.2	33.1	28.5	24.5	13.0
ASIAN							
1986	29.3	16.4	3.9	–	–	5.6	9.7
1996	41.5	18.4	4.6	3.1	7.8	7.9	5.7
2001	38.6	17.4	7.9	10.3	5.6	2.8	5.0
2004	39.0	25.7	19.7	16.2	8.4	9.8	4.4
2009	51.6	11.8	10.2	5.9	7.5	5.8	4.8
HISPANIC							
1986	23.8	14.8	8.7	12.8	1.5	8.1	8.9
1996	30.5	19.5	13.3	9.0	8.9	7.5	7.2
2001	28.0	15.9	15.1	11.8	4.8	11.7	8.0
2004	32.0	16.7	14.7	16.3	8.6	6.6	6.7
2009	36.8	27.2	15.1	15.2	12.9	11.8	8.9

– Represents or rounds to zero.
1 Race and Hispanic origin were collected differently in earlier years compared with 2004 and 2009. In 2004 and later, respondents could mark all race groups they chose, while in earlier years they had to choose just one group. In 1986, 1996, and 2001, Asian includes Pacific Islanders, while in 2004 and 2009 it does not. In 2004 and 2009, Black, White, and Asian include those who marked only the category indicated.
Note: A small percentage of all women in 1986 were missing on marital status (.07 percent of all women).
Source: U.S. Census Bureau, Survey of Income and Program Participation (SIPP), 1986, 1996, 2001, 2004, and 2008 Panels, Wave 2 Topical Module. For information on sampling and nonsampling error, see <www.census.gov/sipp/source.html>.

2009 in the percentage never married was higher for Black women than non-Hispanic White women in just two age groups—50 to 54 years and 55 and over. While the percentage of non-Hispanic White women aged 50 to 54 who had never married in 2009 was 3 times what it was in 1986, the increase was 4 times for Black women of the same age group. For women aged 55 and over, there was no

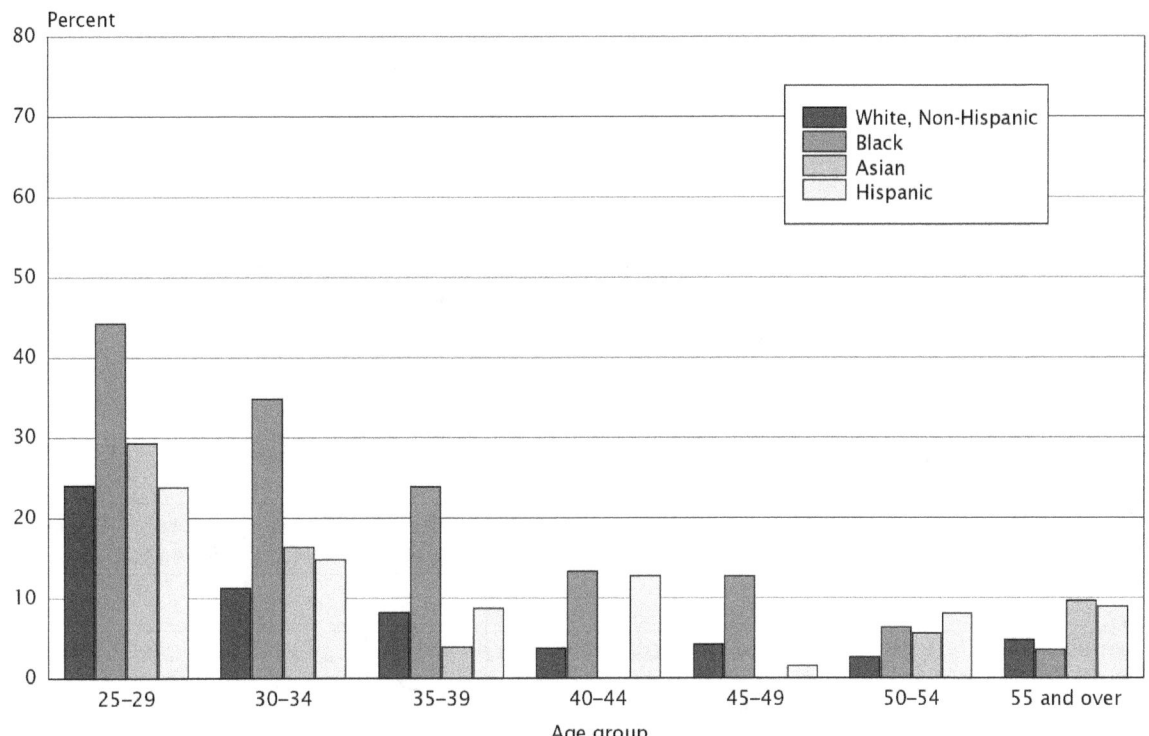

Figure 12.1 Percentage of Women Never Married by Age, Race, and Hispanic Origin: 1986
Source: U.S. Census Bureau, Survey of Income and Program Participation (SIPP), 2008 Panel, Wave 2 Topical Module. For information on sampling and nonsampling error, see <www.census.gov/sipp/sourceac/S&A08_W1toW3(S&A-12).pdf>.

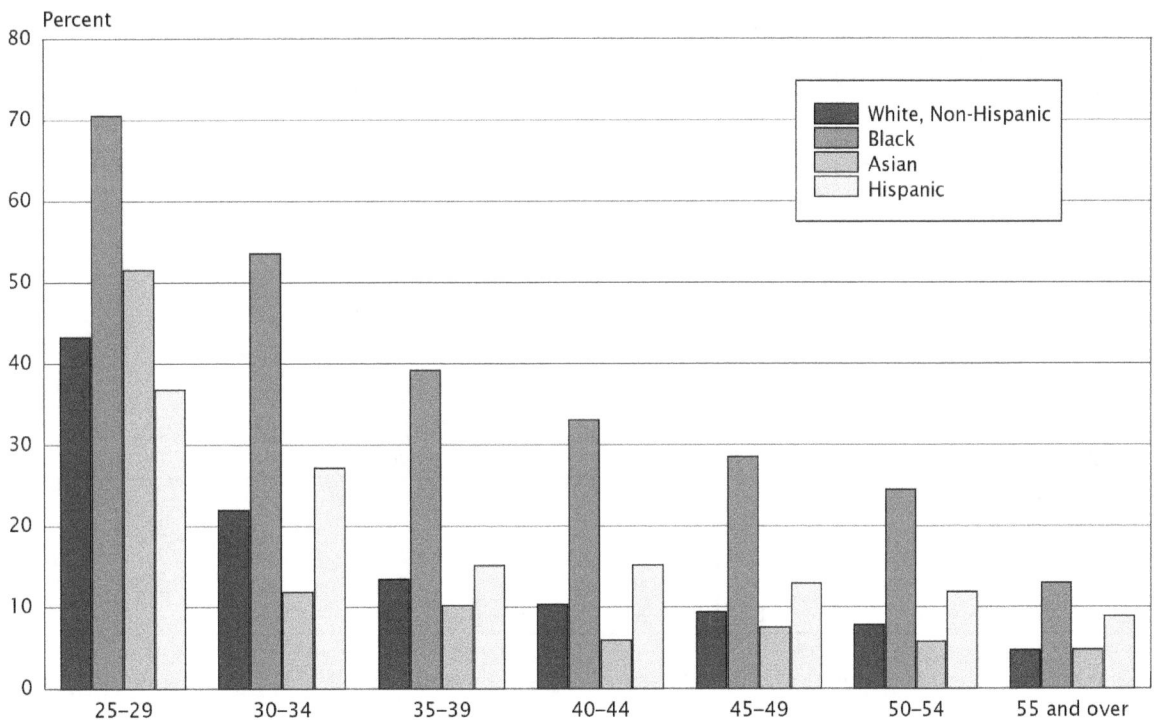

Figure 12.2 Percentage of Women Never Married by Age, Race, and Hispanic Origin: 2009
Source: U.S. Census Bureau, Survey of Income and Program Participation (SIPP), 2008 Panel, Wave 2 Topical Module. For information on sampling and nonsampling error, see <www.census.gov/sipp/sourceac/S&A08_W1toW3(S&A-12).pdf>.

increase for non-Hispanic White women, but the percentage for Black women was 3.7 times as high in 2009 as in 1986. The difference in the magnitude of the increase suggests that a higher percentage of Black women than non-Hispanic White women may never marry.

Another change in marital patterns during 1996 through 2009 was the leveling of the divorce rate, after it had decreased from a high around 1980. Percentages of ever-married women shown in Table 12.2 who had ever divorced, shown grouped by age, reflect this leveling. The table also shows that while percentages for ever divorced generally increased between 1996 and 2009 for older age groups (50 to 59, 60 to 69, and 70 and over), the percentage ever divorced decreased for younger

Table 12.2. Percent Ever Divorced for Ever-Married Women by Age, Race, and Hispanic Origin,[1] for Selected Years: 1996 to 2009

Year	25 to 29 years	30 to 34 years	35 to 39 years	40 to 49 years	50 to 59 years	60 to 69 years	70 and over
TOTAL							
1996	18.8	25.6	32.4	40.5	36.4	27.1	17.5
2001	18.9	23.7	33.3	39.6	41.5	29.6	18.3
2004	11.9	22.0	30.6	38.5	44.1	33.7	18.7
2009	13.8	21.3	27.4	35.6	41.1	36.7	22.3
WHITE							
1996	19.7	26.1	32.2	40.8	36.1	26.6	17.2
2001	19.9	24.4	33.5	40.6	41.8	29.6	18.0
2004	12.4	23.2	30.5	39.1	44.3	33.9	18.1
2009	14.2	22.1	27.6	36.3	41.1	36.9	21.9
WHITE, NON-HISPANIC							
1986	20.5	27.4	33.2	41.6	36.6	26.8	17.0
1996	22.1	26.4	34.7	42.3	42.5	29.9	17.9
2001	13.9	24.9	32.1	41.0	45.6	34.7	18.0
2004	15.2	23.5	30.3	38.6	42.4	38.1	21.7
2009							
BLACK							
1996	14.7	28.0	40.7	44.5	42.0	35.6	21.9
2001	20.6	24.5	37.3	42.2	44.7	33.8	25.4
2004	11.0	20.1	37.1	39.0	47.8	37.2	26.7
2009	14.6	23.9	32.7	35.0	48.2	40.3	27.8
ASIAN							
1996	9.3	12.0	14.3	22.8	23.2	4.9	8.5
2001	4.1	10.7	18.1	17.5	22.7	9.9	5.0
2004	1.9	6.1	11.4	20.1	19.9	9.6	9.1
2009	1.3	7.8	13.2	20.6	18.5	16.0	11.3
HISPANIC							
1996	15.5	17.4	24.0	33.2	31.7	25.6	20.3
2001	12.5	15.5	26.5	28.5	34.0	26.5	21.5
2004	8.8	16.3	24.7	24.4	33.1	23.9	19.5
2009	10.5	16.3	18.1	23.7	30.2	25.0	24.2

1 Race and Hispanic origin were collected differently in earlier years compared with 2004 and 2009. In 2004 and later, respondents could mark all race groups they chose, while in earlier years they had to choose just one group. In 1996 and 2001, Asian includes Pacific Islanders, while in 2004 and 2009 it does not.
In 2004 and 2009, Black, White, and Asian include those who marked only the category indicated.
Source: U.S. Census Bureau, Survey of Income and Program Participation (SIPP), 1996, 2001, 2004, and 2008 Panels, Wave 2 Topical Module. For information on sampling and nonsampling error, see <www.census.gov/sipp/source.html>.

groups of women over the same time period. This is because women in the older age groups in 2009 were the ones who were married during the time when divorce rates were increasing to their height at the end of the 1970s.

As marriage rates have decreased and cohabitation has become more common, marriage has become more selective of adults who are better off socioeconomically and have more education, and divorce rates have leveled.[7] These changes are reflected here in decreasing proportions ever divorced for ever-married women at younger ages. While 19 percent of ever-married women aged 25 to 29 had divorced in 1996, 14 percent had divorced in 2009—a decrease of about 30 percent. The percentage ever divorced decreased about 20 percent for women aged 30 to 34, from 26 percent to 21 percent ever divorced over the same time period. Despite these decreases, the prevalence of divorce in the United States remains higher than in most European countries.[8]

Age at First Marriage

Since the 1950s, the median age at first marriage has risen for both men and women, increasing from 23 for men and 20 for women in 1950, to 28 for men and 26 for women in 2009.[9] Table 12.2 shows the percentages of men and women who were ever married, ever divorced, or married two or more times by selected ages. Data are shown for 5-year birth cohorts, from 1940 to 1944 through 1980 to 1984. Reflecting the rise in the median age at first marriage, the percentages of men and women born in 1980 to 1984 who were married by age 20 (7 percent and 16 percent, respectively) were about one third the percentages of those born in 1940 to 1944 (22 percent and 48 percent, respectively).

Table 12.2 shows the historical decline in the percentages of men and women ever married by age and birth cohort. The percentage of men ever married by age 35 declined 14 percentage points between the 1940 to 1944 birth cohort and the 1965 to 1969 birth cohort. The corresponding decline for women was 10 percentage points. While some people marry for the first time when they are over 35, the current level of these proportions for men and women born in the late 1960s (75 percent and 80 percent, respectively) suggests that it may be unlikely they will reach the same 90 percent plus level achieved by the first baby boom cohorts of the 1940s.

Median Age at Marriage and Divorce

Table 12.5 shows the median age for marital events associated with first and second marriages for people who had ever experienced these events by 2009. These medians reflect the cumulative marital experience of the population as of 2009 and do not represent the ages of people who married or divorced in 2009. Estimates of that type will be discussed in the section on marital events that occurred during 2008. These medians represent only a portrait of the population at a given point in time and

---

7 Cherlin, Andrew, *The Marriage-Go-Round: The State of Marriage and the Family in America Today*, Random House, New York, 2009.

8 See Table 25 in the *Demographic Yearbook* published by the United Nations, available at <http://unstats.un.org/unsd/demographic/products/dyb/2000_round.htm>.

9 Estimates of the median age at first marriage can be found on the Census Bureau Web site. See "Families and Living Arrangements," Table MS-2 at <www.census.gov/population/www/socdemo/hh-fam.html>.

Table 12.3. Percent Intermarried for Currently Married Women in Their First Marriage: 2009

Characteristic	Number of marriages (in thousands)	Percent interracial or Hispanic/non-Hispanic	Margin of error[1]
Total.	48,779	8	0.5
RACE AND HISPANIC ORIGIN			
White alone	41,251	5	0.5
Non-Hispanic	34,808	5	0.5
Black alone	3,614	7	1.8
Asian alone	2,706	23	3.4
Hispanic (any race)	6,988	11	1.6
AGE			
15 to 24 years	2,060	13	3.1
25 to 34 years	9,440	11	1.3
35 to 44 years	11,150	10	1.2
45 to 54 years.	10,821	7	1.0
55 years and over	15,308	4	0.7
EDUCATIONAL ATTAINMENT			
Less than high school	4,646	4	1.2
High school graduate	12,736	7	1.0
Some college	15,150	9	1.0
Bachelor's degree or more	16,247	8	0.9

1 This number, when added to and subtracted from the estimate, provides the 90 percent confidence interval.
Source: U.S. Census Bureau, Survey of Income and Program Participation (SIPP), 2008 Panel, Wave 2 Topical Module. For information on sampling and nonsampling error, see <www.census.gov/sipp/sourceac/S&A08_W1toW3(S&A-12).pdf>.

are influenced not only by the current age structure of the population, but also by past marital patterns, which may not reflect current behavior.[14]

Among people in 2009 who had ever been married, the median age at first marriage was about 22 for non-Hispanic White women and 23 for Black and Hispanic women.[15] The median age at separation from first marriage for these groups was 29, and the median age at divorce from first marriage was 30 for non-Hispanic White and Hispanic women and 31 for Black women. Comparing within race or Hispanic origin group, men were about 2 to 3 years older than women when they married, separated, and divorced from their first marriage. Asian men and women had a higher age at first marriage than other population groups—25 for women and 28 for men.

Half of those who remarried following a divorce from a first marriage had done so by their mid-thirties. Among those who had remarried by 2009, the median age at second marriage was 36 for men and 33 for women.

The median age at widowhood from first marriage was lower for Black men and women (54 years) than for non-Hispanic White men and women (61 years).[16] This difference reflects higher mortality rates for Black men and women compared with non-Hispanic White men and women.[17]

---

14 State-level estimates of the median age at first marriage, as well as estimates by race, are available from the 2008 ACS and later, accessible through American Fact Finder at <http://factfinder.census.gov/home/saff/main.html?_lang=en>. The median is estimated since there is no question about age at first marriage—unlike in SIPP, where this is asked directly.

15 Median age at first marriage differs significantly for Black and Hispanic women.

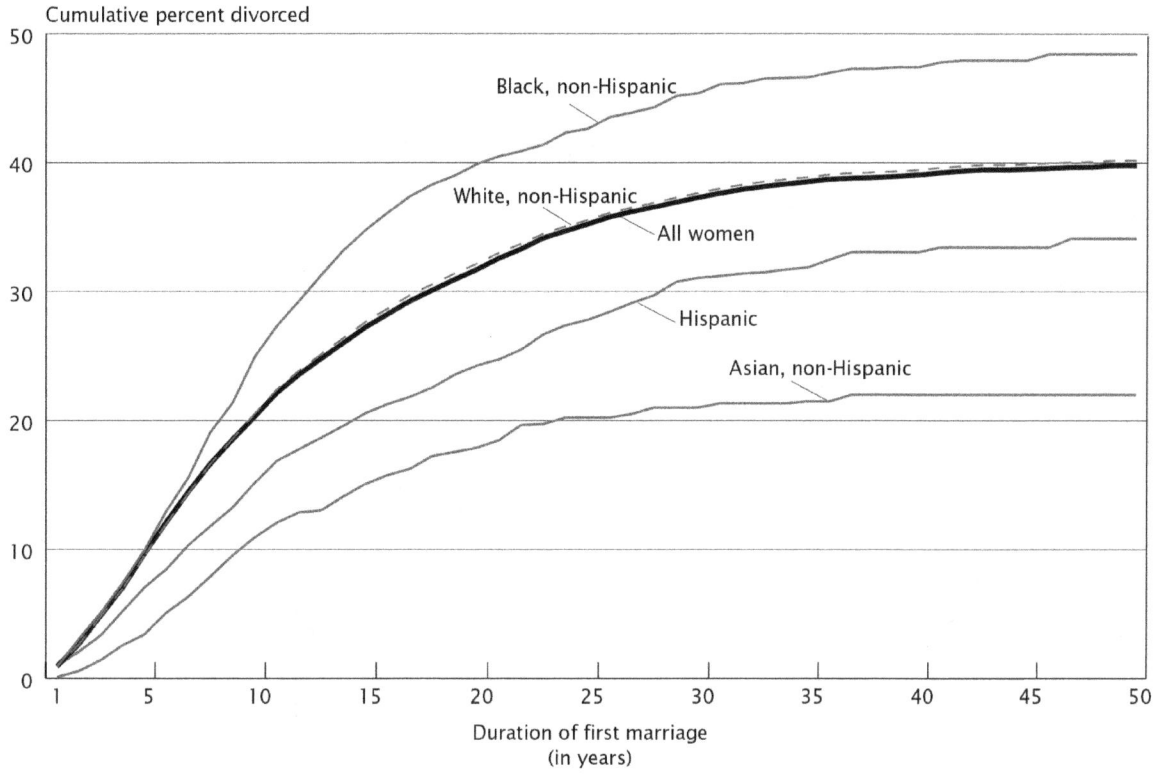

Figure 12.3 Source: U.S. Census Bureau, Survey of Income and Program Participation (SIPP), 2008 Panel, Wave 2 Topical Module. For information on sampling and nonsampling error, see <www.census.gov/sipp/sourceac/S&A08_W1toW3(S&A-12).pdf>.

Duration of Terminated Marriages and Median Time to Remarriage Following Divorce

How long do marriages last and how quickly do people remarry? Table 12.6, profiling the marital experience of the population as of 2009, shows that first marriages which ended in divorce lasted a median of 8 years for men and women overall. The median time from marriage to separation was shorter—about 7 years.

Table 12.5 also shows the median duration of time between the divorce from a first marriage and a second marriage. Half of the men and women in all of the race and Hispanic-origin groups who remarried after divorcing from their first marriage did so within about 4 years. The median duration of second marriages that ended in divorce did not differ from that for first marriages.

Duration of Current Marriages: 2009

While previous sections examined the intervals between different marital events among people who had experienced a marital disruption by 2009, this section looks at the duration of the most recent marriage for couples who were currently married at the time of the survey in 2009. Table 12.7 shows

---

16 Estimates for men and women are not statistically different.

17 Arias, Elizabeth, United States Life Tables, 2006, *National Vital Statistics Reports,* Vol. 58, No. 21, National Center for Health Statistics: Hyattsville, MD, 2010.

Table 12.4. Marital History for People 15 Years Old and Over by Age and Sex: 2009

Characteristic	Total, 15 years and over		15 to 17 years	18 to 19 years	20 to 24 years	25 to 29 years	30 to 34 years	35 to 39 years	40 to 49 years	50 to 59 years	60 to 69 years	70 years and over
	Estimate	Margin of error[1]	years	years	years	years	years	years	years	years	years	Estimate
MALE												
Total (in thousands)	115,797	1,024	6,559	4,311	10,152	10,567	9,518	9,995	21,504	19,568	12,774	10,849
Percent												
Never married	33.0	0.6	98.3	97.5	87.5	59.7	35.6	23.5	16.4	10.8	4.6	3.4
Ever married	67.0	0.6	1.7	2.5	12.5	40.3	64.4	76.5	83.6	89.2	95.4	96.6
Married once	52.3	0.6	1.5	2.5	12.5	38.8	59.4	66.9	65.8	63.4	64.8	72.3
Still married[2]	42.5	0.6	1.0	1.8	11.2	34.2	52.2	56.1	52.2	50.4	53.5	54.0
Married twice	11.6	0.4	0.2	–	–	1.5	4.8	8.7	14.8	20.0	22.1	18.9
Still married[2]	9.0	0.4	0.1	–	–	1.3	4.0	7.4	11.3	15.5	17.5	13.2
Married 3 or more times	3.1	0.2	–	–	–	0.1	0.2	1.0	3.0	5.8	8.5	5.4
Still married[2]	2.3	0.2	–	–	–	0.1	0.2	0.8	2.2	4.3	6.5	3.8
Ever divorced	20.5	0.5	0.4	0.1	0.8	5.0	10.5	17.9	28.5	35.7	36.5	23.4
Currently divorced	9.1	0.4	0.3	0.1	0.7	3.7	6.2	9.5	14.2	15.5	12.4	7.2
Ever widowed	3.6	0.2	0.3	0.5	0.1	0.3	0.2	0.5	1.3	2.5	6.4	22.6
Currently widowed	2.6	0.2	0.2	0.5	0.1	0.3	0.1	0.3	0.9	1.6	3.9	17.4
FEMALE												
Total (in thousands)	123,272	1,022	6,259	4,219	10,158	10,408	9,645	10,267	22,119	20,702	14,288	15,207
Percent												
Never married	27.2	0.5	98.9	95.5	77.3	46.8	26.7	17.3	13.0	9.1	6.0	4.3
Ever married	72.8	0.5	1.1	4.5	22.7	53.2	73.3	82.7	87.0	90.9	94.0	95.7
Married once	57.5	0.6	1.1	4.5	22.4	50.8	64.5	69.3	67.4	65.5	67.7	76.1
Still married[2]	40.6	0.6	0.5	3.9	19.7	43.2	54.5	55.8	51.6	47.5	45.7	30.1
Married twice	12.1	0.4	0.1	–	0.3	2.3	8.0	11.6	15.8	19.5	20.1	15.2
Still married[2]	7.9	0.3	1.0	–	0.2	2.0	6.9	9.1	11.3	13.4	13.2	5.2
Married 3 or more times	3.2	0.2	–	–	–	–	0.8	1.9	3.8	5.9	6.2	4.4
Still married[2]	1.9	0.2	–	–	–	–	0.7	1.4	2.5	4.1	3.6	1.4
Ever divorced	22.4	0.5	0.2	0.2	1.8	7.3	15.6	22.7	31.0	37.3	34.5	21.4
Currently divorced	11.3	0.4	0.1	0.2	1.5	5.3	8.1	11.8	16.4	18.6	16.0	9.9
Ever widowed	10.0	0.4	0.4	0.2	0.1	0.2	0.6	1.4	2.6	6.5	17.0	51.2
Currently widowed	8.9	0.3	0.4	0.2	0.1	0.1	0.4	0.8	1.8	4.9	13.9	48.3

– Represents or rounds to zero.
1 This number, when added to and subtracted from the estimate, provides the 90 percent confidence interval.
2 Includes those currently separated.
Source: U.S. Census Bureau, Survey of Income and Program Participation (SIPP), 2008 Panel, Wave 2 Topical Module. For information on sampling and nonsampling error, see <www.census.gov/sipp/sourceac/S&A08_W1toW3(S&A-12).pdf>.

the number and percentage of married couples in 2009 who had reached various anniversaries. In 2009, 83 percent of all currently married couples had achieved at least their fifth anniversary, 55 percent had been married at least 15 years, and 35 percent had reached their twenty-fifth anniversary. A small percentage of currently married couples had passed their golden (fiftieth) wedding anniversary—6 percent. These percentages are only 1 to 2 percentage points higher than they were in 1996, reflecting both the leveling of divorce rates and the increases in life expectancy.[18]

Table 12.5. Median Age at Marital Event for People 15 Years and Over by Sex, Race, and Hispanic Origin: 2009 (Median age in years for those who experienced the specified event. Numbers in thousands)

Characteristic	Total	White alone		Black alone	Asian alones	All remaining races and combinations	Hispanic (any race)
		Total	Non-Hispanic				
MEN							
Total.	43.3	44.2	46.0	39.3	40.3	37.3	35.6
First Marriage							
Age when married	24.5	24.3	24.2	26.1	27.8	23.9	24.6
Age when separated[1]	30.8	30.6	30.6	32.4	34.6	30.4	30.3
Age when divorced	32.0	31.8	31.8	33.9	35.4	31.3	31.8
Age when widowed	61.1	62.1	62.7	54.3	58.8	61.9	49.4
Second Marriage		35.6	35.6	37.6	37.6	35.1	35.3
Age when married	35.8	39.0	38.9	40.3	(B)	37.4	39.5
Age when separated[1]	39.0	42.1	42.2	41.9	(B)	41.8	40.3
Age when divorced	42.0	61.4	61.3	63.2	(B)	(B)	(B)
Age when widowed	61.4						
WOMEN							
Total.	45.0	45.9	47.5	41.2	41.0	39.5	37.3
First Marriage							
Age when married	22.3	22.1	22.0	23.3	25.3	21.6	22.5
Age when separated[1]	28.8	28.7	28.7	29.5	30.9	27.6	28.6
Age when divorced	30.1	29.8	29.8	31.3	32.2	28.9	29.9
Age when widowed	59.4	60.7	61.2	54.1	57.5	46.6	53.8
Second Marriage							
Age when married	33.3	33.0	33.0	35.5	36.3	32.2	32.8
Age when separated[1]	36.4	36.1	36.2	39.3	(B)	35.5	36.3
Age when divorced	39.3	39.1	39.1	41.2	(B)	37.8	40.2
Age when widowed	60.3	60.9	61.1	59.2	(B)	52.5	58.6

– B Base less than 75,000. Median not calculated.
1 For those who divorced.
Source: U.S. Census Bureau, Survey of Income and Program Participation (SIPP), 2008 Panel, Wave 2 Topical Module. For information on sampling and nonsampling error, see <www.census.gov/sipp/sourceac/S&A08_W1toW3(S&A-12).pdf>.

The percentage reaching particular anniversaries was generally lower for Black and Hispanic women than for non-Hispanic White women.[19] Higher rates of divorce for Blacks and the more youthful age distribution for Hispanics contribute to this difference.

---

18 See Table 7 in the P70–80 report for 1996 estimates. The report is available on the Census Bureau Web site at <www.census.gov/prod/2002pubs/p70-80.pdf>.

19 The percentages of non-Hispanic White women and Black women reaching their fiftieth anniversary do not differ significantly.

Table 12.6. Median Duration of Marriages for People 15 Years and Over by Sex, Race, and Hispanic Origin: 2009 (Duration in years)

Duration	Total	White alone		Black alone	Asian alone	All remaining races and combinations	Hispanic (any race)
		Total	Non-Hispanic				
Duration of first marriage for those whose first marriage ended in divorce							
Men	8.0	7.8	7.8	8.6	8.2	8.6	8.1
Women	8.0	7.9	7.9	8.3	8.3	7.2	8.0
Duration between first marriage and first separation for those who divorced							
Men	6.7	6.6	6.6	7.0	6.6	7.4	6.5
Women	6.6	6.7	6.7	6.4	7.1	5.8	6.3
Duration between first separation and first divorce for those who divorced							
Men	0.8	0.8	0.8	1.1	0.8	0.8	0.9
Women	0.9	0.8	0.8	1.1	1.1	0.9	0.9
Duration between first divorce and remarriage for those whose first marriages ended in divorce and who had remarried							
Men	3.8	3.8	3.7	4.3	4.1	3.6	4.0
Women	3.7	3.6	3.6	4.7	4.4	3.5	4.1
Duration of second marriage for those whose second marriage ended in divorce							
Men	8.5	8.7	8.7	7.9	(B)	6.4	7.4
Women	8.0	7.9	7.8	8.7	(B)	8.1	9.0

B Base less than 75,000. Median duration not shown.
Source: U.S. Census Bureau, Survey of Income and Program Participation (SIPP), 2008 Panel, Wave 2 Topical Module. For information on sampling and nonsampling error, see <www.census.gov/sipp/sourceac/S&A08_W1toW3(S&A-12).pdf>.

Number of Times Married for Those Currently Married

Not all newlyweds begin married life with the same marital history. One or both spouses may have been married previously, which means some couples enter the marriage with children and commitments from previous marital unions. Table 12.8 takes a more detailed look at the number of times wives and husbands had been married when surveyed in 2009. While both spouses were in their first marriage in 72 percent of all currently married couples in 2009, this situation occurred for just 65 percent of the couples who had married within the previous year.[20]

Six percent of all currently married couples involved a wife who was in her second marriage and a husband who was in his first marriage, while another 8 percent of all currently married couples involved a husband who was in his second marriage and a wife who was in her first marriage. Eight percent of currently married couples and couples married within the previous year involved spouses

---

20 Estimates labeled "within the last year" in Table 12.8 were reported as having occurred during calendar year 2008.

Table 12.7. Currently Married Women Who Had Reached Stated Anniversaries by Race and Hispanic Origin: 2009

Anniversary of current marriage	Total	White alone		Black alone	Asian alone	Hispanic (any race)
		Total	Non-Hispanic			
NUMBER (in thousands)						
Total currently married.	62,140	52,704	45,220	4,721	3,086	8,137
5th	51,233	43,802	38,036	3,638	2,499	6,227
10th	42,102	36,416	32,034	2,794	1,937	4,724
15th	34,100	29,697	26,486	2,166	1,483	3,456
25th	21,912	19,300	17,627	1,298	874	1,812
35th	13,141	11,686	10,804	750	457	935
50th	3,851	3,549	3,429	157	97	125
PERCENT						
Total currently married.	100.0	100.0	100.0	100.0	100.0	100.0
5th	82.5	83.1	84.1	77.0	81.0	76.5
10th	67.8	69.1	70.8	59.2	62.8	58.1
15th	54.9	56.3	58.6	45.9	48.0	42.5
25th	35.3	36.6	39.0	27.5	28.3	22.3
35th	21.2	22.2	23.9	15.9	14.8	11.5
50th	6.2	6.7	7.6	3.3	3.1	1.5

Note: Currently married includes married, spouse present and married, spouse absent, excluding separated.
Source: U.S. Census Bureau, Survey of Income and Program Participation (SIPP), 2008 Panel, Wave 2 Topical Module. For information on sampling and nonsampling error, see <www.census.gov/sipp/sourceac/S&A08_W1toW3(S&A-12).pdf>.

Table 12.8. Number of Times Married for Currently Married Wives and Their Husbands: 2009
(Numbers in thousands)

Number of times wife has been married	Number of times husband has been married							
	All current marriages				Married within the last year[1]			
	Total	Married 1 time	Married 2 times	Married 3 or more times	Total	Married 1 time	Married 2 times	Married 3 or more times
Total.	60,607	47,699	10,271	2,637	2,232	1,648	440	144
Married 1 time	48,779	43,340	4,705	734	1,696	1,447	224	24
Married 2 times	9,551	3,814	4,533	1,205	422	163	167	92
Married 3 or more times	2,276	545	1,034	698	114	37	50	27
PERCENT OF MARRIAGES								
Total.	100.0	78.7	16.9	4.4	100.0	73.8	19.7	6.4
Married 1 time	80.5	71.5	7.8	1.2	76.0	64.9	10.0	1.1
Married 2 times	15.8	6.3	7.5	2.0	18.9	7.3	7.5	4.1
Married 3 or more times	3.8	0.9	1.7	1.2	5.1	1.7	2.2	1.2

[1] Includes marriages that occurred during calendar year 2008.
Note: This table includes only people who are married, spouse present.
Source: U.S. Census Bureau, Survey of Income and Program Participation (SIPP), 2008 Panel, Wave 2 Topical Module. For information on sampling and nonsampling error, see <www.census.gov/sipp/sourceac/S&A08_W1toW3(S&A-12).pdf>.

Table 12.9. Characteristics of People 15 Years and Over With a Marital Event During 2008
(Data include first and higher order events. Numbers in thousands)

Characteristic at time of interview	Men					Women				
		With a marital event during 2008					With a marital event during 2008			
	Total	Marriage	Separation	Divorce	Widowhood	Total	Marriage	Separation	Divorce	Widowhood
Total	115,797	2,398	815	792	401	123,272	2,392	870	942	694
PERCENT	100.0	100.0	100.0	100.0	100.0	100.0	100.0	100.0	100.0	100.0
RACE AND HISPANIC ORIGIN										
White alone	81.8	82.1	81.2	82.9	82.6	80.1	82.4	79.4	82.7	83.9
Non-Hispanic	68.4	64.0	68.3	69.3	74.7	68.2	65.7	67.4	68.9	77.1
Black alone	11.2	11.2	14.2	13.1	13.3	12.8	9.2	14.9	12.7	10.2
Asian alone	3.8	3.0	1.3	1.2	3.2	4.0	3.8	1.0	1.5	3.7
Hispanic (any race)	14.8	20.9	14.2	14.0	7.9	13.1	19.1	13.7	14.6	6.7
AGE										
15 to 24 years	18.2	18.6	7.6	5.8	4.5	16.7	25.3	14.6	9.9	1.7
25 to 34 years	17.3	43.2	22.5	23.6	2.1	16.3	41.7	29.3	30.7	1.3
35 to 44 years	17.6	18.5	32.9	31.0	4.1	16.9	16.1	28.9	29.0	4.2
45 to 54 years	18.7	11.1	24.7	27.5	8.9	18.3	10.1	19.0	20.5	8.8
55 to 64 years	14.2	5.4	8.4	7.1	15.0	14.4	4.8	7.9	9.1	19.2
65 years and over	14.0	3.3	3.8	5.0	65.4	17.4	1.9	0.4	0.8	64.8
Median age (in years)	43.3	31.4	41.5	41.8	71.8	45.0	29.5	37.0	37.4	72.0
EDUCATIONAL ATTAINMENT										
Less than high school	17.1	13.4	12.9	9.3	19.0	15.5	10.3	10.8	8.3	18.3
High school graduate	26.2	27.8	32.2	28.7	31.2	25.7	21.8	27.9	25.7	38.9
Some college	31.7	31.2	30.5	36.7	25.5	33.9	36.9	38.1	40.4	28.7
Bachelor's degree or more	25.0	27.6	24.4	25.3	24.2	24.9	31.0	23.3	25.6	14.1
EMPLOYMENT STATUS[1]										
Worked full-time last month	53.9	72.4	70.2	74.1	19.2	39.3	50.5	56.4	57.2	12.7
Worked part-time last month	11.2	9.3	5.5	6.3	5.4	16.1	16.0	12.4	15.1	8.8
Did not work last month	34.8	18.3	24.4	19.6	75.4	44.6	33.5	31.2	27.7	78.5
POVERTY LEVEL										
Below poverty level	10.5	10.4	12.7	12.0	10.7	12.5	11.0	25.5	24.3	14.0
100–199 percent of poverty level	17.3	18.0	17.9	16.2	22.6	19.6	17.0	24.1	22.1	36.0
200+ percent of poverty level	70.3	70.8	63.2	66.1	66.1	65.9	71.2	46.7	50.4	49.4
Income not reported	1.9	0.8	6.2	5.7	0.5	2.0	0.8	3.8	3.2	0.6
HOUSEHOLD RECEIVES PUBLIC ASSISTANCE										
Cash assistance	7.0	5.6	5.7	6.7	7.3	7.9	5.8	9.6	10.0	7.5
Noncash assistance[2]	25.2	29.8	30.3	26.0	19.2	29.3	30.6	45.5	49.6	20.5
TENURE										
Owns home	70.5	51.3	55.5	55.0	82.3	69.9	50.4	48.4	53.3	78.3
Rents home[3]	29.5	48.7	44.6	45.0	17.7	30.2	49.6	51.6	46.7	21.7
FAMILY STATUS[4]										
Not living with own children under 18	75.6	69.8	78.8	75.5	96.3	69.9	60.6	45.9	47.8	96.8
Currently living with own children under 18	24.4	30.2	21.2	24.5	3.7	30.1	39.4	54.1	52.2	3.2
Currently living with own children 1–17	23.3	25.1	20.8	23.7	3.7	28.8	34.6	52.3	49.0	3.2
Currently living with own children under 1	2.5	8.0	0.8	1.3	–	2.8	8.8	4.6	5.7	–

– Represents or rounds to zero.
1 Full-time includes those who usually work 35 or more hours per week; part-time includes those who usually work 1–34 hours per week; those who did not work last month include individuals who were unemployed or were not in the labor force.
2 Noncash benefits include food stamps, Women, Infants, and Children (WIC), Medicaid, rent for public housing, lower rent due to government subsidy, energy assistance, and free or reduced-price lunches or breakfasts.
3 Those who occupy without cash payment are included with renters.
4 For the purposes of this table only, "own children" refers to biological or adopted children. The table excludes stepchildren.
Source: U.S. Census Bureau, Survey of Income and Program Participation (SIPP), 2008 Panel, Wave 2 Topical Module. For information on sampling and nonsampling error, see <www.census.gov/sipp/sourceac/S&A08_W1toW3(S&A-12).pdf>.

who were both in their second marriage.²¹ A very small percentage of all currently married couples (1 percent) consisted of a husband and wife who had both been married 3 or more times.

Because the National Center for Health Statistics (NCHS) no longer publishes detailed marriage statistics by marriage order, it is difficult to determine recent trends in these indicators. Based on the SIPP data in Table 12.8, the percentage of couples married in the previous year in which both were entering their first marriage was 65 percent—higher than the 54 percent for couples who married in 1990, based on the last data published by the NCHS.²² These percentages are both lower than the 69 percent reported by NCHS in 1970. The SIPP figure of 65 percent for 2009, however, is not statistically different from the percentage of first-time marriages in 1973 (65 percent) and 1974 (63 percent).²³ The SIPP data also show that 15 percent of couples married in the previous year involved both spouses marrying for at least the second time, compared with the NCHS estimate of 24 percent in 1990. The SIPP 2009 estimates are again not statistically different from those for 1970, in which 16 percent of marriages involved both previously married spouses.²⁴ Although difficult to consistently determine, it appears that the proportion of first-time marriages of both spouses declined from 1970 to 1990 but subsequently increased in more recent years.

MARITAL EVENTS WITHIN THE PREVIOUS YEAR

This section of the report provides basic information about people who have had marital events in the year before the interview, updating data published in the previous report (P70–97) which analyzed the 2001 SIPP marital history data and the tables published from the SIPP 2004 marital history data.²⁵ This section shows characteristics of men and women who had a marriage, separation, divorce, or were widowed in calendar year 2008.

National estimates of the total number of marriages in the 2008 calendar year from the SIPP were higher than estimates shown in the vital statistics reports published by NCHS. For the year ending April 2009, NCHS estimated the total number of marriages at 2,156,000.²⁶ SIPP data yielded 2.4 million marriages for men and women, about 11 percent higher than the NCHS estimates.²⁷ SIPP estimated 792,000 divorces for men and 942,000 divorces for women during 2008.

---

21 The percentage of couples involving a wife who was in her second marriage and a husband who was in his first marriage did not differ statistically from either the percentage of couples involving a husband who was in his second marriage and a wife who was in her first marriage or the percentage of couples involving spouses who were both in their second marriage.

22 Clarke, Sally C., "Advance Report of Final Marriage Statistics, 1989 and 1990," *Monthly Vital Statistics Report*, Vol. 43, No. 12(S), Table 7, July 14, 1995, National Center for Health Statistics, Hyattsville, MD. See <www.cdc.gov/nchs/data/mvsr /supp/mv43_12s.pdf>.

23 The SIPP estimate for 2009 does not differ statistically from the NCHS statistics for 1973 and 1975.

24 Clarke, Sally C., "Advance Report of Final Marriage Statistics, 1989 and 1990," *Monthly Vital Statistics Report*, Vol. 43, No. 12(S), Table 7, July 14, 1995, National Center for Health Statistics, Hyattsville, MD.

25 The 2004 tables can be accessed on the Census Bureau Web site at <www.census.gov/hhes/socdemo /marriage/data /sipp/2004/tables.html>, and the 2001 report at <www.census.gov /prod/2005pubs/p70-97.pdf>.

26 For additional explanation, see the NCHS Web site at <www.cdc.gov/nchs>, or "Births, Marriages, Divorces and Deaths: Provisional Data for 2009," *National Vital Statistics Reports*, Vol. 58, Number 9, December 2009, <www.cdc.gov /nchs/data /nvsr/nvsr58/nvsr58_09.pdf>.

27 NCHS no longer publishes an estimate of the number of divorces, since it no longer receives data from enough states.

SIPP is one of few sources that can provide a look at changes in the characteristics of those with a recent marital event over recent decades. The following discussion of Table 12.9 includes some comparisons back to similar tables in the earlier reports which analyzed 1996 and 2001 SIPP Panel marital history data.[28]

Compared with men and women who had recently married in 1996, the recently married in 2009 were more likely to be Hispanic and less likely to be non-Hispanic White. While about 75 percent of recently married men and women in 1996 were non-Hispanic White, this decreased to about 65 percent in 2009. Conversely, the proportion of the recently married who were Hispanic rose from about 1 in 10 in 1996 to about 1 in 5 in 2009.

The majority of men and women recently widowed are older than most of the men and women who had other marital events. While the median age of men and women who recently married, divorced, or separated was under 50 years, the median age of the men and women who were widowed in the last year was 72 years (Table 12.9).[29]

Age is also especially important when looking at employment status, housing tenure, and family status. The majority of recently married men and women were under age 35 (62 percent of men and 67 percent of women), with a median age of 31 for men and 30 for women. Half or more had at least some college. The percentage of recently married women who had at least a bachelor's degree was higher in 2009 (31 percent) than in 1996 (21 percent). About half of recently married men and women owned their homes. While 30 percent of recently married men lived with their children under 18, about 40 percent of recently married women did. A higher percentage of recently married men lived with their children under 18 in 2009 than in 1996 (25 percent), although the corresponding percentage for women was not different (36 percent in 1996).

The majority of recently separated and divorced men were aged 35 to 54 and the majority of separated and divorced women were aged 25 to 44. While half of these women lived with their own children under 18 (54 percent of separated women and 52 percent of divorced women), one-quarter of recently separated or divorced men (21 percent of those separated and 25 percent of those divorced) lived with their own children under 18.

The data show that marital disruption results in much poorer economic circumstances for women than for men. Thirteen percent of recently separated men were below the poverty level, compared with 26 percent of recently separated women. While 26 percent of recently divorced men or someone in their household received noncash public assistance, 50 percent of recently divorced women or someone in their household received noncash public assistance.

SOURCE OF THE DATA

The population represented (the population universe) in the 2008 Survey of Income and Program Participation (SIPP) is the civilian noninstitutionalized population living in the United States. The SIPP is a longitudinal survey conducted at 4-month intervals. The data in this report were collected

---

28 Both of the earlier reports are available on the Census Bureau Web site. See Table 8 in the 1996 report, <www.census.gov/prod/2002pubs/p70-80.pdf>. See Table 9 in the 2001 report, <www.census.gov/prod/2005pubs/p70-97.pdf>.

29 The median age of men and women widowed in the last year does not differ statistically.

from January through April 2009 in the second wave (interview) of the 2008 SIPP. The data highlighted in this report primarily come from the core and the marital history topical module. Although the main focus of the SIPP is information on labor force participation, jobs, income, and participation in federal assistance programs, information on other topics is also collected in topical modules on a rotating basis. The institutionalized population, which is excluded from the population universe, is composed primarily of the people in correctional institutions and nursing homes (91 percent of the 4.1 million institutionalized people in Census 2000).

ACCURACY OF THE ESTIMATES

Statistics from surveys are subject to sampling and nonsampling error. All comparisons presented in this report have taken sampling error into account and are significant at the 90 percent confidence level unless otherwise noted. This means the 90 percent confidence interval for the difference between the estimates being compared does not include zero. Nonsampling errors in surveys may be attributed to a variety of sources, such as how the survey was designed, how respondents interpret questions, how able and willing respondents are to provide correct answers, and how accurately the answers are coded and classified. The Census Bureau employs quality control procedures throughout the production process, including the overall design of surveys, wording of questions, review of the work of interviewers and coders, and statistical review of reports to minimize these errors.

The Survey of Income and Program Participation (SIPP) weighting procedure uses ratio estimation, whereby sample estimates are adjusted to independent estimates of the national population by age, race, sex, and Hispanic origin. This weighting partially corrects for bias due to undercoverage, but biases may still be present when people who are missed by the survey differ from those interviewed in ways other than the age, race, sex, and Hispanic origin. How this weighting procedure affects other variables in the survey is not precisely known. All of these considerations affect comparisons across different surveys or data sources.

For further information on the statistical standards and the computation and use of standard errors, go to www.census.gov/sipp/sourceac/S&A08_W1toW3(S&A-12).pdf, or contact Benjamin Reist of the Census Bureau's Demographic Statistical Methods Division at <Benjamin.M.Reist@census.gov.

Additional information on the SIPP can be found at the following: www.census.gov/sipp (main SIPP Web site), www.census.gov/sipp/workpapr/wp230.pdf (SIPP Quality Profile), and www.census.gov/sipp/usrguide.html (SIPP User's Guide).

Chapter 13

The American Myth of Divorce

By William C. Spohn

"Don't stay together just for the sake of the children." "If divorce is better for you, it will be better for your kids."

Barbara Dafoe Whitehead's *The Divorce Culture* analyzes the history and social significance of divorce. More importantly, she raises troubling ethical questions about the practice.

First, the factual profile: From 1965 to 1975, the rate of divorce doubled in the United States. It peaked in 1979 at 22 per thousand married women and then stabilized at the 1994 rate of 20 per thousand. Since 1974, 1 million children a year have seen their parents divorce, and 45 percent of all American children can expect their families to break up before they reach the age of 18.

This historic increase in divorce evoked minimal public anxiety or debate, unlike previous eras when the divorce rate rose, as it did between 1910 and 1920, and after World War II. Dafoe charges that this change in attitude resulted from a change in the ethical frame of reference applied to divorce.

Instead of looking at marital breakup in terms of an ethic of obligation to others, Americans began to see it in terms of an ethic of obligation to the self. In other words, no longer were the parents' interests presumed to be subordinate to their children's; instead, individual happiness became the new standard by which a marriage was judged.

According to Dafoe, this shift was a result of the psychological revolution of the 1960s and '70s, which changed "the locus of divorce from the outer social world to the inner world of the self." In this view, "the family, once the realm of the fettered and obligated self, [became] a fertile realm for exploring the potential of the self, unfettered by roles and obligations."

The first wave of literature on the new divorce culture, largely written by relatively affluent and recently divorced women, celebrated these trends as liberating for women and children. After the mid-1980s, however, popular advice books began to challenge some of the earlier assumptions.

William C. Spohn, "The American Myth of Divorce," *Issues in Ethics*, vol. 9, no. 2. Copyright © 1998 by Santa Clara University, Markkula Center for Applied Ethics. Reprinted with permission.

A more troubling picture emerged from studies of larger populations and from tracing the effects on children over time. It turned out there was no trickle down of psychological benefits from mothers to their children. Even though 80 percent of men and 50 percent of women felt their lives were better after divorce, the effects on children were disastrous. By almost every measure, children in divorced families fared worse: emotional problems, early sexual experimenting, dropping out of school, delinquency, teen pregnancy, and drug use.

Remarriage was no solution; children in stepfamilies were two to three times more likely than their counterparts to suffer emotional and behavioral problems and twice as likely to have learning problems.

Long-term studies by Judith Wallerstein and others argue that the impact of divorce on children is cumulative. Even 15 years after their parents' divorce, many children are emotionally troubled, occupationally aimless, and unable to sustain a relationship with someone of the opposite sex. Their parents' inability to sustain the relationship that counted most to them and the subsequent loss of connection to their fathers seem to have eroded these young peoples' sense of identity and ability to trust others and commit themselves.

In the ethos of expressive individualism, where self-fulfillment is the central moral norm, the parents are the only stakeholders in the marriage. But once we pay attention to the children, it becomes impossible to pretend that divorce is primarily an individual's choice rather than a profoundly social event.

Dafoe questions whether our reluctance to blame individuals who divorce has stifled ethical criticisms of the divorce revolution. She writes, "The truth is that divorce involves a radical redistribution of hardship, from adults to children, and therefore cannot be viewed as a morally neutral act."

So, should we stay together for the sake of the children? Dafoe argues that in most cases the answer is yes. Divorce makes sense in the 10 percent to 15 percent of troubled marriages that involve high-level and persistent conflict with severe abuse and physical violence.

But the case is not so clear in marriages marked by marital dissatisfaction, emotional estrangement, boredom, or another romantic interest. In these instances, adults, who are more resilient than children, can be expected to sacrifice some of their own interests in order to preserve the stable and caring home necessary for their offspring to flourish. Traditionally, spouses were obligated not merely to stay in a troubled marriage for the sake of the children but to improve it.

Society also has a stake in parents' remaining committed: "It is the experience of dependable and durable family bonds that shapes a child's sense of trust and fosters development of such traits as initiative, independence, and even risk-taking," Dafoe writes. "Without these traits, it is extremely difficult to cultivate other personal characteristics such as resourcefulness, responsibility, and resilience, which are essential in a pluralistic society and a demanding global economy."

The American discussion of divorce seems to be moving back to the conviction that divorce has ethical and social dimensions. There are calls to retrieve some traditional standards: Children have moral priority; the social cost of divorce has to be counted even more than the benefit to the individual spouse; society has a stake in keeping marriages together; fathers are not dispensable. Such appeals may be able to counter the ethos of expressive individualism that has redefined marriage as an institution for the self-fulfillment of adults.

Chapter 14

Adultery or Divorce—Is There a Right Answer?

By Mark D. White

Is getting divorced "better" than cheating? Maybe not ...
Published on March 29, 2010 by Mark D. White, Ph.D. in Maybe It's Just Me, But ...

One persistent theme in the (largely *fantastic* and immensely *gratifying*) comments* to my post on the ethics of adultery was the option of leaving the relationship altogether, which means divorce in the case of married couples.

Several commenters (including me) noted that while that may be an obvious and relatively costless alternative for some (particularly unmarried couples), factors such as children and financial constraints may make divorce more difficult for others. In turn, this hardship may serve (at least in part) to justify adultery in the case of an extraordinarily dysfunctional relationship from which escape is just as extraordinarily difficult.

(Note my use of the word "may" above—every situation is different, and each person must use his or her judgment to make a decision he or she is ethically comfortable with, such as whether divorce will have a net positive or negative impact on his or her children.)

But I think an even more interesting question is this: even in the absence of children and financial ties, is divorce an *ethical* alternative to adultery? I presume most would say "of course," but I'm not so sure, and exploring that uncertainty is the subject of this post.

---

* I really cannot say enough how much the readers here at PT have come mean to me in my relatively short time here. I've had some success with popular (as opposed to academic) writing before, and I blogged elsewhere, but blogging here provides a level of instant feedback that I've never known before. After the post on the ethics of adultery became so successful—thanks to all of you—I shared the news with some of my academic colleagues, who envied the ability that this blog gives me to "reach the people" to such a degree. The current post, in fact, was originally a sketch for an academic paper that, were it ever finished and published, would be read by perhaps dozens of people over my lifetime. Now, publishing it here, it will be read by dozens of people in the first few minutes—simply amazing, and as I said above, immensely gratifying. *Thank you.*

Mark D. White, "Adultery or Divorce—Is There a Right Answer?" *Psychology Today.* Copyright © 2010 by Mark D. White. Reprinted with permission.

First, let's be clear what we're talking about here. We're not talking about mutually voluntary (bilateral) divorce, in which both spouses agree that dissolution of the marriage is the best option for all concerned. And we're not talking about unilateral divorce (initiated by one spouse against the wishes of the other) for other reasons (besides adultery). We are talking about unilateral divorce, initiated for the purpose of pursuing a romantic and/or sexual relationship with another person, as opposed to remaining married and engaging in adulterous acts.

You may wonder what got me thinking about this (which I've been doing for a while, long before I became a PT blogger). In the last post, I explained that one deontological argument against adultery centered on the breaking of a promise (the wedding vow). But doesn't divorce do the same thing? You know, all that "for better or for worse" and "til death do we part" language (or the rough equivalents)?

Divorce is legal, of course (at least according to civil law if not religious law, which may be as important, if not more important, to some), and in most states does not require a demonstration of fault, but that doesn't settle the ethical issue. For example, I doubt many people base their opinions on the morality of abortion, same-sex marriage, or torture on its legality at any given moment. (But the legality aspect will pop up again later.)

So why is breaking the "staying together" part of the wedding vows OK, but not the "forsaking all others" part—especially when divorce (by definition) ends the marriage, whereas infidelity may not?

Let's start with what's wrong with adultery, but approached differently than we did in the last post. The "wrongness" of adultery is usually traced to three sources: 1) injury or harm to the relationship from the deception usually associated with adultery, 2) injury or harm to the relationship from the adulterous act itself, and 3) the breaking of the marital vow, promise, or commitment. (I treat all three of those as components of harm to the spouse, which is why that is not a separate, fourth category.) In the terms of the previous post, the first two categories would be utilitarian in nature, while the third is deontological (with some utilitarian overtones), but those categories are of less use here.

So let's look at these issues, one at a time:

If the main issue is **deception**, then divorce does look better, since it does not involve deception (except possibly regarding motive) whereas infidelity often does.

If the main issue with adultery is **promise-breaking**, then divorce seems to be just as bad, unless one part of the promise is considered more important than another (which it clearly is in different cultures, as discussed in the comments to the last post).

If the main issue with adultery is **harm to the relationship**, then divorce imposes the same harm—in fact, on the average it does more harm to the relationship, since by definition a marriage cannot survive divorce (unless the couple gets remarried), but a marriage can survive adultery (and, if it doesn't, it ends in divorce anyway). Of course, some would claim that adultery can improve the marriage—if we accept this, at least in some (relatively rare) cases, this makes divorce look even more harmful to the relationship compared to adultery. But even if we doubt the benefits to marriage of adultery, divorce still does more damage to marriages on the average than adultery does.

If the above is correct (and doesn't leave anything crucially important out), then we can't make a clear-cut determination that divorce is an ethically preferable alternative to adultery. Compared to adultery, divorce is less deceptive (a good thing), represents a roughly equal threat to promise-keeping (a wash), and threatens greater harm to the relationship (a bad thing). So in *some* cases, divorce may be less ethical than adultery, which goes against (what I take to be) common intuition.

So, is there a right answer? No, not in terms of one right answer for everybody, but each person can come up with an answer that is right for him or her. But, you may ask, in what sense is such an answer "right" if we can't appeal to some higher moral authority for verification? Well, it has to be "right" in the sense that we have reasons for that decision that reflect our integrity or character, which in part is based on our moral beliefs, as well as life experiences, past decisions, and so on. In other words, *you* have to believe that you have found the right answer, and you have be able to defend that answer to *yourself*—sincerely, like you're having a conversation with your conscience, not in the sense of rationalization.

For instance, if you value your marriage, the relationship itself, very highly, the fact that divorce poses the greatest threat to that marriage may lead to decide that divorce is not the right answer to an unacceptable marriage (which does not imply that adultery is either, of course, but that's a separate decision discussed in the previous post). Or, if you value honesty very highly, then divorce may be the better way to deal with an unacceptable marriage than adultery is. Or, if there is another factor we have not considered here that is very important to you, such as your religious tradition and what it says about divorce, as well as things we assumed away at the beginning, like children and financial ties, then your right answer will depend on that.

One final question: if what we said above about divorce and adultery is correct, then why is divorce so often regarded as the obvious ethical choice? Does this imply that fidelity within the marriage is regarded as more important than the marriage itself? (Several commenters to the last post focused on this.) People often say, "if you want to have sex with someone else, the honorable thing to do is get a divorce first." Divorce is more honest, true, but it may also give up on the marriage too quickly; after all, many marriages do survive adultery (whether or not they are better off for it).

Here's one possible explanation (and feel free to offer more): Divorce may be seen as more ethically acceptable (outside certain faiths) simply because it *is* legal. I said above that legality can't settle questions of morality, but it certainly affects our perception of the morality of behavior. Divorce is an institution in Western countries, and to choose divorce is, in some sense, to "play by the rules," whereas adultery represents breaking the rules.

(On the negative side, precisely because it's legal, divorce can more easily be used as a threat—"if you don't do what I want, I'll divorce you"—allowing one spouse to exploit the marital relationship for private gain, especially if the other spouse values the marriage more. It isn't pretty, but it happens.)

All I'm trying to say is that divorce should not be assumed to be *always* ethically better than adultery—it may be in some cases, but not in all cases. In the end, we must each use our judgment, based on our values and experience, to arrive at what we believe--what we *must* believe—to be the right answer.**

Let me know what you think!

** The concept of the "right answer" comes originally from the legal philosophy of Ronald Dworkin (particularly from his book *Taking Rights Seriously*), which I am incorporating into a theory of judgment and character in my scholarly work—more on that to come.

FURTHER READINGS

Amato, Paul R., and Jacob Cheadle. "The Long Reach of Divorce: Divorce and Child Well-Being Across Three Generations." *Journal of Marriage and Family 67* (February 2005): 191–206.

Cherlin, Andrew J. *The Marriage-Go-Round: The State of Marriage and the Family in America Today.* New York: Random House, 2010.

Furstenberg, Frank F. "Divorce and the American Family." *Annual Review of Sociology 16* (1990): 379–403.

Heath, Melanie. *One Marriage under God: The Campaign to Promote Marriage in America.* New York: New York University Press, 2012.

Stevenson, Betsy, and Justin Wolfers. "Marriage and Divorce: Changes and Their Driving Forces." *The Journal of Economic Perspectives* 21, no. 2 (2007), 27–52.

Modern Trends in Family: The Future of Marriage

Chapter 15

Marriage as a Public Issue

By Steven L. Nock

Following several decades of sweeping demographic, social, and legal changes that have minimized the importance of marriage in U.S. society, a wide-ranging assortment of Americans-religious activists, family practitioners, therapeutic professionals, educators, and state and federal officials—is now conspicuously promoting marriage. Public discussions of family formation often support the goal of having all children raised in healthy, married families. Social science research offers evidence that marriage, unlike other family structures, confers special benefits on both adults and children. Public policymakers promote stable marriages and discourage unmarried births. Congress has declared out-of-wedlock births, reliance on welfare assistance for raising children, and single-mother families contrary to the national interest. This article reviews this renewed national interest in marriage, focusing first on the demographic trends behind the debate and then on the scientific evidence about the consequences of marriage for the economic well-being and health of Americans. It next identifies the primary actors and activities involved in the marriage-promotion effort, and concludes by considering the significance of this renewed national focus on marriage.

Marriage as a Public Issue

Marriage is no stranger to national debate in the United States. It has been at the center of a variety of American social, religious, and political movements over the nation's history. Past political activists, most at the state level, have worked to deny access to marriage to certain groups-slaves, people of certain races, certain categories of immigrants, or homosexuals-or to grant married women greater legal rights or to liberalize divorce laws. Social and religious activists have typically focused on such matters as reducing divorce. What is new-and remarkable-about the current marriage movement is that its purpose is to promote matrimony. In certain respects,

Steven L. Nock, "Marriage as a Public Issue," *The Future of Children, vol. 15, no. 2,* pp. 13–32. Copyright © 2005 by The Trustees of Princeton University, (CC BY-ND 3.0).

today's marriage movement may seem surprising. After all, most Americans value marriage highly, and the overwhelming majority marry at some point in their lives. Indeed, by international standards they marry at high rates and divorce at lower rates than they did two decades ago. But the institution of marriage has recently undergone dramatic transformation. Rapid demographic and social changes in the United States over the past four or five decades have fundamentally disrupted traditional marriage and family patterns. What once forcefully organized American life no longer does so. In many respects, the current debate about marriage represents the nation's attempt to interpret and make sense of these wrenching social changes.

Demographic Trends

The chief demographic and cultural trends driving the marriage debate have been the weakening link between marriage and parenthood, the declining significance of marriage as an organizing principle of adult life, and the increasingly accepted view that marriage and parenthood are private matters, relevant only to the individuals directly involved.

Andrew Cherlin provides a full discussion of the demographic shifts over the past half-century in the way Americans organize their households and families. The most significant for my discussion are the following. First, people now postpone marriage to later ages. They often live in their parents' homes, with friends, or with unmarried partners, thus increasing the time adults spend unmarried. Second, more couples now live together without getting married, either as a precursor or an alternative to marriage or as an alternative to living alone. The availability of such alternatives naturally makes marriage less central to domestic life. Third, high divorce rates and births to un-married mothers leave more households headed by single parents, increasing the time both adults and children spend outside married-couple families. Fourth, because more women, especially more married women, are in the labor force, the prevalence of one-wage-earner, two-parent families-what has been called the "traditional" family-has declined. Finally, delayed and declining fertility and increasing longevity result in fewer children, smaller families, and longer lives, adding to the time parents spend "post-children" and to the number of married couples without children.

These five demographic trends reflect other important social and economic changes, including increasing equality between the sexes, the legalization of abortion, increasing tolerance for diverse lifestyles, and liberalized laws governing divorce. Perhaps the most important change, however, has been the development of effective birth control.

Gaining Control of Fertility

The centrality of marriage in American culture and law during the nineteenth and twentieth centuries can be understood, in part, as a consequence of poorly controlled fertility. As long as sexual intercourse naturally resulted in births, marriage (or engagement) was the only permissible venue for sex. Marriage was an institutional and societal arrangement that allocated responsibility for children. No alternative civil or religious arrangement could accomplish that task, except in extraordinary circumstances. By restricting sex to marriage, communities were able to reduce births of children for whom no male kin were obviously and legitimately responsible.

Children born outside marriage were denied certain legal rights, such as inheritance and claims on paternal assets. These children-and their mothers-were also stigmatized in the eyes of the community.

By such means, communities effectively limited the number of births outside marriage. But once effective contraception uncoupled sex from fertility, this social justification for marriage became irrelevant. The convention of "shotgun" weddings, for example, gradually disappeared. Before the advent of effective contraception and legal abortion, a wedding to avoid the stigma of an illegitimate birth typically followed a premarital pregnancy. That it no longer does so illustrates the changing under-standing of the importance of marriage for births.

The birth control pill was introduced in 1960. Within a decade, more than a third of all married women in America were using oral contraception. There was also a note-worthy increase in voluntary sterilization among women older than age thirty. Indeed, by 1970, six in ten American married women were using medical, effective, non-coitus related methods of birth control. Ten years earlier, wives had extremely limited access to contraception, and much of what existed was ineffective. These technological innovations in birth control have been described as a "contraceptive revolution" or a "reproductive technology shock" because of their pro-found implications for social customs and norms.

Sex Becomes a Private Matter

The contraceptive revolution made sex a private matter legally and essentially re-moved it from state control. A series of U.S. Supreme Court decisions during the 1960s had major implications for the legal and cultural meaning of sex and childbearing. In the most important case, Griswold v. Connecticut (1965), the Court declared unconstitutional a state law forbidding the use of contraceptive devices, even by married couples. Writing for the Court majority, Justice William O. Douglas explained that various guarantees of the Bill of Rights "create zones of privacy," making "the very idea of prohibiting the practice of birth control . . . repulsive to the notions of privacy surrounding the marriage relationship." Griswold and subsequent Court decisions established a constitutional right to privacy in matters of sexual behavior among consenting adults, married or single, and, most recently, heterosexual or homosexual.

Before Griswold, sexual matters had never been completely private because of their potential public consequences. Communities prohibited sexual freedoms because adultery and illegitimacy disrupted family lines, some-times creating collective obligations for the care of offspring. Premarital and extramarital sexual intercourse were illegal. The ability to separate intercourse from reproduction re-moved the rationale for such regulations. Sexual intercourse was long the legal symbolic core of marriage; consummation defined its de facto creation. Sexual exclusivity was the basis for a range of legal restrictions surrounding marriage. Adultery, for example, provided grounds for lawsuits by the aggrieved spouse. A married person's consortium, the legally protected emotional stakes a spouse has in his or her marriage, was protected in family law. Those who damaged a marriage by adultery or by luring a married partner into an extramarital relationship (enticement) were subject to tortuous legal actions for damages to consortium.

Such "heart balm" claims are now more a curiosity than a conspicuous feature of domestic relations law, except when physical injury is involved. Most jurisdictions have abolished or limited such suits. That such actions are now pursued so infrequently (in the few remaining states where they are still permitted) attests to the declining legal significance of sexual exclusivity in marriage. Similarly, the rapid spread of no-fault divorce laws since 1970 has effectively eliminated adultery as a condition for divorce. Culturally, once sexual relations came to be viewed as private decisions unrelated to marriage, so did reproduction choices. In other words, once sex and procreation could be separated, so could sex and marriage. But so, too, of course, could reproduction and marriage, as they increasingly have been.

Both the social stigma and the legal consequences of having an "illegitimate" child have virtually vanished in recent years. In a series of decisions between 1968 and 1978, the U.S. Supreme Court declared unconstitutional the legal distinctions associated with the marital status of a child's parents. In this as in most areas of domestic relations, American family law has shifted its primary focus from the married couple to the individual. The marital status of parents is legally irrelevant from the perspective of either generation.

In short, now that fertility can be controlled, parenthood and marriage are less institutionalized and much less predictably connected. A once near-universal insistence on an adult social script governing marriage has given way to an expanding range of acceptable, though less traditional, life course options, such as cohabitation. Living together in a sexual relationship, once taboo, is now so acceptable that a majority of Americans cohabit before they marry. And yet the practice is still so novel that it lacks a vernacular name. Nor, importantly, is it yet governed by norms or explicit laws. Like many social changes fostered by sexual freedom, cohabitation is not yet institutionalized, not yet integrated fully into the nation's culture or law.

The old rules have changed, but new standards have yet to emerge. The new living arrangements are often incompatible with old customs and conventions. Even more vexing, the new arrangements offer fewer traditional solutions when problems arise, because many of the problems themselves are the result of nontraditional arrangements. Cohabiting couples, for example, have little tradition to follow when dealing with the informal equivalent of their "in-laws." Relations with the older generation are strained as a result. Predictably, when a stable system of social conventions is so quickly altered, some will react by seeking to restore it. Today's marriage movement is one such reaction. ...

The Consequences of Marriage

For well over a century, researchers have known that married people are generally better off than their unmarried counterparts. As early as 1897, sociologist Emile Durkheim was theorizing about why married adults have lower suicide rates than unmarried adults. In a recent survey David Ribar notes that links between marriage and better health in children and adults "have been documented in hundreds of quantitative studies covering different time periods and different countries."

The accumulated research shows that married people are typically healthier, live longer, earn more, have better mental health, have better sex lives, and are happier than their un-married counterparts. They have lower rates of suicide, fatal accidents, acute and chronic illness, alcoholism, and depression. (...)

Despite abundant evidence documenting such correlation, however, a question recurs: is marriage the cause of the health and happiness enjoyed by married people, or are healthier and happier people the ones most likely to marry? If people who are less healthy, happy, or successful are also less attractive as potential spouses, then they will be less likely to be selected into marriage. The ranks of the unmarried will thus contain a disproportionate number of such people. On the other hand, if marriage actually causes people to have better health, happiness, or success, then the unmarried would, again, be less happy, healthy, or successful. Because both the "selection" and the "causal" arguments lead to the same empirical results, debate has continued for many years.

It is impossible to settle the issue definitively through a rigorous scientific experiment: people cannot be randomly assigned to marry or remain single, divorce or remain together. Before the 1970s, researchers relied on cross-sectional data (either a single survey or one point in a long-term data series) that simply compared the married with the unmarried on various outcomes. But cross-sectional associations do not make a convincing case that marriage has beneficial effects. They may be confounded by omitted variables that influence both the likelihood of being married and of enjoying better outcomes, or by reverse causation (for example, better health leading to marriage rather than vice versa).

Since the 1970s marriage researchers have been using long-term data that follow the same group of people as they move into and out of marriage. If changes in marital status (marrying, divorcing, remarrying) are consistently correlated with comparable changes in health or economic well-being, this is strong evidence for the plausibility of a causal connection. Such a long-term data design is as close to a true experiment as researchers can hope to get. These studies have provided evidence for both causal and selection arguments, with the causal argument sometimes seeming stronger and sometimes weaker in its effects.

Theoretical Underpinnings

Before I review the research findings, it is worth considering why married adults might differ (especially in beneficial ways) from their unmarried counterparts. What theory would predict or explain such differences? A variety of such explanations exist and can be grouped under three broad themes: marriage as a social institution, specialization, and the domesticating role of marriage.

The institutional perspective argues that marriage changes individuals in positive ways, both to the extent that others treat them differently and to the extent that they come to view themselves differently. The marital relationship carries with it legal, moral, and conventional assumptions about what is right and proper. It is, in other words, institutionalized and defined by social norms. It is culturally patterned and integrated into other basic social institutions like education, the economy, and politics. In this sense, married individuals have a tradition of solutions to rely on when they confront problems. For many matters in domestic life, marriage supplies a template.

Moreover, the institutional nature of marriage implies that others will treat married people differently because of the cultural assumptions made about husbands and wives. Employers may prefer married to unmarried workers, for example, or may reward married employees with greater opportunities and benefits. Insurers may discount policies for married people. And the law gives married partners legal rights vis-a-vis each other that are not granted to unmarried people. Economists refer to this aspect of marriage as its "signaling" function. Economic signals- are activities or attributes of a person that convey information to others. The most effective economic signals are those that involve significant cost to the sender. A classic example is a college degree, which transmits, for ex-ample to an employer, valuable information about the sender. Because marriage, like a college degree, has significant costs attached, it serves as an economic signal of those things culturally associated with marriage: commitment, stability, and maturity, among other things. Friends, relatives, and employers will be inclined to assume such things about married people. To the extent they do, married people will benefit. Because cohabitation is relatively costless (in signaling theory, cohabitation is "cheap talk"), it does not convey the same positive signal marriage does. Thus, for example, it is not surprising that cohabiting men earn less than married men, even when other aspects of their relationships are similar.

Regardless of what marriage may mean to an individual in a relationship, it has broader implications in what it means to others. This is a core assumption of the institutional argument about marriage.

The institution of marriage also involves what Andrew Cherlin calls "enforceable trust." "Marriage still requires a public commitment to a long-term, possibly lifelong relationship. ... Cohabitation, in contrast, requires only a private commitment which is easier to break. Therefore, marriage, more so than cohabitation, lowers the risk that one's partner will renege on agreements that have been made." Many observers now believe that this aspect of marriage has become less central as the private, individualized view of marriage has become increasingly dominant.

The second theory about why married people might differ from unmarried people is specialization. When two people marry and merge households, they not only gain obvious economies of scale but also tend to develop an efficient division of labor. To the extent that spouses have different skills, preferences, or abilities, marriage allows each to concentrate on those in which he or she has a relative advantage. Such efficiencies have traditionally implied that wives would focus on nonmarket labor, such as child care and homemaking, because women's wages were so much lower than men's. But even in contemporary marriages, efficiencies from a division of labor still arise. For example, married parents with young children sometimes stagger their work hours to permit one to deliver the children to school and the other to be home when school is out. This simple strategy reduces the demand for expensive day care. As couples refine their division of tasks, the household benefits to the extent that each partner's productivity increases. Such specialization produces greater interdependencies and lowers divorce rates. The interdependencies also have economic value ("marriage-specific capital") and have been protected in tort law as consortium. Such specialization diminishes the wife's earning potential in the market to the extent that her skills or credentials, or both, decay. Still, even in contemporary marriages, in which the large majority of wives are employed, couples continue to divide household tasks. Cohabiting couples are less likely to do so.

The third theory about differences between married and unmarried people involves marriage's domesticating role. Men are thought to change more when they marry than women do because unmarried men live less healthy lives than unmarried women do and therefore have more room in their lives for positive change. Specifically, once men are married, they are much less likely to engage in risky behaviors such as drinking heavily, driving dangerously, or using drugs. They are also more likely to work regularly, help others more, volunteer more, and attend religious services more frequently. Durkheim argued that such changes occur because marriage integrates men into social groups of like-minded others and, by doing so, establishes acceptable boundaries around their behaviors. Others have made similar arguments about how marriage "domesticates" men by fostering a sense of responsibility for their families, orienting them toward the future and making them sensitive to the long-term consequences of their actions, and providing someone to offer advice, schedule medical appointments, or encourage pro-social behaviors (the so-called nagging factor). And both partners' mental health appears to benefit from the support and understanding they share (more in marriage than in cohabiting relationships).

Economic Changes Associated with Marriage

As noted, the correlation between marriage and economic outcomes involves both selection and causal factors. Men with favorable expected earnings are more likely to marry and less prone to divorce. But research has found that marriage also improves earnings, at least for men. The so-called marriage premium is the additional income that men generate once they marry. Men's earnings, not only in America but in other developed countries, increase once they marry (over and above any change associated with age or experience), and their earnings increase faster than those of comparable unmarried men. And the marriage premium is lost when men divorce. The generally accepted explanation is that men's productivity increases after marriage, largely because of specialization.

After replicating, and thus validating, earlier findings of a marriage premium for men, especially in the first years of marriage, economists Sanders Korenman and David Neumark examined employment records that included performance evaluations and other 20 indicators of productivity. They found that married men had higher performance ratings than unmarried men and that their higher productivity was largely responsible for their higher earnings.

Women's earnings consistently fail to increase as a result of marriage. But they do not consistently drop, either. Rather, marriage-linked changes in women's earnings are probably due more to fertility. Both married and un-married women who have children earn less, as a result.

Research that controls for selectivity typically finds somewhat smaller marriage earnings premiums for men, but it nevertheless finds a premium. (For women, the situation is less clear.) Such findings, as well as new evidence that marriage is increasingly viewed as something to postpone until one is already financially stable (that is, reverse causality), mean that it is probably true that both causal and selection effects operate for both sexes in matters of marriage and economic well-being.

Health Changes Associated with Marriage

People who are involved with others typically enjoy better health than those who are socially isolated. Because marriage is a form of social integration, it is not surprising that married people are healthier. Almost without exception, long-term studies of health find that marriage (especially when it is satisfying or long term, or both) is associated with better health and increased longevity. With respect to physical health and mortality, most people adopt a healthier lifestyle once married, thereby avoiding illness or death caused by harmful behavior such as excessive drinking. A spouse is likely to encourage healthier behaviors in his or her partner, such as smoking or drinking less, going to the doctor when ill, having regular checkups, and visiting the dentist. And marital interactions typically reduce stress, thereby contributing to better health.

There is some, albeit limited, evidence of selectivity with respect to health. For example, good health appears to make unemployed women—but not working women—more likely to get married. Research in the Netherlands found that poor health increased the chances of divorce, though it did not affect entry into marriage. Such a line of research offers minimal support for the "selection" argument.

Overall, both causal and selection arguments are probably true in matters of health. Healthier people are more likely both to marry and to avoid divorce. At the same time, marriage promotes healthier lifestyles and reduces the chances of death. Research indicates that the positive effects of marriage seem stronger for men than for women. The most likely explanation for such findings is that unmarried men lead more unhealthy lives and take greater risks than unmarried women do.

The Marriage Movement: E Pluribus Unum

Based in part on research showing that marriage is good for adults and children, strengthening marriage has become a goal of both public and private initiatives in recent years.

Proponents of strengthening marriage form a diverse group. Many are in religious communities, especially conservative Protestant denominations. Their aim is to rebuild a traditional model of lifelong monogamous marriage. Others—practitioners and professionals in various fields—are motivated by concerns about rising divorce rates or about the welfare of couples, individual adults, and children. Many are therapy-oriented and seek to educate or counsel people about strategies and skills to build healthy relationships, whether through marriage or otherwise. Others belong to fatherhood groups concerned about absent fathers. Still others are state government officials concerned about the problems of the poor. Most of these latter are affiliated with programs targeting unmarried parents, many growing out of changes in welfare law in the late 1990s.

Religious Mobilization

The dramatic transformation of American households and families from the late 1960s through the late 1980s came on the heels of one of the most homogeneous cultural periods of U.S. history in matters of marriage and living arrangements. The postwar era of the 1950s featured historically high fertility rates, low divorce rates, and youthful ages at marriage. The postwar economy and veterans' programs significantly expanded the middle class. Attendance at religious services was high. Culturally, it was the most "familistic" decade of the century: the family was understood as the crucial social institution, both for the individual and for society as a whole. Familism, an ideology that emerged during the seventeenth and eighteenth centuries, associated the prevailing family principles of marriage, childbearing, motherhood, commitment, and sacrifice for family with a sense of sacredness. It stressed sexual fidelity in marriage, chastity before marriage, intensive child-rearing, a commitment to a lifelong marriage, and high levels of expressive interaction among family members.

Against this backdrop, the demographic and cultural trends of the 1960s and 1970s raised grave concern among conservative religious communities, who saw most of these trends as signs of decay. Feminism, the sexual revolution, legalized abortion, divorce, cohabitation, homosexuality, and open challenges to authority energized the rise of a religiously affiliated movement to restore the basic features of 1950s familism. The new Christian Right, which included such groups as Jerry Falwell's Moral Majority, Beverly LaHaye's Concerned Women for America, and James Dobson's Focus on the Family (later the Family Research Council), became a powerful political force, mobilizing millions of voters and establishing lobbying groups with close ties to Republican leaders and conservative members of Congress. More generally, conservative Protestantism has been, and remains, an important force in matters of the family because its adherents are very active, devoting more time and money to their churches and affiliated organizations than any other major religious group in America.

With increased sexual freedom driving many of the liberalizing trends of the later twentieth century, it is not surprising that sexual matters were the focus of much of the reaction. As Karen Armstrong notes in her historical review of conservative religious movements, the fundamentalists of the 1970s and 1980s "associated the integrity and even the survival of their society with the traditional position of women." Feminism, homosexuality, and abortion were central themes in a religious movement to restore family values.

Professional Mobilization

Others involved in the marriage debate include professionals, practitioners, and social scientists with an interest in divorce and marital stability. Psychologists have analyzed interpersonal behaviors and strategies associated with various outcomes of relationships and have identified styles of conflict resolution, coping, and communication as critical elements in marriage. Demographers and sociologists have identified background traits such as cohabitation, parental divorce, young age at marriage, and low levels of religiousness as strong predictors of divorce.

About twenty-five years ago, a field now known as couples education or marriage education began integrating such research into therapeutic approaches to helping couples prepare for or prevent problems in relationships. Couples education, offered in class-like settings, teaches both individuals and couples strategies to avoid the known risks to marriage.

Yet another group of professionals launched programs to promote and help fathers. Fatherhood programs, many in state government, focus on pregnancy prevention (most target young men), child support enforcement and the establishment of paternity, visitation issues, and services for poor fathers, especially those unable to comply with child support orders. Many national organizations support fatherhood. The National Fatherhood Initiative, founded in 1994, seeks to increase the involvement of fathers with their children through a range of educational and training programs. The National Center for Fathering, founded in 1990, sponsors seminars for corporations and schools to encourage greater family involvement by fathers. The Families and Work Institute's Fatherhood Project works with corporations, government agencies, and local fatherhood groups to develop father-friendly programs and policies, such as paternity leave. Other groups supporting fatherhood include the National Partnership for Community Leader-ship and the National Practitioners Network for Fathers and Families. Several independent professionals, national professional organizations, and educational and research institutions have also launched efforts on behalf of marriage. (...)

Conclusions and Recommendations

The seemingly endless array of contemporary public and private efforts to promote marriage, reduce out-of-wedlock births, encourage responsible fatherhood, and persuade unmarried parents to marry would have made little sense to Americans living just fifty years ago. For them, marriage was the central and defining feature of adult identity; for them, such goals were elemental moral principles. Not so for today's Americans, who find themselves far removed from such a marriage-centered culture and struggling to re-define the role that marriages and families play in society.

Sociologists refer to historical moments such as our own, when technology has advanced much more rapidly than the institutions surrounding it, as periods of culture lag. The technological advance in this case was effective fertility control. When scientists discovered how to control the link between sex and reproduction, they set off prodigious changes in the institutions of marriage and the family. Many Americans are now engaged in the contemporary marriage debate precisely because they are struggling to understand the meaning of the wrenching dislocations in American social and family life over the past half-century.

Champions of marriage have thus far had few victories. Perhaps it is still too early. More likely, the related goals of promoting marriage and discouraging divorce or out-of-wedlock births will fare about as well as other national attempts to alter large social trends.

At the moment, most marriage-promotion efforts focus on individuals and the choices they make. It may be possible to convince poor women that it is best to get married before having children. It may be possible to convince them that marriage is better than cohabitation. It may be possible to teach couples how to resolve problems that jeopardize their relationships. Evidence suggests that most poor women already understand many of these things. Given how little researchers and professionals know about helping couples get or stay married, however, our expectations of policies in these areas should be modest, at best. Despite the lack of effective strategies to accomplish these goals, there nevertheless appears to be an emerging political, cultural, and scientific consensus about the consequences of different family structures for children's well-being. Increasingly, Americans appear to understand that the best arrangement for children is with two loving parents even if we have yet to develop ways always to achieve that goal. Our current efforts reflect this uncertainty about how to strengthen families.

Attempts directed toward changing or "fixing" individuals reflect a psychological behaviorist assumption that the root "problem" lies within the person, not his or her society or environment. If one adopts this perspective, then the obvious solution is something like education or training-couples education, for example, or counseling. Again, if one adopts this perspective, then the assessment of such solutions lies in measuring individual change, as studied through such strategies as random-assignment experiments. But if the problem is viewed as larger than the individual, and if it is seen as endemic to an entire historical era, then it cannot be addressed solely at the individual level. One way to begin to address it would be to engage in a prolonged and sometimes painful national discussion. Such a discussion would take place in public among lawmakers, clergy, teachers, journalists, opinion leaders, and intellectuals-and in private between partners, between parents, and among family members. Such a national conversation would interpret and make sense of the changing roles played by marriage and families in society. This is how social change is managed and understood. And this, I believe, is how to understand today's debate over the value of marriage.

FURTHER READINGS

Bengtson, Vern L., Timothy J. Biblarz, and Robert E. L. Roberts. *How Families Still Matter: A Longitudinal Study of Youth in Two Generations*. New York: Cambridge University Press, 2002.

Blankenhorn, David. *The Future of Marriage*. New York: Encounter Books, 2009.

Coontz, Stephanie. "The Future of Marriage." *Cato Unbound: Journal of Debate*, January 14, 2008.

Dickson, Lynda. "The Future of Marriage and Family in Black America." *Journal of Black Studies* 23, no. 4 (1993): 472–91.

Fraser Hodder, Harbour. "The Future of Marriage: Changing Demographics, Economics, and Laws Alter the Meaning of Matrimony in America." *Harvard Magazine*, November-December, 2004.

Modern Trends in Family: Family Planning

Chapter 16

Abortion

By Jeffrey Balancio, Ph.D.

If you have ever participated in or have been within earshot of a discussion about whether abortion should be legal you know that people can be passionate about their positions. You may also know that rarely does anyone change anybody's mind during these discussions.

This article does not take a side or promote a position on the abortion issue. The intention is to help the reader determine if abortion is an ethical choice for her or him personally.

When we talk about evaluating an activity as ethical we are not measuring it against statutes, we are measuring it against principles of morality, conceptions of right and wrong or codes of behavior expected by the group to which the individual belongs. Morals are the principles on which one judges right and wrong; ethics are the principles of right conduct. They are closely related and often interchangeable. Three of the four assumptions built into this article are: people have an inner moral compass; ethics drives actions and decisions that are consistent with one's moral compass; and an action or decision is unethical when it is not consistent with one's moral compass.

Debates about the legality of abortion rarely change opinions because the parties involved are anchored by their core principles. Legality is the state of being in conformity with the law whereas ethics is a system that determines conformity with one's moral principles. Laws usually apply equally to all people. Ethics are not universal and are not necessarily synchronized with laws. For example, recently it became legal to smoke marijuana in Colorado yet some people may decide, after engaging their internal moral compass, that it is not an ethical behavior and therefore not appropriate to participate. Others will make the opposite decision. In a similar manner, all readers here are asked to bring their moral principles and conceptions of right and wrong to the table. In return, the article provides a variety of positions to measure them against. The conclusions each reader may reach regarding abortion should then be as personal, based on his/her moral compass, as the decisions being made by individual Coloradans regarding whether or not to smoke marijuana.

Regardless of the government's position on legality, important abortion considerations include rights; most notably the rights of the woman and the rights of the zygote / embryo/ fetus within her. A woman is a person and a person definitely has some rights. Is a zygote, embryo or fetus a person? Does it matter if a zygote, embryo or fetus is a person? That should be considered because inducing an abortion involves extinguishing the life of a zygote, embryo or a fetus. Those three terms represent discrete phases in the first trimester of gestation, which is the name given to the period of time between conception and birth.

The zygote, which contains all of the genetic information needed to become a baby—half of the DNA from each parent – results when a sperm fertilizes an egg cell (moment of conception). After one week of development the term embryo is used. Development continues during the embryonic period as the embryo experiences organogenesis. By the end of the eighth week all major body parts, heart beat and brain waves are present and the embryo matures into a fetus, the term used to describe the developing baby until the moment of birth. For the balance of this article the word 'fetus' will be inclusive of zygote, embryo and fetus.

One inarguable right a person in America has is the right to life. What is not inarguable in America, however, is agreement as to the time at which human life begins. At one end of the opinion spectrum human life is said to begin at the 'moment of conception'. At nearly the other end it is believed to begin at the 'moment of birth'. I say nearly at the other end of the spectrum because some argue that at the 'moment of birth' the baby is not yet a person. This theory contends that in order to be a person one has to have the capacity of self-awareness and that capacity does not occur until some undefined number of months following birth.

What constitutes and defines a 'person' varies greatly from culture to culture, entailing different rights, duties, kinship bonds, and titles. Most attempts to define personhood recognize that the human person must extend beyond a merely biological basis to include some form of consciousness or rationality.

In some Western cultures metaphysical questions are raised regarding the identity of consciousness over time, about the identity of states of consciousness with particular bodies, and about how we differentiate ourselves from what is not ourselves. It also raises ethical questions. The concept of personhood allows us to isolate appropriate objects of moral concern i.e. persons, as opposed to anything else worthy of moral recognition. The notion of personhood also allows us to differentiate among those who are appropriate because personhood may consist of degrees. Can one human being be more or less a person than another? Should a patient in a coma be considered less of a person than a fully conscious one? Should a fetus be considered less a person than an infant? Some people reject this last view, arguing that by any definition of 'person', a fetus qualifies.

Personhood in some Eastern cultures is more a process than a state or category of being. The person, they believe, embodies part of his or her ancestral past. Some of these cultures believe in reincarnation as a means through which the person continues through generations. The idea of spiritual continuation, however, is not part of some Western cultures that believe each soul to be individual and unique, the inhabitant of only one body.

The idea of a person as having an inner life and inner consciousness arose largely through a Christian tradition which held that every person has a soul regardless of legal or social status. Christianity helped to establish the idea of the person as not only a legal, but also a moral entity. Many of those who believe life begins at the 'moment of conception' believe it is at that moment ensoulment or "hominization" occurs, the moment that human life begins. One extension of this thinking is it is as immoral to kill a fetus in the womb as it is to kill a person who is outside of the womb.

Some Jewish sects, citing that Adam did not become a living being until God breathed life into him, believe that fetuses / infants do not become persons until they take their first breath. One extension of this thinking is that abortion is morally permissible at any time during the pregnancy. It should be noted, however, that none of the denominations of Judaism allow indiscriminate abortion without justifiable case.

In his Encyclical Letter Pope Paul VI provided a different perspective to Christians. "We are obliged once more to declare that the direct interruption of the generative process already begun and, above all, all direct abortion, even for therapeutic reasons, are to be absolutely excluded as lawful means of regulating the number of children".

> Above excerpted from Chapter 2, Section 14 of 1968 Encyclical Letter entitled "Humanae Vitae (Human Life). http://www.vatican.va/holy_father/paul_vi/encyclicals/documents/hf_p-vi_enc_25071968_humanae-vitae_en.html

Pope John Paul II reinforced this position in his Encyclical Letter. "Certainly, from the moral point of view ... abortion destroys the life of a human being; ...directly violates the divine commandment "You shall not kill".

> Above excerpted from Chapter 1, Section 13 of 1995 Encyclical Letter entitled "Evangelium Vitae" (Gospel of Life). http://www.vatican.va/holy_father/john_paul_ii/encyclicals/documents/hf_jp-ii_enc_25031995_evangelium-vitae_en.html

Others focus on 'personhood' and contend that personhood requires basic characteristics. The most common being the capacity to have conscious experiences (sentience), to feel emotions, to be able to reason, to have the ability to communicate, to have self-awareness and to control one's behavior through moral principles or ideals. One extension of this thinking is to kill a non-sentient fetus is no more immoral than to kill a non-sentient animal. Another extension of this thinking is that at birth the baby is a 'potential person' which does not become a person until he/she achieves self-awareness.

Utilitarians define sentient beings as those who can experience pain. The pain threshold is a milestone most doctors agree is achieved by the fetus by the 13th week. Another developmental criteria used for personhood is the presence of brainwaves which, the medical profession tells us, begins at about the sixth week.

The Roe v. Wade ruling placed emphasis on 'viability', the point at which the fetus is able to sustain life outside of the mother's womb, with or without the assistance of artificial support. At the time of the Roe v. Wade decision (1973) viability was believed to occur in the third trimester, usually at 28 weeks (seven months) but may occur at 24 weeks (six months). In the 41 years since the Roe v. Wade decision medical advances have reduced viability to approximately 20-21 weeks (five months). These advances were officially recognized in a 1992 case (Planned Parenthood v. Casey) where the US Supreme Court held that due to advances in life-preserving medicines the point at which a fetus might become 'viable' could occur before the third trimester.

The title of this article asks if abortion is ethical and we began with a comment about passionate, disparate and firm opinions articulated and held during discussions about whether abortion should be legal. Divergent views should not be surprising in conversations among Americans because we live in a country where ethnic, religious, political and cultural variety is a hallmark. Christians, Jews, Agnostics, Buddhists, Muslims, Hindus, Atheists, followers of Eastern cultures, subscribers to Western cultures and many others are all involved in the abortion conversation. Each person has an individual moral compass.

The moral compass is developed over time and represents the aggregation of principles we've internalized that help us define right and wrong. Principles, perhaps, that were initially developed through the influence of parents and family (when we were passive recipients of external influences); then refined through religion, education, social and political affiliations, exposure to outside influences including media, entertainment, science and the press (when we were active evaluators of external influences); and ultimately solidified through personal initiative and reflection (when we became critical thinkers).

It may be presumptuous to assume the abortion decision is one that confronts an adult who has achieved the ability to engage in critical thinking but it is the fourth assumption made here nonetheless. Why? Because if the decision confronts an immature or unstable person the expectation for evaluation and consideration based on ethics and morality would be a moot point.

Ethics and morality are important because, unlike buying durable or nondurable goods such as a car, house, clothes, appliances or food, the abortion decision involves a broader variable set with more serious, potential life-altering implications. The lists below represent 'influences' presented by both sides of the decision. The sources are listed below each citation for those who would like to read the entire, unedited, articles.

Pro-Life—10 Arguments Against Abortion

1. Since life begins at conception, abortion is akin to murder as it is the act of taking human life. Abortion is in direct defiance of the commonly accepted idea of the sanctity of human life.
2. No civilized society permits one human to intentionally harm or take the life of another human without punishment, and abortion is no different.
3. Adoption is a viable alternative to abortion and accomplishes the same result. And with 1.5 million American families wanting to adopt a child, there is no such thing as an unwanted child.
4. An abortion can result in medical complications later in life; the risk of ectopic pregnancies doubles, and the chance of a miscarriage and pelvic inflammatory disease also increases.
5. In the instance of rape and incest, …abortion punishes the unborn child who committed no crime; instead, it is the perpetrator who should be punished.
6. Abortion should not be used as another form of contraception.
7. For women who demand complete control of their body, control should include preventing the risk of unwanted pregnancy through the responsible use of contraception or, if that is not possible, through abstinence.
8. Many Americans who pay taxes are opposed to abortion; therefore it's morally wrong to use tax dollars to fund abortion.
9. Those who choose abortions are often minors or young women with insufficient life experience to understand fully what they are doing. Many have lifelong regrets afterwards.
10. Abortion frequently causes intense psychological pain and stress.

Pro-Choice—10 Arguments For Abortion

1. Nearly all abortions take place in the first trimester, when a fetus cannot exist independent of the mother…cannot be regarded as a separate entity as it cannot exist outside her womb.
2. The concept of personhood is different from the concept of human life...
3. Adoption is not an alternative to abortion, because it remains the woman's choice whether or not to give her child up for adoption. Statistics show that very few women who give birth choose to give up their babies—less than 3% of white unmarried women and less than 2% of black unmarried women.
4. Abortion is a safe medical procedure…. Medical abortions have less than 0.5% risk of serious complications and do not affect a woman's health or future ability to become pregnant or give birth.
5. In the case of rape or incest, forcing a woman made pregnant by this violent act would cause further psychological harm to the victim.
6. Abortion is not used as a form of contraception... Only 8% of women who have abortions do not use any form of birth control due more to individual carelessness than to the availability of abortion.
7. The ability of a woman to have control of her body is critical to civil rights.
8. Taxpayer dollars are used to enable poor women to access the same medical services as rich women, and abortion is one of these services...
9. Teenagers who become mothers have grim prospects for the future….
10. Like any other difficult situation, abortion creates stress. Yet the American Psychological Association found that stress was greatest prior to an abortion, and that there was no evidence of post-abortion syndrome.

Source: "About Abortion—Thinking About Abortion and Making the Abortion Decision." http://womensissues.about.com/od/reproductiverights/a/AbortionArgumen.htm

Another example of abortion decision advice is provided in an article containing a brief summary of abortion along with a 7-step approach to decision making.

How To Decide…

An abortion is the removal or expulsion of an embryo or fetus from the uterus, resulting in or caused by its death. … Deciding whether or not to get an abortion can be one of the toughest choices that a pregnant woman has to go through. Several things need to be factored in during the decision making process. This period can be very stressful and emotional.

1. Discuss with your close friends and family. Your close friends and family will be able to provide their opinions and thoughts that may help you in determining whether or not to complete an abortion.
2. Consider your morals and beliefs. Your morals and beliefs may play a big part in your decision about whether or not to have an abortion. However, you may also decide that you are not in a state where you could care for your child, in or out of the womb. Think about it; and make up your own mind and once you know what you want to do, tune out everyone else. …
3. Consider the costs of raising a child. …It is estimated that to raise a child from birth to age 17, a parent will spend nearly $269,520.
4. Consider putting the child up for adoption….

5. Consider both the medical side effects of having an abortion and the effects of going though with the pregnancy. After having an abortion, many mothers receive side effects such as sickness, varying degrees of bleeding, depression and, in some extreme cases, death. Similarly, giving birth will carry some risk of sickness or death.
6. Consider the costs of an abortion. …You should expect to pay anywhere from $400—$2,000 to get an abortion.
7. Remember that in the end, the decision is yours to make. While it is good to listen to other people's opinions and advice about getting an abortion or keeping the baby, make sure that you (and the baby's father, if applicable) are the one who actually makes the choice.

Source: "How to Decide Whether or Not to Get an Abortion." http://www.wikihow.com/Decide-Whether-or-Not-to-Get-an-Abortion

The above are typical of how advice is proffered regarding abortion. It is usually presented as 'pro-life', 'pro-choice' or 'neutral factors'. Frequently the advice of one directly contradicts the advice of others. The bottom line is always the same, an individual has to weigh all the variables and make a personal decision.

So, how should a person make the abortion decision? The 'passive recipients' will probably do as they are told; the 'active evaluators' may seek consensus of peers and colleagues and the 'critical thinkers' will rely on their well developed internal moral compasses.

You can begin the decision process by weighing all the factors—the opinions of your peers and colleagues, the mores of your social clubs and business organizations, political influences, religious teachings, scientific findings, personal economics, medical impacts and various definitions of justifiable case. In the end, however, the factors that drive the decision, the factors that make the decision 'ethical' or 'moral' are your personal principles of morality, your conceptions of right and wrong and your definition of right conduct.

One might say the decision is made in your gut…and that just might be where your moral compass is located.

ATTRIBUTION

Thank you to the following website contributors, each of which I reviewed during my research for this article:

1. www.jme.bmj.com
2. www.libchrist.com
3. www.vatican.va
4. www.atheism.com
5. www.thecatholicthing.org
6. www.ramblingdc.net
7. www.womensissues.about.com

Also helpful during my research: *Analyzing Moral Issues* (Fifth Edition), Judith A. Boss. McGraw-Hill, 2010.

Chapter 17

Advocating Equal Protection for Men in Reproductive Rights and Responsibilities

By Illya D. Lichtenberg and Jack Baldwin Leclair

ARTICLE I. INTRODUCTION

In the society of today, and for nearly the 40-years since Roe v. Wade, reproductive rights have been synonymous with a woman's right. It is uncontested that women exclusively carry the physical burden of a child for a nine-month gestation period. It is also uncontested that there are important issues attached to pregnancy concerning individual rights and social welfare. Yet nine months do not make an adult of an infant nor do the temporary burdens of pregnancy entitle women to impose a form of involuntary servitude upon the opposite sex.

Section 5.02 Abortion and Decision Making

The decision of whether to have an abortion has been established solely as a woman's choice. She possesses unfettered decision-making power. If she chooses to carry the child to term, she may do so without any legally recognized objection from the father. If she chooses to have an abortion, she may also do so without any legally recognized objection from the father. In determining whether the woman has an abortion, she has total control and decision-making power until the fetus reaches viability. The father's desires in such circumstances are not legally recognized. He has no legal standing and no voice in the decision.

CHILD SUPPORT AND DECISION MAKING

If the woman has carried the child to term, choosing not to have an abortion, the next step where decision-making powers are involved is the support of the child. The father again is left without

---

Illya D. Lichtenberg and Jack Baldwin LeClair, "Advocating Equal Protection for Men in Reproductive Rights and Responsibilities," *Southern University Law Center,* vol. 38, no. 1, pp. 53-78. Copyright © 2010 by Southern University Law Review. Reprinted with permission by the authors and the Southern University Law Center.

any decision-making power. The man who impregnates the woman and whose request for an abortion is unilaterally denied must support the child regardless of the potential detriments to his life. This support of the child is not limited to the years he or she is a minor, but it can also be extended to include a college education. The social utility, which supports this argument, holds that society cannot afford to have unsupported single mothers dependent upon the state for sustenance.

Responsibility for support is then placed on the father. The mother, in this circumstance, also faces similar obligations to the child, namely providing support and care for the child, but this does not compensate for the earlier inequalities, it only exacerbates them. She chose to bear the child and therefore voluntarily chose to take-on the responsibility of care and support, he has not. The only decision he has made was to have intercourse with a woman after that he is nothing more than a unit of economic production in the eyes of the law, part bank roll, and part machine.

As demonstrated in this section, having sex or preventing conception is currently the point at which all decision-making power for the male is terminated. After conception from intercourse, an instinctual necessity, the male remains powerless to make reproductive decisions or voluntarily accept or refuse paternal responsibilities. On the other hand, the female retains complete decision-making power over whether a child is born, the pregnancy terminated, and a host of other decisions regarding the pregnancy and child. She literally has months to make the abortion decision, a right that is often exercised.

Clearly, there is nothing "equal" concerning either the legal or social arrangements of men and women in the reproductive process. In addition, there is no "protection" for the man, at least in the legal arrangement of decision-making powers.

To offer an equal protection alternative to men in reproductive decision-making, there appears only one way in which this can be accomplished. It does not offer men equal protection, but the proposed solution offers men token compensation for the long history of injustice to which they have been subjected. Certainly the option of a male abortion would provide a compensatory mechanism, but nature has demanded that only one party be capable of bearing a child, making this a physical impossibility.

A "symbolic abortion" by the male may be within the realm of human, social, and legal design. Where this "symbolic abortion" takes place must still be resolved. The fertilization stage offers little from which a "symbolic abortion" could occur, and thus altering current practices provides little opportunity for creating a remedy.

The abortion decision, on the other hand, provides more fertile ground from which an equitable solution can be derived. Unfortunately, other interests are at stake when considering the abortion decision as the point for compensatory equal protection in reproduction decisions, namely those privacy interests of the woman in her own body. Providing the male the legal authority to compel an actual abortion would intrude upon the control and individual sanctity of the woman's body. Even without considering the privacy issue, there is little in the way of a realistic solution in the abortion decision making stage. A conflict would naturally arise over who has more decision making powers. If the father-to-be requests the abortion and the mother-to-be desires to carry the child-to-be to term, or vice-versa, the two sides would at best have equal standing. Who would prevail if both are equal? If the status of each party were determined by other criteria, what would the criteria be? At the decision making stage of abortion there is little room for providing equal protection without intruding upon an area where women have a significant and superior privacy interest to the male.

The support stage appears as the only area in which a reasonable solution can be found. It is the point at which the male's "symbolic abortion" can take place without invading other privacy interests. Although the proposed solution may influence decisions of women at the abortion stage, the male's decisions would have no legal standing to invade the privacy of the woman's body. Whatever influence the father-to-be's decision has over the mother-to-be's decision is based solely on the importance the mother-to-be attributes to his decision.

The proposed solution is simple. The father-to-be would reserve the right to refuse support for the child. The father-to-be could simply abort himself from the situation by stating that he has no interest in the child-to-be, for whatever reason, and thus will not support the child. Similar to the female abortion, the male aborts himself from the post-pregnancy situation, as though it never existed.

This of course would allow the male to remove himself at any point from child support, an inequity in itself. The mother-to-be obviously has a limited window of time in making her abortion decision; the father-to-be could potentially make this decision at anytime. Once the child becomes viable, the woman may no longer lawfully abort. To prevent the solution from creating an inequity, both interested parties need to be placed in a similar position. The woman has until the child is viable to decide on the abortion, so the male should be placed in a similar position as the female. The following illustrates an example of the practical operation of the proposed solution.

1. If the woman decides to have an abortion she can do so with or without the consent of her partner.
2. If the mother-to-be desires to keep the child, she informs the father-to-be and allows adequate time for him to properly consider his feelings directed towards her pregnancy. The father-to-be informs the mother-to-be of his decision. The mother-to-be, having all information available to her, then decides whether an abortion is appropriate.
3. After the decision is made, it is final. For example, if the father-to-be aborts himself from the situation, he cannot claim parental rights at a later point should the mother carry the child to term. Nor can the aborted father simply change his mind and decide that he would like to contribute support at a later point and thus justify involvement with his aborted child. There does not seem to be any reason to refuse the father, the ability to contribute support at some later point if the mother should agree to it, similar to a voluntary abortion. Of course, consent of the mother would be the central tenant of this decision.
4. The father-to-be who has agreed to take on his parental responsibilities is not eligible to withdraw support at a later point. The decision is final, like the mother's, and his duty continues until the child reaches adulthood.

This proposed solution to the lack of rights offered to men in the Roe decision raises other concerns, particularly in regard to the social impact. Perhaps the social costs are too high to justify this proposed solution. Are there going to be a larger number of children who do not receive support from their fathers in the United States if such a constitutional right were created? The answer to this question has not been empirically tested. The following proposed solution could perhaps relieve some social anxieties that might be caused by the creation of such a constitutional right.

1. Females might become more responsible in using birth control as a result of knowing that the male will not be forced into supporting the child. Many girls and young women may have fallen

victim to a false romanticization of reproduction. They may not realize the responsibilities beyond the pregnancy itself.

Also the woman would not have the option of blaming the male leaving her in an impoverished state; she would have to accept full responsibility for her actions and life conditions, as she would be aware well in advance of the man's intentions.

2. This proposal might lead to better communication between partners as to their future intentions for family and other long-term commitments. The newly created constitutional right might result in couples making better informed decisions. This would force couples to discuss future plans in advance; something they should be doing already.
3. Many men might deceive women as to their intent for child-rearing responsibilities so as to gain continued sexual access or other motives traditionally assumed immoral. This proposal would offer women a better understanding of a man's true intentions should she become pregnant.
4. Currently, there exists a large number of "dead beat dads." It is unlikely that this contributes a great deal to the current social problems, and it may in fact help alleviate some of them. The majority of the empirical evidence suggests that "dead beats" are unable, rather than unwilling to pay.
5. The compulsion of law to force people to fulfill a social responsibility should be reserved as a last resort. The law gains support from the people because it is consistent with widely held social mores, not a forceful compulsion. Thus, the vast majority of men should fulfill their social obligations, with or without the force of law. If men on a mass scale flee from the social responsibilities of child support because of this new decision-making power, it becomes a symptom of a society in ill-health, rather than an individual wrong-doer who should be subjected to the punitive control of the state.

Although there is not a great deal of support for these proposed benefits, little exists to suggest that they are harmful either. Would social costs be high if there were any social costs at all? It is doubtful, and if there were social costs perhaps the finger could be pointed in the opposite direction for a change.

FURTHER READINGS

Camosy, Charles C. *Beyond the Abortion Wars: A Way Forward for a New Generation*, Wm. B. Grand Rapids, MI: Eerdmans Publishing, 2015.

Eig, Jonathan. *The Birth of the Pill: How Four Crusaders Reinvented Sex and Launched a Revolution.* New York: W. W. Norton & Company, 2014.

Gensler, Harry J. "A Kantian Argument Against Abortion." *Philosophical Studies: An International Journal for Philosophy in the Analytic Tradition* 49, no. 1 (1986): 83–98.

Roberts, Dorothy. *Killing the Black Body: Race, Reproduction, and the Meaning of Liberty*, New York: Pantheon Books, 1997.

Sawhill, Isabel V. *Generation Unbound: Drifting into Sex and Parenthood Without Marriage.* Washington, DC: Brookings Institute Press, 2014.

UNIT VIII

Modern Trends in Family: Parenthood

Chapter 18

Rights of Children, Rights of Parents, and the Moral Basis of the Family

By Ferdinand Schoeman

Philosophers debate whether children especially infants, are the kinds of beings who can have moral rights; whether rights talk in general has any point unless the being whom rights are exercise choice (which infants are not); and whether ascribing some rights to beings commits us to ascribing others (i.e., must one have a whole packet of general rights or none at all, or may one ascribe certain rights to one kind of being and other rights to other kinds of beings?).[1] Not only have many of these abstract philosophical issues about rights been argued inconclusively, but for the most part we can do without talk about children's rights and can express ourselves instead in terms of the needs and welfare of (small) children and the duties

---

1 It is perhaps worth mentioning two related conceptual proposal for thinking about rights of children in response to the worries just indicated. First of all, Bruce Hafen has suggested that we distinguish between two kinds of legal rights: (1) legal rights which protect one from undue interference by the state and from the harmful acts of others; and (2) legal rights that permit persons to make choices which have significant long-term consequences—choices which seem to require mature capacities. These latter rights, called 'choice rights,' are not, Hafen argues, appropriately ascribed to children. Consequently, children's rights include the right to be protected from their own immaturity. Arguing to a similar effect, Jeffrey Murphy has distinguished between 'autonomy rights' and 'social contract rights.' While the role of autonomy rights is to make out the special kind of treatment which is appropriate toward autonomous rational persons whose choices are to be respected, the role of social contract rights is to guarantee legally the satisfaction of certain moral claims—ones rational agents under a veil of ignorance would find morally reasonable to insure. The child's right to paternalistic treatment, argues Murphy, loses its sense of paradox when understood as a social contract right (see Bruce Hafen, "Children's Liberation and the New Egalitarianism: Some Reservations about Abandoning Youth to Their 'Rights "*Brigham Young University Law Review* 1976 [1976]: 605- 58,esp. pp. 644- 70; 644-70; and Jeffrey Murphy, "Rights and Borderline Cases," *Arizona Law Review* 19 [1977]: 228-41). For the debate on the general nature of rights and the grounds for the meaningful ascription of rights, see H. L. A. Hart, "Are There Any Natural Rights?" *Philosophical Review* 64 (1955): 175-91; David Lyons, "Rights, Claimants, and Beneficiaries," *American Philosophical Quarterly* (1969): 173-85; Joel Feinberg, "Duties, Rights, and Claims," *American Philosophical Jurisprudence: Second Series*, ed. A. W. Simpson (Oxford: Oxford University Press, 1973), pp. 171-201; R. Flathman, *The Practice of Rights* (Cambridge, Mass.: Harvard University Press, 1976); and A. I. Melden, *Rights and Persons* (Berkeley: University of California Press, 1977), pp. 166-224.

Ferdinand Schoeman, "Rights of Children, Rights of Parents, and the Moral Basis of the Family," *Ethics*, vol. 91, no. 1, pp. 6–19. Copyright © 1980 by University of Chicago Press. Reprinted with permission.

of their parents. I shall regard it as given that parents have a duty to protect their children from abuse and neglect, both physical and emotional, recognizing that what should count as abuse or neglect for legal purposes is difficult to determine and may even change from context to context.[2] Also I shall assume that, if a parent or guardian fails to promote the child's interest at some threshold level of adequacy, a form of intervention, ranging from counseling to imprisonment of the parent as well as loss of parental rights to the child, may be legitimate.

There is a different and more practical reason for hesitating to stress the rights of infants vis-a-vis their parents. We typically pay attention to the rights of individuals in order to stress their moral independence—the fact that one individual constitutes a limit on what others, whether well intentioned or not, may legitimately do. In other words, the language of rights typically helps us to sharpen our appreciation of the moral boundaries which separate people, emphasizing the appropriateness of seeing other persons as independent and autonomous agents. While such emphasis constitutes an important point when it comes to structuring relationships between older children and their parents, it may obscure the real point of moral criticism intended in the case of parent-infant relationships. When we are tempted to admonish parents for morally failing in their relationship to their young children, it is presumably and usually because we find them not furnishing the love, attention, and security we think it every parent's duty to provide. We find them short on caring and intimacy and insensitive to the state of dependency and vulnerability into which children are born and remain for several years.

Ideally the relationship between parent and infant involves an awareness of a kind of union between people which is perhaps more suitably described in poetic-spiritual language than in analytic moral terminology. We *share our selves* with those with whom we are intimate and are aware that they do the same with us.[3] Traditional moral boundaries, which give rigid shape to the self, are transparent to this kind of sharing. This makes for nonabstract moral relationships in which talk about rights of others, respect for others, and even welfare of others is to a certain extent irrelevant.[4] It is worth mentioning that the etymology of 'intimate' relates it to a verb meaning 'to bring within,' and that the primary meanings of 'intimate' focus on this character of being innermost for a person. It is also worth mentioning that establishing such relationships tends to be the primary reason adults in our culture give for wanting and having children.[5]

The danger of talk about rights of children is that it may encourage people to think that the proper relationship between themselves and their children is the abstract one that the language of rights is forged to suit. So, rather than encouraging abusive parents to feel more intimate with their children, it may cause parents in intimate relationships with their infants to reassess the appropriateness of their

---

2 See Michael Wald, "State Intervention on Behalf of 'Neglected' Children: A Search for Realistic Standards," *Stanford Law Review* 27 (1974-75): 985- 1040 (reprinted in *Pursuing Justice for the Child*, ed. Margaret K. Rosenheim [Chicago: University of Chicago Press, 1976]; page references are to *Stanford Law Review*); and "Symposium: Juvenile Justice," *Boston University Law Review* 57 (1977): 663-731.
3 See Martin Buber, "Dialogue," in *Between Man and Man,* ed. Martin Buber (London: Routledge & Kegan Paul, 1949); Robert Burt, "The Limits of the Law: Can It Regulate Health Care Decisions?" *Hastings Center Report* 7 (1977): 29-32.
4 See Hegel, *Philosophy of Right,* secs. 158-64. But note that for Hegel, once civil society makes its appearance, the abstract relations which aim at social well-being come to predominate over rights of intimacy and privacy (see secs. 238-341). Aristotle, though generally subordinating family relationships to the goals of the polis (*Politics* 1:13.15 and 7.16- 17), does describe children as "another self" of the parents (*Nichomachean Ethics* 8.12) and also says that justice is irrelevant between friends (ibid., 8.1).
5 Lois Hoffman, "The Value of Children to Parents—a National Sample Survey" (paper read at the meeting of the American Public Health Association, Los Angeles, October 1978).

blurring the boundaries of individual identity and to question their consciousness of a profound sense of identification with, and commitment toward, their families. Emphasis on the rights of children might foster thinking about the relationship between parent and child as quasi-contractual, Limited, and directed toward the promotion of an abstract public good. Such emphasis unambiguously suggests that the relationship is a one-way relationship aimed almost solely at promoting the best interest of the child.

There are many circumstances when the independence of children, primarily older ones, ought to be stressed; for these circumstances, stress on children's rights makes sense, But when it is the dependence and vulnerability of the child that we want to emphasize, as we unfortunately must at times do, some different moral strategy would be more appropriate. And when we become conscious of the possibilities that intimacy here, as in other relations, is a two-way sharing of benefits, primary emphasis on the rights perspective becomes even more distorting. To avoid misunderstanding, however, I wish to reiterate that in recommending a different moral strategy I am not to be taken as denying that infants have rights, either in relation to their parents or in relation to abstract others. Rather, I am questioning the moral advantages of extolling the rights of infants in our consciousness of their most important relationships.

Let me try now to articulate briefly the principles at which we have arrived and then proceed to describe and execute the objective of this paper. As persons, children ought to he thought of as possessing rights; but as infants in relationship to their parents, they are to be thought of primarily as having needs, the satisfaction of which involves intimate and intense relationships with others. As against society, we might yet think of infants and parents as having rights to conditions which permit or encourage, or at least do not discourage, the social and material conditions conducive to parent-child intimacy—a point we will return to in Section 111. What I want to discuss primarily is the moral basis for thinking that biological parents have a presumptive right to keep their children under their care in the setting of privacy, autonomy, and responsibility which is usually accorded the family.

For purposes of this paper, I shall mean by 'family' an intense continuing and intimate organization of at least one adult and child, wherein the child is extensively and profoundly dependent on the adult, in which the adult supplies the child with its emotional and material needs, and in which the parent is dependent on the child for a certain certain rights of privacy and autonomy. The right of privacy entitles the adults of the family to exclude others from scrutinizing obtrusions into family occurrences. The right to autonomy entitles the adults of the family to make important decisions about the kinds of influences they want the children to experience and entitles them to wide latitude in remedying what they regard as faults in the children's behavior. Neither the right to privacy nor the right to autonomy associated with the family is absolute. These rights are to be conceived as rights against society at large. In relation to the children, they impose upon parents the duty to employ considered judgments in taking into account each child's needs, and eventually his rights. But in large part, such duties are unenforceable by the state because of the rights of privacy and autonomy already mentioned.

Just how much discretion should be left to the parents—how wide should their latitude be in structuring the environment of their children? For theoretical reasons to be advanced in Section III, I follow Michael Wald and others in setting strict threshold conditions (amounting to a clear-and-present-danger criterion) which must be met before coercive state intervention is permitted. Wald argues that coercive intervention should be authorized only if (1) serious physical or emotional harm to the child is imminent and (2) the intervention is likely to be less detrimental than the status quo.[6] Wald cites several practical factors in justifying his recommended policy of restraint. (1) Typically, good alternatives to unfortunate family circumstances are not available. (2) It is difficult to predict which circumstances will have harmful long-range effects. (3) There is a lack of consensus about proper methods of child rearing and the ideal end product of child rearing. (4) Our social commitment to diversity of life-styles requires a great deal of tolerance in what should be permitted.

While such factors reflect important desiderata, it is notable that concern for the parent appears to be irrelevant in Wald's article, as in much of the legal literature of recent vintage.[7] Though I find this exclusion of the parents' perspective peculiar, very widespread, and in need of remedy, it is to a certain extent understandable. For the infant, the family as here defined involves an intimate relationship with at least one adult. Since the psychological evidence suggests that children need this type of relationship for their cognitive and emotional well-being,[8] we may conclude that children must be provided with such an arrangement (or, if you prefer, that they have a right to it). But from the child's perspective it does not matter whether the adult who will become its psychological parent is also its biological parent.

In what follows, I shall focus on the parents' perspective and attempt to address this question: Why should the biological parents be thought to have a right to raise their child in an intimate setting even before it is determined that their child will fare best under their care and guidance (*however* 'faring best' is defined)? Ultimately, what I shall want to emphasize is that the functional, efficiency-oriented approach to the family found in much of the literature defending family autonomy represents neither the only nor the best assessment of the moral basis of the family.

It should, however, be noted that not all social theorists see the family as an institution worth preserving. For not only does it provide a context for abuse and brutality in which the law has traditionally declined to take an interest, it also interferes with what might be called 'equality of opportunity' because it makes children depend on the spiritual and material resources of the family they happen to be born into.[9] Though these points do constitute genuine moral worries which are theoretically inseparable from family institutions, pursuing such worries is not part of my present interest, though they will be touched on in the final portion of the paper.

II

Since surprisingly little philosophical attention has been devoted to the moral meaning of intimate relationships such as arise in family settings,[10] it should prove a useful exercise to see just what can be said in behalf of the biological parents' rights to raise their offspring, obvious though it may appear.

---

6   Wald, "State Intervention . . . pp. 992-93, 1005.
7   Amy Gutmann has trenchantly discussed the paternalistic and nonpaternalistic basis of parental rights within liberal theory in "Children, Paternalism, and Education: A Liberal Argument," photocopied (Princeton, N.J.: Princeton University).
8   Urie Bronfenbrenner, *A Report on Longitudinal Evaluation of Preschool Programs*, vol. 2, *Is Early Intervention Effective?* DHEW Publication no. (OHD), 75-25 (Washington, D.C.: Government Printing Office, 1975); and Joseph Goldstein, Anna Freud, and Albert Solnit, *Beyond the Best Interest of the Child* (New York: Free Press, 1973).
9   John Rawls, *A Theory of Justice* (Cambridge, Mass.: Harvard University Press, 1971), p. 511; Charles Fried, *Right and Wrong* (Cambridge, Mass.: Harvard University Press, 1978), pp. 150-55; and Lorenne Clark, "Privacy, Property, Freedom and the Family," in *Philosophical Law*, ed. Richard Bronaugh (London: H. Greenwood & Co., 1978), pp. 167-87.
10   Notable exceptions include Francis Schrag, "Justice and the Family," *Inquiry* 19 (1976): 193-208; Melden; and Fried.

The right of biological parents (hereinafter referred to as just 'parents') with which I am concerned is not a right to certain services from their children, but a right against all the rest of society to be indulged, within wide limits, to share life with each child and thus inevitably to fashion the child's environment as they see fit, immune from the scrutiny of and direction from others.

It might be impatiently suggested that parents' rights to raise their children stem from an evolutionary phenomenon: parents' natural affections for their offspring and their infants' needs make for something like a preestablished harmony of interests. Since everyone, or almost everyone, benefits from this arrangement, and since provisions can be made for those few biological anomalies in which natural passions and natural needs do not correlate, what better basis could there be for our traditional arrangement? The suggestion might be given added weight by calling to mind the reported deleterious effects of impersonal, institutional efforts at raising children.

Three comments are in order in response. First, it has been observed that parental attachments may be more the result of enculturation than we naively suppose.[11] Second, there is sufficient evidence to suggest that not all alternative modes of distributing children involve impersonal institutions in which children languish emotionally and intellectually.[12] Third, and philosophically most significant, I wish to consider what we would think parents' rights would amount to if means equal or superior to those parents can typically supply could be found for benefiting the child outside the biological parents' domain. Would parents still have a claim on their children, as against society? And if so, what would its basis be? Is the parents' right to their children contingent on the biological family's being the most efficient arrangement for benefiting children? Or is there some less incidental account of parental prerogative? (As indicated above, most recent proponents of family autonomy and state restraint have argued that promoting the child's interest is the primary or sole basis of their advocacy.[13] Though I am in agreement with these policy recommendations, I find that more needs to be said about their justification.)

One not very plausible account for the parents' right, despite the fact that the account can be traced back to Aristotle, involves looking at the child as the property of the parent, analogous to teeth and hair which have fallen out.[14] Since the child is the product of material and labor supplied prenatally by the mother, the child would seem to be the natural possession par excellence but for the fact that this product is a person. (I suppose that those who think that the newborn infant is not yet a person would have an easy time thinking of the parent as entitled to the infant in Aristotelian fashion.)[15]

Another justification for our current arrangements might follow these lines: as long as children are adequately cared for under our present practices, we can take into account parental preferences. True, these preferences as such do not constitute rights, but in our way of allocating benefits, once children's

---

11 P. Aries, *Centuries of Childhood: A Social History of Family Life* (New York: Alfred A. Knopf, Inc., 1962), pt. 1, chap. 2; and Arlene Skolnick, *The Intimate Environment* (Boston: Little, Brown & Co., 1973), pp. 60-62.
12 Bronfenbrenner, pp. 46-48.
13 Hafen, p. 651; Wald, "State Intervention . . ."; Goldstein et al., pp. 7, 25.
14 Aristotle adopts the view that the child is the parent's possession, actually comparing the child to a tooth and a piece of hair (*Nichomachean Ethics* 8.12). But since Aristotle also thinks that slaves are possessions toward which the master owes nothing, and since vis-a-vis their children Aristotle's view is that parents ought to make their benefit primary (*Politics* 3.6.7), it is not the best of analogies that Aristotle picked to represent his own views of parent-child relationships. For *a critical discussion of Locke's treatment of this view, see Robert Nozick, *Anarchy, State, and Utopia* (New York: Basic Books, 1974), pp. 287-91. It may be worth noting that we often use the possessive idiom to indicate a special relationship to something and not legal or moral proprietorship. An architect might say of a building, "That's mine!" or a child might say of a teacher, "That's my teacher," without suggesting ownership.
15 Michael Tooley, "Abortion and Infanticide," *Philosophy and Public Affairs* 2 (1972): 37-65.

needs are satisfied—a precondition we have set into our scheme—preferences should count in our determination of which claims will be recognized as entitlements.

This account of the basis of parental rights is not contingent solely on the fact of benefiting children but also makes essential reference to parents as persons with preferences which must be considered as long as the child's basic needs are met. But ultimately this justification of parental right is not satisfying, for all that would be necessary to override it would be a showing of some increased benefit to children in nonparental settings. True, the needs of the children and the preferences of the parents go some way toward showing that it is the parents, and not someone else, that should be accorded rights over their children. But if marginally more good resulted for children from alternative setups, this fact could immediately outweigh parental preferences and militate against according parents' rights. I take it as a given that a parent's stake in her relationship to her children is based on something more profound than parental preferences, even when we add to such preferences a realistic skepticism about the state's competence to distribute children in a manner more advantageous to them.

In discussing sources of authority, Elizabeth Anscombe has recently proposed that institutionalized practices which carry out important tasks thereby gain legitimization or authority.[16] Anscombe suggests that the parent's rights to obedience from her child and respect for her exercise of discretion from others outside the family evolve from the manifestly crucial functions parental authority performs. So long as families maintain their position of being necessary conditions for the performance of such functions, Anscombe's argument captures common sense and preserves family entitlements. But the emergence of alternative, possibly superior (relative to the child), means of rearing children would deprive the family of its position of being necessary and hence undermine its claim to rightful autonomy, except on a customary basis.

We must note that these last two theories are by no means clearly false or even clearly wanting. Whether they are fully adequate must be judged in light of alternative dimensions we can manage to elaborate.

III

We have yet to supply the justification of three institutions which we, for the most part, take for granted. Why should the family be accorded rights to privacy and autonomy? Why should the family be given extensive responsibilities for the development of children? Why should the *biological* parent be thought entitled to be in charge of a family? I believe that the notion of intimacy supplies the basis for these presumptions and would like now to elaborate an account more successful than those mentioned in the preceding section. But I shall try to show first why intimacy requires privacy and autonomy as its setting, and second why we should recognize a right to intimate relationships. I shall then argue that the parent's right to raise her children in a family stems naturally from the right to engage in intimate relationships, even when recognition of this right involves some comparative cost to the child.

At an earlier point in this paper, I described an intimate relationship as one in which one shares one's self with one or more others. It was suggested that, via intimate relationships, one transcends abstract and rather impersonal associations with others and enters personal and meaningful relationships

---

16   Elizabeth Anscombe, "On the Source of Authority of the State," *Ratio* 20 (1978): **1-28.**

or unions. Such relationships are meaningful because of the personal commitments to others which are constitutive of such relationships. For most people, not only are such unions central to defining who one is, but human existence would have little or no meaning if cut off from all possibility of maintaining or reestablishing such relationships. Though such relationships are undoubtedly culturally dependent in the form they take, they constitute one's roots in life or attachment to living, even when the concerns of the relationship are independent of, or hostile to, the values of the culture and the welfare of others.[17]

Practically speaking, the strength or very possibility of intimate relationships varies inversely with the degree of social intrusion into such relationships generally tolerated.[18] The prospect of state intervention into a relationship depresses the sense of security of the relationship. It makes people hesitant to see their interests fused with those of another.[19] The intimate sharing described as part of these close unions presupposes limited sovereignty on the part of those reaching out to and sharing with others to determine the conditions of the relationship. Without privacy and autonomy, the relationship would be neither secure nor on the parties' own terms.

Privacy and autonomy provide the moral space within which concrete personal relationships can be formed independently of general social concerns. To give the state authority to regulate such relationships would inevitably result in a redirection or 'socialization' of these relationships. We see evidence of this shift in doctor-patient relationships, wherein doctors are seen increasingly to have direct responsibilities for the health of the population and not for the comfort of specific patients.[20] While it would be presumptuous of me to declare, without marshaling evidence, that such shifts in loyalties ought on balance to be forestalled, it should be recognized and made part of our reckoning that systems of meaning can be uprooted in the process of realigning commitments.

Lon Fuller has devoted considerable attention to understanding principles of human association and the law's varying capacities to regulate diverse kinds of relationships.[21] He distinguishes two different principles of association, the relative mix of which in any particular relationship determines what the relationship is. One principle is shared commitment, the other is the legalistic. The legalistic aspect is that which makes explicit rules of duty and entitlement.[22] While the former principle, shared commitment, is concerned with conditions of mind and degrees of inner resolution, the latter is concerned with overt, clearly definable acts.[23] As the legalistic principle comes to dominate the parties' image of their relationship with one another, the element of shared commitment tends to sink out of sight. State intervention into a relationship, Fuller argues, tends to shift the emphasis of the

---

17 Though Aristotle observed that the aims of friendship and political association differed, the former aiming at common social life and the latter at the good life, he regarded friendship as on a lower moral plain than political association and as a means to the good life (see *Politics* 3.9.9- 15 and 1.1.1).

18 Aries argues that our modern notion of the intimate family emerged as sociability (neighborly relations, friendships, and traditional contacts) diminished and presupposed a sense of the importance of privacy (see esp. pp. 398-407).

19 Goldstein et al.

20 Charles Fried, *Medical Experimentation: Personal Integrity and Social Policy* (Amsterdam: Elsevier, 1974), represents a critical discussion of such proposals.

21 Lon Fuller, "Two Principles of Human Association," in *Nomos XI: Voluntary Associations,* ed. J. R. Pennock and J. W. Chapman (New York: Atherton Press, 1969), pp. 3-23, and "Human Interaction and the Law," *American Journal of Jurisprudence* 14 (1969): 1-36.

22 Fuller, "Two Principles of Human Association," pp. 6-8.

23 Ibid., p. 14.

relationship in the direction of formality and abstractness.[24] The very act of precisely sorting things out in conformity with the legalistic paradigm tends to wring out aspects of inner commitment.[25]

Fuller's analysis helps to indicate why intimate relationships must be accorded privacy and autonomy and why they deserve social and legal respect. Friendship, love, and family represent institutions in which intimacy is central to the relationships. Because of the importance of these relationships to the self-image and meaningful existence of most people, the state, before intruding, should impose high standards like the clear-and-present-danger test suggested above. The state should be very chary in trying to alter the terms of such relationships to serve social ends. As has been noted by others, while the state is quite limited in its ability to promote relationships, it can do much to destroy them.[26] The state threatens relationships by requiring the parties to think of themselves as primarily serving public ends and as having public duties. This intrusion beclouds the integrity of the trust and devotion that can arise between people. Though it may be that important ends are served by such intrusion, as, for example, when doctors are required to report suspected cases of child abuse, we should be willing at the very least to acknowledge the cost of such intrusions. Parenthetically, it is worthwhile noting that the state does find certain relationships privileged, like the lawyer-client relationship, even at some possible cost to public welfare.

Yet to show the importance of intimate relationships, even family relationships as characterized in this paper, is not yet to show that parents have any rights to their children. After all, adults can establish intimate relationships with other consenting adults. Insuring that children become part of an intimate and secure setting is not the same as assuring the biological parents of these children that they (the parents) will be part of this same setting.

The alternative to the natural and customary distribution of children to their parents is some kind of social decision determining who goes with whom. Such distribution schemes are not necessarily, from the perspective of the infant, inimical to intimacy, as the institution of early adoption establishes. But it does or may preclude such kinds of intimacy for those who are determined by popular social criteria to be not maximally fit or not maximally competent to really provide children with all that they need or can use. But such a preclusion would, I believe, represent an interference with a practice from which intimacy and with it life meaning typically emerge.

Once this is acknowledged, I am not sure what else would have to be added before we could come to speak of such structures of meaning as investing individuals with a moral right to be free from intentional interferences. Presumably, part of what would be required would include a moral comparison of various elaborated social structures. Because I am not equipped to articulate such comparisons, I shall speak of moral claims as distinct from moral rights, claims being justified on the basis of their importance to our present conditions. So, rather than arguing that we have a moral right to family autonomy or that we should have a positive legal right to such autonomy, I will be content in encouraging a kind of appreciation for the meaning of the family over and above the recognition of its accomplishments as an institution dedicated to the production of future citizens.

Though the infant is nonconsenting, it does not represent a denial of its rights for it to be entrusted to its parents even if better surroundings are available, since we are assuming that minimal conditions for adequate upbringing will be met. (We are, after all, utilizing something like the

---

24 Ibid., p. 21.
25 Fuller, "Human Interaction and the Law," p. 34.
26 Joseph Goldstein, "Finding the Least-detrimental Alternative," *Psychoanalytic Study of the Child* 27 (1972): 626-41, esp. p. 637.

clear-and-present-danger test to protect children from abuse and neglect, though of course such standards raise problems of their own.)[27] To set terms for emotional parenting more stringent than required for the protection of children from abuse and neglect constitutes an interference in a person's claim to establish intimate relations except on the society's terms. We have already indicated reasons for thinking that such regulation transforms relationships into less intimate ones. Such allocation schemes could redefine the parenting role as one in which the objective is abstract social well-being, not intimacy and the kind of meaning found in commitment to particular others.

The practice of entrusting children to their parents ultimately limits the control of society to determine the life-style and beliefs of persons because it means there would be one important relationship a person could be in without the requirement of prior social approval. Since society cannot determine and should not try to determine who may have intimate relationships with whom, if a person chooses to have his relationships in a family setting, society should not interfere, since that kind of choice is essential to intimate relationships in general.

Thus, as a way of transcending oneself and the boundaries of abstract others, as a way of finding meaning in life, and as a means of maintaining some kind of social and moral autonomy, the claim to freedom from scrutiny and control in one's relations with others should be thought of as a moral claim as important as any other that can be envisioned. It must not be up to society in general, without there being some special cause, to decide whom one can relate to and on what terms. Other things being equal, parents consequently are entitled to maintain their offspring and seek meaning with and through them.

Though there are many questions which plague the account of family privacy advanced here, there is one in particular I would like to raise and address because of the direction it suggests for further reflection. The problem is: Given the subjective basis of the importance of intimate relationships, how can it be used to defend privacy and autonomy within families in general, since the members of many families manifestly fail to invest their relationships with the requisite kind of personal meaning? And looked at the other way, there are surely many relationships in which personal meaning is sought and found but to which the law is and, as things stand, ought to remain oblivious. If we distinguish the substance from the structure of an intimate relationship, we can see the question as requiring that we justify our practice of according privacy and autonomy to people who comply only in form to meaningful relationships while denying them to other people who may be far more committed to one another but who fail to establish the formal, institutional accoutrements of close relationships.

In responding, we need to note that the state cannot employ the subjective or substantial criterion when judging whether privacy and autonomy are appropriate for a particular relationship. The state is unequipped to investigate souls, and even were it so equipped it could set its standards and make its particular findings only at the expense of just the kind of intrusions which shatter the very relationships it would be seeking to protect. Consequently, it is essential that there be formal or ritualized means of 'privatizing' a relationship, on the basis of overt acts or habits, even though inevitably there

---

27 "Synopsis: Standards Relating to Abuse and Neglect," *Boston University Law Review* 57 (1977): 663-68; R. Bourne and E. Newberger, "'Family Autonomy' or 'Coercive Intervention'? Ambiguity and Conflict in the Proposed Standards for Child Abuse and Neglect," *Boston University Law Review* 57 (1977): 670-706; R. McCathren, "Accountability in the Child Protection System: A Defense of the Proposed Standards Relating to Abuse and Neglect," *Boston University Law Review* 57 (1977): 707-31; Robert Burt, "Developing Constitutional Rights of, in, and for the Children," in Rosenheim; and Wald, "State Intervention . . . ."

will result two tragic consequences: abuses of privileged privacy and intrusions into some morally deserving relationships.

Ultimately, what is being suggested here is that it is important for states to respect relationships the very point of which is to insulate the people so related from ordinary forms of social and legal control. The state needs to be cognizant of those means—culture specific and conventional, though not necessarily popular—that people have for finding meaning; and it must do so by means of clearly structured and easily recognizable institutions of relating. It can do neither more nor less without changing the nature or possibility of such relationships. Any effort to gauge the meaning of a particular relationship that goes beyond superficially based presumptions will involve distorting intrusions. Consequently, what is important about the biological relationship between parents and children is the *conventional meaning* given to it within our culture. Since people do in fact vest the biological relationship with meanings of intimacy, the state must not interfere with that relationship unless the danger is serious, clear, and immanent.

Most justifications of family autonomy that one finds in the literature have concentrated on the child's perspective and stressed the point that families, as we know them, represent the least-detrimental means we have of child rearing. In contrast, my arguments on behalf of the family, though concerned with the well-being of children, have had as their chief focus an idea of human relationships. Consequently, even if someone could demonstrate that there were some more efficient and effective institution for promoting the interests of children than the traditional family, I would still think that the family would have a strong, though rebuttable, moral presumption in its favor. The implications of such a presumption extend beyond requiring high threshold conditions before the state intervenes coercively into family affairs. The presumption would seem to imply that the state should not, to the extent possible, make the family and parental responsibility otiose through the provision directly to children of services which parents are in a position to supply.

One final point. Some people have argued recently that, while the family deserves the privacy and autonomy suggested above, in case the state is presented with a claim of rights violation by a child, the state is in a situation in which it must either find for the child or find for the parent, and that accordingly it should make its decision by regarding the interests and rights of the parents and child as being on a par. However plausible this picture of restricted options appears, it ignores one crucial alternative. Parents can be seen as representing the interests of the family as an integrated whole in addition to representing their own particular interests. Though entrusting individuals with the responsibility of making judgments for the common good when their own interests are involved does not accord well with modern constitutionalist conceptions, we should not discount on a priori grounds the prospects for such an arrangement's being feasible in certain contexts. The context in which such kinds of representation can work are those in which people in fact conceive their roles and their very identity as requiring such an attitude. Informal custom rather than formal institutional means of resolving conflict of interest generally sufficed in ancient and medieval government, imbued with notions of virtue and right as they typically were.[28]

Given social expectations and governmental noninterference, important ends are served by relegating to parents the right to decide important issues for the family, even when what is at

---

28 Fritz Kern, *Kingship and Law in the Middle Ages* (Oxford: Blackwell Scientific Publications, Ltd., 1948); and Otto Gierke, *Political Theories of the Middle Ages* (Cambridge: Cambridge University Press, 1922). John Garvey has argued that this policy toward the family is consistent with Supreme Court decisions in "Child, Parent, State, and the Due Process Clause: An Essay on the Supreme Court's Recent Work," *Southern California Law Review* 51 (1978): 769-822.

issue is a conflict in interests between the parent as individual and the child as individual. I have been suggesting that if the state takes the attitude that conflicts within families are the same as conflicts anywhere, the state will be adding considerable impetus to the evolution of the family as a nonintimate structure.

Chapter 19

Mothers but Not Wives: The Increasing Lag

By Christina Gibson-Davis

Marriage behaviors among all women have changed dramatically over the past half century. Although the vast majority of women eventually marry (up to 90%, according to one recent estimate; Goldstein & Kenney, 2001), the age at first marriage has increased by more than 25% since 1960, from 20 to 25 years (U.S. Bureau of the Census, 2004). This delay in marriage most likely contributes to the decline in marriage rates, particularly for less well-educated and Black women, who have been found to be significantly less likely to marry than are better educated or White women (Ellwood & Jencks, 2004).

In addition, marriage behaviors in response to a pregnancy have also changed. The increasing rate of nonmarital births attests to the willingness of individuals to have a birth outside of marriage. Fewer individuals marry in response to a birth as so-called shotgun marriages have become increasingly rare. (…)

In the United States of 50 years ago, when abortion was illegal, contraception was difficult for unmarried women to obtain, and societal norms censured out-of-wedlock sexual activity and childbearing, marriage and fertility were closely linked. Individuals who desired to live in a romantic relationship with an opposite-sex partner or who faced an unplanned pregnancy had little option but to marry. Today, the family formation landscape is quite different, and fertility behaviors that were once considered the sole province of marriage (e.g., contraception, sexual intimacy, childbearing) are now normative outside the bounds of marriage. As a result, marriage and fertility have become increasingly disconnected, as one is no longer necessary for the other.

Scholars have also noted that as the practical ties between marriage and fertility have weakened, the motivations and expectations regarding each have diverged.

As marriage has become less commonplace and its practical import has declined, it has taken on an increased symbolic importance that was absent in years past. Marriage has become associated with a set of relational and economic standards, including good jobs, significant savings, and

Christina Gibson-Davis, "Mothers but Not Wives: The Increasing Lag," *Journal of Marriage and Family*, vol. 73, no. 1, pp. 265-267, 275-276. Copyright © 2011 by John Wiley & Sons, Inc. Reprinted with permission.

enough money to afford a mortgage, and couples who marry publicly demonstrate that they have met or exceeded these standards. These standards have not been found to adhere for other family-formation activities, such as cohabitation or fertility. Research among low-income unwed mothers, in fact, has suggested that some mothers view economic resources as largely orthogonal to the decision to have a child. Instead, women had children because they had relatively few vocational or educational opportunities, and they looked to childbearing as a way to provide meaning to their lives. They therefore felt no need to delay childbearing, even as they put off marriage.

Scholars have also suggested that changes in unwed mothers' marital behaviors have arisen because the economic gains to marriage have declined. The wages of men, particularly those with less education, have decreased in real value. Traditional models of family formation, as Becker (1981) first laid out, predicted that this decline in real wages should lead to a decrease in marriage rates, as men with lower earnings were less able to provide market goods to their families. In addition, participation in the welfare system could alter marriage trends among unwed mothers. The Aid to Families with Dependent Children (AFDC) program, which began to accept large numbers of unwed mothers in the mid-1960s, discouraged marriage by greatly restricting eligibility for two-parent married households and by counting the resources of any non-biological cohabiting man against the mother's cash grant (Moffit, 2002). Temporary Aid to Needy Families (TANF), the policy that replaced AFDC in the welfare reform act of 1996, eased eligibility restrictions for two parent households. Even under TANF, though, marriage disincentives remain in place, insofar as two-parent families receive less benefits than they would as two single adults.

The explanatory power of men's earnings and welfare participation on unwed mothers' marriage behavior remains a matter of scholarly debate. Although male earnings correlate positively with marriage rates, the decline in marriage far outweighs what a decline in male earnings alone can account for. Studies of AFDC have reported either very small or null effects of welfare participation on marriage behavior (for reviews, see Moffitt, 1992, 1998). Moreover, research has found that poor unmarried mothers were not any more likely to marry under TANF than they were under AFDC, which suggests that cash welfare policies have had little effect on their marital behavior.

Nevertheless, all these factors—marriage and fertility as distinct end points, declining economic benefits to marriage, and welfare participation—suggest that unmarried mothers are less likely to marry than they were in the past.

There may also be an increased delay in marriage if mothers are waiting longer to marry until they have achieved the economic prerequisites of marriage. In addition, differences across time are likely to be larger in magnitude for mothers with low levels of human capital. As noted above, less well-educated women have had greater declines in their marriage rates than have better educated women. Declines in marriage rates for mothers, who face a particularly proscribed marriage pool, may be even more pronounced. Racial differences may also exist, insofar as *Nonmarital Births and Marriage* 267 race and class are closely correlated. Moreover, the decline in financially viable men has been particularly acute in the Black community, and Black women may have more difficulty than White women in locating suitable matches. (…)

I hypothesize that the unwed mothers of today are less likely to marry than were unwed mothers of 40 years ago and that the time between first birth and first marriage has increased substantially. I also hypothesize that declines and delays are more pronounced for Black and less well-educated women; it is unclear, however, whether educational differences will be greater than racial differences. Models also control for woman's age at birth, as teenage mothers may be less likely to marry, and age is positively correlated with marriage.

It should be noted that, because of relatively high rates of cohabitation, many of today's unwed mothers are likely to live with the father of the child. Approximately half of all nonmarital births in the United States are to cohabiting parents, with larger fractions for women of color and mothers older than age 20. Scholars believe, however, that in the U.S. context, cohabitation is not a substitute for marriage, insofar as it has not been associated with the same advantages for children. Higher levels of instability, lower quality relationships, and lower levels of financial resources mark cohabiting unions, as compared to marriages. Perhaps it is not surprising, then, that promoting marriage—and not just two-parent households—remains the primary objective of policy makers concerned about family formation.

An emerging sociocultural view of out-of wedlock childbearing and marriage has suggested that women view births and marriages as distinct end points. In part because of changing social norms that sanction sexual intimacy and childbearing outside of marriage, the once-close connection between marriage and fertility has loosened. This decreased connection has led individuals to develop different motivations and expectations regarding marriage and fertility. Marriage, though highly desired, has become associated with a set of relational and economic standards, and it can be delayed until those standards have been achieved. Individuals can also delay marriage as long as they wish without forgoing sexual intimacy and childbearing.

Childbearing, in contrast, may be viewed as a meaning-making activity and is not held to the same set of economic standards as marriage is. Individuals, therefore, do not delay childbearing, but they delay marriage until they feel they have met its economic prerequisites.

This theoretical perspective has suggested that increased delays between childbearing and marriage should mark trends in marriage among unwed mothers but that mothers should not be forgoing marriage altogether. The results found here were consistent with that interpretation, as delays in marriage (with the exception of less well-educated Blacks) are arguably more pronounced that declines in marriage. As compared to mothers who gave birth in the 1960s, mothers who gave birth in the 1990s and early 2000s are much less likely to marry in the years immediately following a birth. The percentage of White women who married within 3 years of an out of wedlock birth decreased by 27%; for Blacks, the decrease was 60%. But excluding lower educated Black mothers, a majority of mothers eventually married, which suggests that mothers are not avoiding marriage entirely. (…)

There were declines in marriage rates overall: less well-educated Whites and Blacks of all educational levels who gave birth between 1989 and 2004 were significantly less likely to marry than were their peers who gave birth between 1960 and 1967. In some cases, the declines are quite substantial: marriage odds for a Black mother in the 1960 – 1967 cohort were twice as great as marriage odds for a Black mother in the 1989 – 2004 cohort. Moreover, the decline in marriage odds for less well-educated women is evident not only when comparing the marital behavior of 1960s mothers to 1990s mothers but also when comparing the marital behavior of mothers in the 1980s to mothers in the 1990s.

Nevertheless, the overall picture that emerges is that many unwed mothers will eventually become wives, but it may take them several years to do so. (…)

I had hypothesized that changes in marital behavior would be greater for less well educated and Black women, who have had marked declines in their overall marriage rates and who have been to be less likely to marry following an out-of wedlock birth. In addition, if mothers are waiting to marry until they have achieved the economic prerequisites, then it may be more difficult for economically marginalized groups to realize those prerequisites. Results confirmed the hypotheses. Marital decline and delay over time were greater in magnitude for less well educated mothers and were more pronounced for Blacks than for Whites.

Yet results also indicated that racial differences were just as pronounced as educational differences because the cumulative marriage rates for better educated Blacks more closely resembled less well-educated Blacks than better educated Whites. Scholars have found that Black mothers were less likely to marry than White mothers, in part because Black women faced a more proscribed marriage pool and had a harder time finding economically viable partners. It is possible that well-educated Black mothers have a particularly difficult time finding suitable matches, but this result bears further investigation.

The results for better educated White mothers were intriguing, insofar as they were the only group with increased odds of marriage over time. The qualitative studies that informed this current work concentrated on the disconnect between first marriage and first births among low-income mothers and had little to say about the marital behavior of women with more education. One possibility is that there have been compositional shifts in the types of better educated White women who have an out-of-wedlock birth. Perhaps births to White, better educated mothers in the 1989–2004 cohort were more likely to be in the context of a committed relationship than were births to mothers with the same demographic characteristics in earlier birth cohorts. (…)

Results suggested, though, that mothers who gave birth in the past decade were relatively more advantaged (in terms of education and age) than mothers who gave birth several decades ago. If the pool of unwed mothers has become less negatively selected over time, then results presented here most likely understate declines and delays in marriage.

In addition, results showed that the marriage odds of mothers continue to decrease, even if the comparison was between mothers giving birth in the 1990s to mothers giving births in the 1980s. (…)

In addition to describing trends in marriage, an additional goal of this study was to highlight how the experiences of children born into unwed parent homes have changed over time.

The median time from first birth to first marriage for Blacks, for example, rose from 8 to 16 years, suggesting that many Black children may be teenagers before their mothers marry. The age at mother's marriage has implications for child well-being, as marriage may affect children differently if that marriage occurs when they are in elementary school rather than high school. As one example, longer exposure to an unwed-parent home may increase the probability that a child experiences family instability.

Family instability has been linked to adverse outcomes for children, with children who experienced multiple transitions particularly at risk. In addition, unmarried mothers, whether cohabiting or single, had higher poverty rates and lower levels of economic resources than married mothers. Later age at mothers' marriage implies that children will spend more time in a potentially poor environment; given the importance of resources in early child development, later age at marriage may not convey the same advantages to children as marriage at an earlier age.

Moreover, the increasing age for children at their mother's first marriage raises important issues and questions for policies aimed to promote marriage. For example, if a primary goal of marriage promotion is to reduce poverty among children, then the results here suggest such a strategy may be of limited effectiveness if the mother waits several years before marriage. The increased delay between first birth and first marriage also raises the issue of whom the mother should marry: From a policy perspective, is it more important that the mother marry the biological father when the child is younger or that she marry a stepfather when the child is older? What if by waiting the mother makes a better match that is more stable? Should we trade off an early marriage for a higher quality marriage when the child is older?

REFERENCES

Akerlof, G. A., Yellen, J. T., & Katz, M. L. (1996). An analysis of out-of-wedlock childbearing in the United States. *Quarterly Journal of Economics, 111*, 278–317.

Allison, P. D. (1984). *Event history analysis*. Bevery Hills, CA: Sage.

Becker, G. (1981). *A treatise on the family*. Cambridge, MA: Harvard University Press.

Bennett, N. G., Bloom, D. E., & Miller, C. K. (1995). The influence of nonmarital childbearing on the formation of first marriages. *Demography, 32*, 47–62.

Brown, S. L. (2000). Union transitions among cohabitors: The significance of relationship assessments and expectations. *Journal of Marriage and the Family, 62*, 833–846.

Buckles, K., & Hungerman, D. M. (2008). *Season of birth and later outcomes: Old questions, new answers* (NBER Working Paper No. 14573). Cambridge, MA: National Bureau of Economic Research.

Bzostek, S., Carlson, M. J., & McLanahan, S. (2009). *Mothers' repartnering after a nonmarital birth* (Working Paper No. 2006-27-FF). Princeton, NJ: Center for Research on Child Wellbeing.

Carlson, M. J., McLanahan, S., & England, P. (2004). Union formation in fragile families. *Demography, 41*, 237–261.

Cavanagh, S. E., & Huston, A. C. (2008). The timing of family instability and children's social development. *Journal of Marriage and Family, 70*, 1258–1270.

Cherlin, A. J. (2004). The deinstitutionalization of American marriage. *Journal of Marriage and Family, 66*, 848–861.

Cherlin, A. J. (2009). The marriage-go-round: *The state of marriage and the family in America today*. New York: Knopf.

Dion, M. R. (2005). Healthy marriage programs: Learning what works. *Future of Children, 15*, 139–156.

Duncan, G. J., Brooks-Gunn, J., Yeung, W. J., & Smith, J. (1998). How much does childhood poverty affect the life chances of children? *American Sociological Review, 63*, 406–423.

Edin, K., & Kefalas, M. J. (2005). *Promises I can keep: Why poor women put motherhood before marriage*. Berkeley: University of California Press.

Ellwood, D. T., & Jencks, C. (2004). The uneven spread of single-parent families: What do we know? Where do we look for answers? In K. Neckerman (Ed.), *Social inequality* (pp. 3–77). New York: Russell Sage Foundation.

Foster, E. M., & Kalil, A. (2007). Living arrangements and children's development in low-income white, black, and Latino families. *Child Development, 78*, 1657–1667.

Gibson-Davis, C. M. (2009). Money, marriage, and children: Testing the financial expectations and family formation theory. *Journal of Marriage and Family, 71*, 146–161.

Gibson-Davis, C. M., Edin, K., & McLanahan, S. (2005). High hopes but even higher expectations: The retreat from marriage among low-income couples. *Journal of Marriage and Family, 67*, 1301–1312.

Goldstein, J. R., & Kenney, C. (2001). Marriage delayed or marriage forgone? New cohort forecasts of first marriage for U.S. women. *American Sociological Review, 66*, 506–519.

Graefe, D. R., & Lichter, D. T. (2002). Marriage among unwed mothers: Whites, blacks and Hispanics compared. *Perspectives on Sexual and Reproductive Health, 34*, 286–294.

Graefe, D. R., & Lichter, D. T. (2008). Marriage patterns among unwed mothers: Before and after PRWORA. *Journal of Policy Analysis and Management, 27*, 479–497.

Gray, J. A., Stockard, J., & Stone, J. (2006). The rising share of nonmarital births: Fertility choice or marriage behavior? *Demography, 43*, 241–253.

Harknett, K., & McLanahan, S. S. (2004). Racial and ethnic differences in marriage after the birth of a child. *American Sociological Review, 69,* 790–811.

Hill, M. S., Yeung, W., & Duncan, G. J. (2001). Childhood family structure and young adult behaviors. *Journal of Population Economics, 14,* 271–299.

Hofferth, S. L., & Anderson, K. G. (2003). Are all dads equal? Biology versus marriage as a basis for paternal investment. *Journal of Marriage and Family, 65,* 213–232.

Kennedy, S., & Bumpass, L. (2008). Cohabitation and children's living arrangements: New estimates from the United States. *Demographic Research, 19,* 1663–1692.

Lerman, R. (2002). *Marriage and the economic well-being of families with children: A review of the literature.* Washington, DC: Urban Institute.

Lichter, D. T., & Graefe, D. R. (2001). Finding a mate? The marital and cohabitation histories of unwed mothers. In L. L. Wu & B. Wolfe (Eds.), *Out of wedlock: Causes and consequences of nonmarital fertility* (pp. 317–343). New York: Russell Sage Foundation.

Lichter, D. T., & Graefe, D. R. (2007). Men and marriage promotion: Who marries unwed mothers? *Social Service Review, 81,* 397–421.

Lichter, D. T., McLaughlin, D. K., & Ribar, D. C. (2002). Economic restructuring and the retreat from marriage. *Social Science Research, 31,* 230–256.

Manning, W. D. (1993). Marriage and cohabitation following premarital conception. *Journal of Marriage and the Family, 55,* 839–850.

Martin, J. A., Hamilton, B. E., Sutton, P. D., Ventura, S. J., Menacker, F., Kirmeyer, S., & Mahews, M.S. (2009). *Births: Final data for 2006.* Hyattsville, MD: National Center for Health Statistics.

Moffitt, R. (1992). Incentive effects of the U.S. welfare system: A review. *Journal of Economic Literature, 30,* 1–61.

Moffitt, R. (1998). The effect of welfare on marriage and fertility. In R. Moffitt (Ed.), *Welfare, the family, and reproductive behavior: Research perspectives* (pp. 50–97). Washington, DC: National Academy Press.

Moffitt, R. (2002). The Temporary Assistance for Needy Families program. In R. Moffitt (Ed.), *Means-tested transfer programs* (pp. 291–363). Chicago: National Bureau of Economic Research.

Osborne, C., & McLanahan, S. (2007). Partnership instability and child well-being. *Journal of Marriage and Family, 69,* 1065–1083.

Parnell, A. M., Swicegood, G., & Stevens, G. (1994). Nonmarital pregnancies and marriage in the United States. *Social Forces, 73,* 263–287.

Popenoe, D. (2009). Cohabitation, marriage, and child wellbeing: A cross-national perspective. *Society, 46,* 429–436.

Rindfuss, R. R., Palmore, J. A., & Bumpass, L. (1982). Selectivity and the analysis of birth intervals from survey data. *Asian and Pacific Census Forum, 8,* 5–10, 15–16.

Schoen, R., Landale, N. S., & Daniels, K. (2007). Family transitions in young adulthood. *Demography, 44,* 807–820.

Smith, H. L., Morgan, S. P., & Koropeckyj-Cox, T. (1996). A decomposition of trends in the nonmarital fertility ratios of blacks and whites in the United States, 1960–92. *Demography, 33,* 141–151.

Smock, P. J., Manning, W. D., & Porter, M. (2005). "Everything's there except money": How money shapes decisions to marry among cohabitors. *Journal of Marriage and Family, 67,* 680–696.

StataCorp. (2009). *Stata statistical software: Release 11 SE.* College Station, TX: Author.

Stevenson, B., & Wolfers, J. (2007). Marriage and divorce: Changes and their driving forces. *Journal of Economic Perspectives, 21,* 27–52.

Thornton, A., & Young-DeMarco, L. (2001). Four decades of trends in attitudes toward family issues in the United States: The 1960s through the 1990s. *Journal of Marriage and Family, 63*, 1009–1037.

U.S. Bureau of the Census. (2004). *Table MS-2. Estimated median age at first marriage, by sex: 1890 to the present*. Retrieved November 30, 2004, from http://www.census.gov/population/socdemo/hh-fam/tabMS-2.pdf.

Wilson, W. J. (1987). *The truly disadvantaged: The inner city, the underclass, and public policy*. Chicago: University of Chicago Press.

Wilson, W. J., & Neckerman, K. A. (1986). Poverty and family structure: The widening gap between evidence and public policy issues. In S. H. Danziger & D. H. Weinberg (Eds.), *Fighting poverty: What works, and what doesn't* (pp. 232–259). Cambridge, MA: Harvard University Press.

Wu, L. L. (2008). Cohort estimates of nonmarital fertility for U.S. women. *Demography, 45*, 193–207.

Chapter 20

Balancing Work and Family Life, Outcomes

By Kim Parker and Wendy Wang

OVERVIEW

The way mothers and fathers spend their time has changed dramatically in the past half century. Dads are doing more housework and child care; moms more paid work outside the home. Neither has overtaken the other in their "traditional" realms, but their roles are converging, according to a new Pew Research Center analysis of long-term data on time use.

At the same time, roughly equal shares of working mothers and fathers report in a new Pew Research Center survey feeling stressed about juggling work and family life: 56% of working moms and 50% of working dads say they find it very or somewhat difficult to balance these responsibilities.

Still, there are important gender role differences. While a nearly equal share of mothers and fathers say they wish they could be at home raising their children rather than working, dads are much more likely than moms to say they want to work full time. And when it comes to what they value most in a job, working fathers place more importance on having a high-paying job, while working mothers are more concerned with having a flexible schedule.[1]

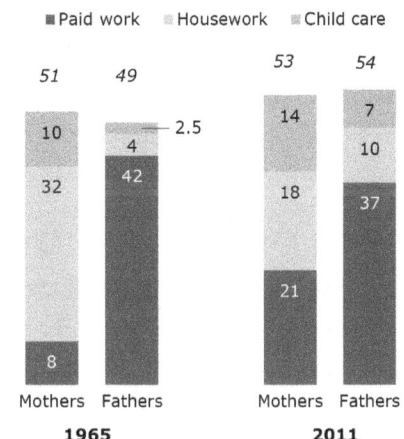

___
1 Unless otherwise noted, references to "parents" and "mothers" or "fathers" throughout this report refer to those with at least one child under the age of 18 and references to "young children" refer to children younger than 18.

Kim Parker and Wendy Wang, from *Modern Parenthood: Roles of Moms and Dads Converge as They Balance Work and Family*, pp. 1–4, 19–26. Copyright © 2013 by Pew Research Center. Reprinted with permission.

However, mothers' attitudes toward work have changed considerably in recent years. Among mothers with children under age 18, the share saying they would prefer to work full time has increased from 20% in 2007 to 32% in 2012. Tough economic times may have ushered in a new mindset, as women in the most difficult financial circumstances are among the most likely to say working full time is the ideal situation for them.

At the same time, the public remains conflicted about what is best for children. Among all adults, only 16% say the ideal situation for a young child is to have a mother who works full time. A plurality of adults (42%) say mothers working part time is ideal, and one-third say it's best for young children if their mothers do not work at all outside of the home.

These findings are based on a new Pew Research survey of 2,511 adults nationwide conducted Nov. 28-Dec. 5, 2012, and an analysis of the American Time Use Survey (ATUS). The ATUS, which began in 2003, is a nationally representative telephone survey that measures the amount of time people spend doing various activities throughout the day. It is sponsored by the U.S. Bureau of Labor Statistics and is conducted by the U.S. Census Bureau. Data collected from 2003 through 2011 include interviews with more than 124,000 respondents. Comparable time diary data are available going back as far as 1965, allowing for an analysis of trends over a nearly 50-year period.[2]

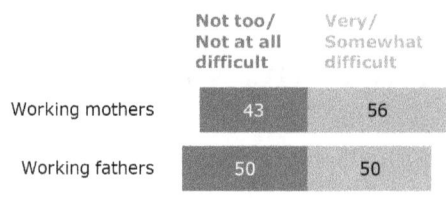

Work-Family Balance Is Challenging for Moms and Dads

% saying it is ... for them to balance the responsibilities of their job and their family

	Not too/ Not at all difficult	Very/ Somewhat difficult
Working mothers	43	56
Working fathers	50	50

Notes: Based on mothers and fathers with children under age 18. "Working" refers to full- or part-time employment. "Don't know/Refused" responses not shown.
PEW RESEARCH CENTER   Q41

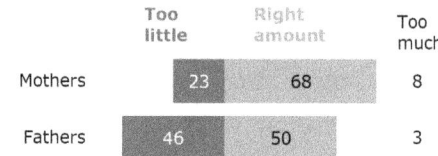

Fathers Conflicted about Time Spent with Children

% saying they spend ... time with their children

	Too little	Right amount	Too much
Mothers	23	68	8
Fathers	46	50	3

Notes: Based on mothers and fathers with children under age 18. "Don't know/Refused" responses not shown.
PEW RESEARCH CENTER   Q26a

Balancing Work and Family

The Pew Research survey finds that about half (53%) of all working parents with children under age 18 say it is difficult for them to balance the responsibilities of their job with the responsibilities of their family. There is no significant gap in attitudes between mothers and fathers: 56% of mothers and 50% of fathers say juggling work and family life is difficult for them.

Feeling rushed is also a part of everyday life for today's mothers and fathers. Among those with children under age 18, 40% of working mothers and 34% of working fathers say they always feel rushed.

With so many demands on their time, many parents wonder whether they are spending the right amount of time with their children. Overall, 33% of parents with children under age 18 say they are not spending enough time with their children. Fathers are much more likely than mothers to feel this way. Some 46% of fathers say they are not spending enough time with their children, compared with 23% of mothers. Analysis of time use data shows that fathers devote significantly less time than mothers to child care (an average of seven hours per week for fathers, compared with 14 hours per week for

---

2 Data from 1965 to 2000 are from Suzanne Bianchi, et al., 2006, Changing Rhythms of American Family Life, which analyzed time diary surveys conducted before the ATUS was established.

mothers). Among mothers, 68% say they spend the right amount of time with their children. Only half of fathers say the same. Relatively few mothers (8%) or fathers (3%) say they spend too much time with their children.

Mothers, Fathers and Time Use

A lot has changed for women and men in the 50 years since Betty Friedan wrote "The Feminine Mystique." Women have made major strides in education and employment, and the American workplace has been transformed. But with these changes have come the added pressures of balancing work and family life, for mothers and fathers alike. Trends in time use going back to 1965 clearly show how the increased participation of women in the workforce has affected the amount of time mothers devote to paid work. In 2011, mothers spent, on average, 21 hours per week on paid work, up from eight hours in 1965. Over the same period, the total amount of time mothers spend in non-paid work has gone down somewhat.

For their part, fathers now spend more time engaged in housework and child care than they did half a century ago. And the amount of time they devote to paid work has decreased slightly over that period. Fathers have by no means caught up to mothers in terms of time spent caring for children and doing household chores, but there has been some gender convergence in the way they divide their time between work and home.

Roughly 60% of two-parent households[3] with children under age 18 have two working parents. In those households, on average, fathers spend more time than mothers in paid work, while mothers spend more time on child care and household chores. However, when their paid work is combined with the work they do at home, fathers and mothers are carrying an almost equal workload.

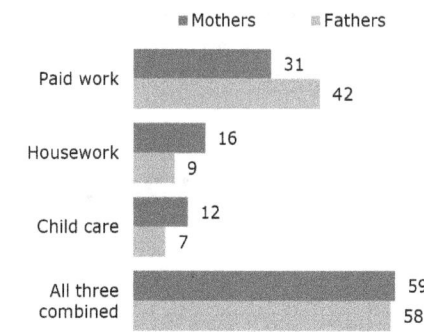

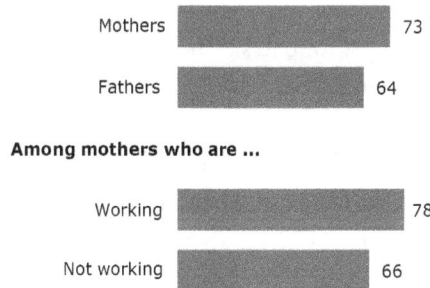

How Do Today's Mothers and Fathers Rate Themselves?

In spite of challenges they face, today's parents give themselves good grades overall for the job they are doing raising their children. Among all parents with children under age 18, 24% say they have done an excellent job, and an additional 45% say they have done a very good job. Some 24% say they have done a good job, and only 6% rate their job as parents as fair or poor.

---

3 In both the Pew Research Survey and the American Time Use Survey, it is possible that some two-parent households are made up of a same-sex couple rather than a mother and father. Due to data limitations, same-sex couples are not analyzed separately.

Mothers give themselves somewhat higher ratings than do fathers: 73% of mothers say they are doing an excellent or very good job as a parent, compared with 64% of fathers.

Working mothers give themselves slightly higher ratings than non-working mothers for the job they are doing as parents. Among mothers with children under age 18 who work full or part time, 78% say they are doing an excellent or very good job as parents. Among mothers who are not employed, 66% say the same.

CHAPTER 2: BALANCING WORK AND FAMILY LIFE

One of the challenges for working parents is finding enough time to do it all. Many say they feel rushed, and more than half say they have difficulty balancing the responsibilities of their job and their family life. While working mothers and fathers divide their time differently—with fathers concentrating somewhat more on paid work and mothers more on home and children—moms and dads are equally likely to find the juggling act challenging.

Feeling Rushed?

Overall, 25% of adults say they "always" feel rushed, and an additional 47% say they "sometimes" feel rushed. Parents with children under age 18 are significantly more likely than adults who do not have children in that age group to say they always feel rushed, even to do the things they have to do (34% vs. 20%, respectively). Only 18% of parents say they almost never feel rushed, compared with 31% of adults with no children under age 18. Similar shares of fathers (32%) and mothers (37%) say they are always in a rush.

Working parents are more likely than non-working parents to say that they always feel rushed. Some 37% of employed parents say they are always rushed, and an additional 47% say they sometimes feel rushed. Among parents who are not employed, 27% say they are always rushed and 45% say they are sometimes in a rush. Among mothers, non-working mothers are more than twice as likely as working mothers (24% vs. 11%) to say they almost never feel rushed.[8]

Parents More Rushed than Non-Parents

% saying they ... feel rushed

■ Always ■ Sometimes ■ Almost never

	Always	Sometimes	Almost never
Has children <18	34	46	18
No children <18	20	47	31

Among adults with children <18 ...

	Always	Sometimes	Almost never
Mothers	37	47	16
Fathers	32	45	22
Married	36	47	15
Unmarried	31	44	25
Working	37	47	15
Not working	27	45	28

Note: "Don't know/Refused" responses not shown.
PEW RESEARCH CENTER   Q4

Married and unmarried parents are about equally liked to say they always feel rushed (36% and 31%, respectively). However, unmarried parents (25%) are significantly more likely than married parents (15%) to say they almost never feel rushed.

Parents who live in dual-income households report feeling busier than those who live in a household where only one spouse or partner is employed. About four-in-ten (39%) parents in dual-earner

---

8   There were too few non-working fathers in the sample to analyze them separately.

partnerships say they are always rushed, compared with 28% of parents for whom either they or their partner is not working.

Managing Work and Family

Mothers and fathers feel equally pressured these days when it comes to managing their time between work and family. Among those with children under age 18, half of working fathers and 56% of working mothers say that balancing the responsibilities of their job with the responsibilities of their family is very or somewhat difficult.

Among all working parents with children under age 18, 15% say it is very difficult and 37% say it is somewhat difficult to balance their work and their family life. About one-third (32%) say it is not too difficult, and 15% say it is not at all difficult.

In the Pew Research survey, this question was asked among employed people who were either parents of children younger than 18 or married. Those who did not have children under age 18 (i.e., who are married with grown children or married without any children) were

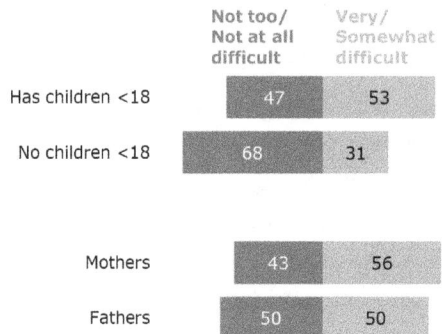

less likely than parents of young children to say it was difficult for them to manage work and family simultaneously—31% of those without children under age 18 say this balance is very or somewhat difficult, compared with 53% of those who have young children.

Parents in dual-income households are no more likely than those in single-income households to say it is very or somewhat difficult to balance the responsibilities of work and family life (54% vs. 49%, respectively).

There is no historical trend for the Pew Research question, so it is difficult to say how the level of difficulty men and women experience in balancing work and family life has changed over time. However, another national survey offers some clues. The Families and Work Institute conducted a survey of the U.S. workforce in 2008 that included questions about work-life balance. This survey found that fathers were more much likely to feel conflicts between their working lives and personal lives in 2008 than they had been in 1977, while mothers experienced only a modest increase in these conflicts over the same period. In 1977, 35% of employed fathers whose spouse or partner worked and 41% of employed mothers in dual-earner couples said they experienced at least some work-life conflict.[9] In 2008, the share of fathers saying this had increased to 60%, while the share of mothers saying so went up only marginally to 47%.[10]

---

9 1977 figures are from surveys conducted by the Institute for Social Research at the University of Michigan.

10 This analysis is based on mothers and fathers with child(ren) younger than 18 who are in dual-earner couples and are employed for at least 20 hours per week. Work-life conflict is measured here using the following question: "How much do your job and your family life interfere with each other—a lot, somewhat, not too much or not at all?" To see the full report from the Families and Work Institute, see, Galinsky, Ellen, K. Aumann, J.T. Bond. 2011. "Times are Changing: Gender and Generation at Work and at Home." Families and Work Institute. August.

Working vs. Staying Home with the Kids

Not only do many working mothers and fathers find it difficult to balance work and family, fully half say they would like to be home with their children, rather than working. Survey respondents were asked which statement best describes how they balance work and family: (1) They would prefer to be at home raising their children, but they need to work because they need the income; or (2) Even though it takes them away from their family, they enjoy their work and want to keep working. Among all working parents with children under age 18, 50% say they would prefer to be home raising their children, while 46% say they want to keep working.

Mothers and fathers have nearly identical views on this question. Roughly half of working mothers (52%) and fathers (48%) say they would prefer to be home with their children but they have to work because they need the income. Some 42% of mothers and 49% of fathers say that even though work takes them away from their families, they enjoy their work and want to keep working. (These differences are not statistically significant.)

NBC News and the Wall Street Journal asked this question of working mothers 12 years ago, and opinions have changed very little since then. In 2000, 48% of working mothers with children under age 18 said they would prefer to be home with their children but needed to work, and 44% said they would like to keep working even though it took them away from their family.[11]

Income and education are strongly correlated with the desire to be at home rather than working. Among working parents with annual household incomes of less than $50,000, fully 63% say they would prefer to be home with their children but need to work because they need the income. This compares with 39% of working parents with incomes of $50,000 or higher. Similarly, working parents who have not attended college are more likely than those who have to say they would prefer to be home with their children (62% vs. 42%).

Working Mothers, Fathers Conflicted about Work and Family

% saying…

	Working mothers	Working fathers
I'd prefer to be home with my children, but I need the income so I need to work	52	48
Even though it takes me away from my family, I want to keep working	42	49
Don't know/Refused	5	3
	100	100

Notes: Based on those who are employed either full or part time. Mothers are fathers are those with children under age 18. Figures may not add to 100% due to rounding. See text for complete wording of items.

PEW RESEARCH CENTER Q44

Income and Education Gaps in Work-Life Balance

% of employed parents with children under age 18 saying they …

	Would prefer to be home, but need income	Enjoy work, want to keep working
Income		
Less than $50,000	63	35
$50,000 or higher	39	55
Education		
No college	62	36
Some college or more	42	53

Note: Based on those who are employed either full or part time. Income based on annual family income. "Don't know/Refused" responses not shown.

PEW RESEARCH CENTER Q44

---

11 In the June 2000 NBC/WSJ trend, the question was asked only of employed women who have children younger than 18 living in their household. This differs slightly from the Pew Research question, which does not take into account the living situation of the children. Fathers were not asked this question in the 2000 survey.

CHAPTER 3: OUTCOMES

How Do Today's Mothers and Fathers Rate Themselves as Parents?

In spite of the challenges they face, today's parents give themselves good grades overall for the job they are doing raising their children. Among all parents with children under age 18, 24% say they are doing an excellent job, and an additional 45% say they are doing a very good job. Some 24% say they are doing a good job, and only 6% say they are doing a fair or poor job as parents.

Mothers give themselves somewhat higher grades than do fathers: 73% of mothers with children under age 18 say they are doing an excellent or very good job as a parent, compared with 64% of fathers.

Married parents with children younger than 18 give themselves higher ratings than do unmarried parents. Some 72% of married parents say they are doing an excellent or very good job raising their children, compared with 63% of unmarried parents.

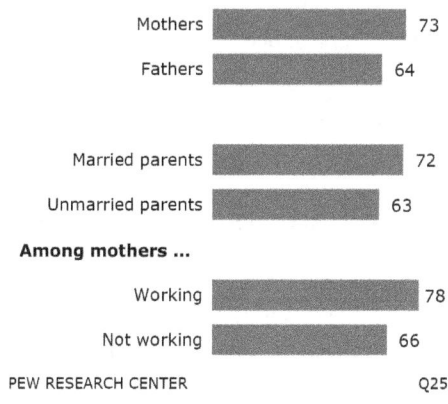

Mothers, Fathers Give Themselves High Ratings for Parenting

% with children under age 18 saying they are doing an "excellent" or "very good" job as parents

- Mothers: 73
- Fathers: 64
- Married parents: 72
- Unmarried parents: 63

Among mothers …
- Working: 78
- Not working: 66

PEW RESEARCH CENTER Q25

Among mothers, those who are working give themselves particularly high ratings—78% of working moms say they are doing an excellent or good job raising their children. Among non-working mothers, 66% say the same.

Whether parents feel they spend enough time with their children has a big impact on how they evaluate their parenting. Parents who think they spend the right amount of time with their children are about three times as likely as parents who say they spend too little time with their children to say they are doing an excellent job parenting (30% vs. 11%). Overall, 77% of parents who say they spend the right amount of time with their kids also say they are doing an excellent or very good job as parents; only 54% of those who say they spend too little time rate themselves as doing an excellent or very good job.

Similarly, parents who say they have difficulty balancing work and family life are harder on themselves when it comes to evaluating their parenting. Among working parents who say balancing the responsibilities of their job and their family is difficult for them, two-thirds give themselves an excellent or very good rating for the job they are doing as parents. By contrast, among working parents who say balancing these responsibilities is not difficult for them, 77% give themselves high marks.

Parents' self-evaluations differ somewhat by key demographic groups. Among parents with children of any age, white and black parents give themselves similar grades for their parenting, while Hispanic parents are much harder on themselves. Only 56% of Hispanic parents say they are doing an excellent or very good

Does More Time Spent with Children Lead to Better Parenting?

% saying they are doing an ... job as parents

■ Excellent ▪ Very good

All parents with children <18: 24 | 45

Time spent with children:

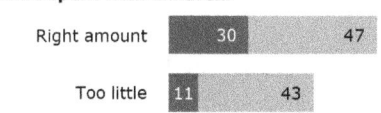

Right amount: 30 | 47
Too little: 11 | 43

Notes: Parents who said they spend "too much" time with children not shown due to small sample size. For all parents, n=643; for parents who spend "right amount," of time n=395; for "too little" time, n=204. "Good," "Only fair," "Poor" and "Don't know/Refused" responses not shown.

PEW RESEARCH CENTER Q25, 26a

job as parents, while 72% of white parents and 67% of black parents give themselves high marks for parenting.[12]

Education is also linked to parents' self-assessments. Among parents with children under age 18, those who have attended or graduated from college rate their parenting more favorably than those who have not attended college: 73% of parents with some college experience say they are doing an excellent or very good job as parents, compared with 63% of those with no college experience.

Some Parents are Happier than Others

The stresses and joys of parenthood are inextricably linked to overall happiness and well-being. It is nearly impossible, using survey data alone, to disaggregate the factors that contribute to happiness. However, some interesting patterns emerge relating to work and family life.

In general, adults with children of any age tend to be somewhat happier than those who do not have children.[13] Three-in-ten parents (31%) say they are "very happy," 48% say they are "pretty happy" and 17% say they are "not too happy." Among adults with no children, 24% say they are very happy, 60% say they are pretty happy and 14% say they are not too happy.

Among parents with children under age 18, mothers (36%) and fathers (30%) report roughly equal levels of happiness. However, a slightly larger share of fathers than mothers say they are not too happy (17% vs. 11%). Married parents are happier than unmarried parents (38% vs. 23% say they are very happy).

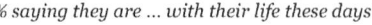

Who's Happy?

% saying they are ... with their life these days

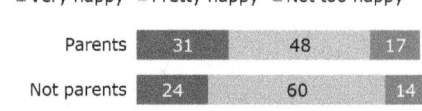

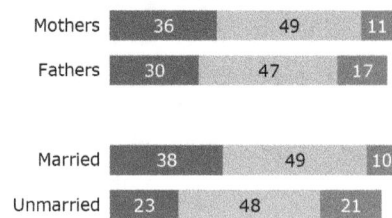

Note: In the first set of bars, parents are adults with children of any age. "Don't know/Refused" responses not shown.

PEW RESEARCH CENTER   Q1

Moms, Marriage, Work and Happiness

% of mothers with children under age 18 saying they are "very happy"

Note: "Working" includes those who work full or part time.

PEW RESEARCH CENTER   Q1

---

12 Analysis of racial and ethnic differences is based on parents with children of any age due to small sample sizes among those with children under age 18.
13 It was cited frequently in psychological research in the past that parents were less happy than non-parents. However, recent studies have suggested that while this was true from the mid-1980s to the mid-1990s, there seems to have been a turn-around in 1995, with parents from then until 2008 happier than non-parents. (USA Today, Sharon Jayson, "Parents today are happier than non-parents, studies suggest," May 2012, and The Atlantic, Hans Villarica, "Study of the Day: Maybe Parents Actually Are Happier than Non-Parents," May 2012.)

There is a significant gap in happiness between married and unmarried mothers. Among married mothers with children under age 18, 43% say they are very happy with their life overall. By contrast, only 23% of unmarried mothers say they are very happy.

There is also a gap in happiness between working and non-working mothers. While 45% of mothers who do not work are very happy with their life, only 31% of working mothers say they are very happy.

Further statistical analysis suggests that marriage trumps employment status when it comes to moms' happiness. When race, ethnicity, educational attainment and income are held constant, marital status is a significant predictor of overall happiness, but work status is not.[14]

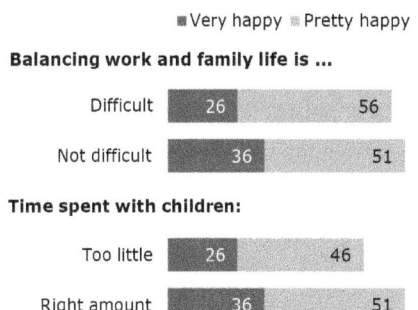

Work-Life Balance and Happiness

While parenthood can be a source of great happiness, the stresses and strains of balancing work and family life may have an impact on overall well-being. Working parents who say they find it difficult to manage the responsibilities of their job and their family are somewhat less happy overall than those who don't have difficulty balancing these things. Only 26% of those who say it's difficult for them to balance work and family say they are very happy, compared with 36% of those who don't have difficulty balancing.

Further analysis shows there is a much stronger correlation between happiness and work-life balance among working fathers than among working mothers. While 23% of working fathers who say it's difficult to balance work and family life are very happy overall, 38% of fathers who don't have difficulty balancing say they are very happy. There is no significant difference in the level of happiness among working women who say balancing work and family is difficult for them (30% are very happy) and those who say it is not (32%).[15]

Similarly, parents who say they do not spend enough time with their children are less happy than those who say they spend the right amount of time with their children. Among those parents who say they spend too little time with their children, 26% say they are very happy overall. This compares with 36% of those who say they spend the right amount of time with their children.

---

14 These findings are based on a multivariate regression analysis which tested the likelihood that a mother would be "very happy," based on a series of variables: employment status, marital status, race, ethnicity, educational attainment and income.
15 For mothers saying it is not difficult for them to balance work and family life, n=96.

Chapter 21

Balance of Work and Family Needs

By Carol Bennett-Speight, Ph.D.

Abstract

The United States workforce and American families were changing in the years before the Family and Medical Leave Act (FMLA) was enacted in 1993. The U.S. was and continues to be in the midst of rapid demographic changes including an aging population, an increase in diverse family types, and more women in the work force and a greater ethnic diversity in the work force. The interplay of these trends significantly influenced the informal arrangement of assistance by employed caregivers. Research indicates that caregiving responsibilities interfered with their social and family relationships, personal free time and work productivity. In addition, surveys indicate that the most endorsed workplace policy is the ability to utilize a flexible work schedule. However, the Family and Medical Leave Act of 1993 provided some provisions for balancing work and family needs. The Act required employers with fifty or more employees within a seventy-five mile radius to offer eligible employees up to twelve weeks of unpaid leave during a twelve month period for a variety of medical reasons such as

- the birth of a child and to care for the newborn child within one year of birth;
- the placement with the employee of a child for adoption or foster care and to care for the newly placed child within one year of placement;
- to care for the employee's spouse, child, or parent who has a serious health condition;
- a serious health condition that makes the employee unable to perform the essential functions of his or her job;
- any qualifying exigency arising out of the fact that the employee's spouse, son, daughter, or parent is a covered military member on "covered active duty;" or
- Twenty-six workweeks of leave during a single 12-month period to care for a covered service member with a serious injury or illness if the eligible employee is the service member's

spouse, son, daughter, parent, or next of kin (military caregiver leave). (United States Department of Labor http://wlow.dol/whd/fmla

King, N (2000) provides an ethical framework for compliance with the FMLA. He uses this framework for Human Resources that leads to some ethical work place choices that enhances the "balance between employer and employee needs and a requirement of consistency and fairness in the treatment of groups of employees with similar family care needs, leading to equitable treatment." However, are we ethically and consistently fair and equitable with the provision of the FMLA of 1993? Does the FMLA allow families to maintain their economic security?

Although the Family Medical Leave Act (FMLA), mandates 12 weeks of job-protected leave to qualified workers, but the leave is unpaid, limited to companies with 50 or more employees and only covers employees who worked at least 1,250 hours in the year before requesting leave. Many do not qualify for the leave. As a result, about 50 percent of surveyed employees reported they met the qualifications to take FMLA, according to DOL's report, which was released. The report *Family and Medical Leave in 2012* consists of survey results compiled by DOL (Department of Labor) by ABI Associates, a Cambridge Mass-based consulting firm. The firm surveyed 1,812 worksites and 2,852 employees in 2012, including both employers and employees who are covered by the FMLA and those who are not. The survey found that 13 percent of all employees, both those who were covered under the FMLA, and those who were not took leave for an FMLA-covered reason in 2012. Among workers who were eligible for FMLA leave in 2012, 16 percent took leave while only 10 percent of ineligible employees did so. Abt Associates (2012–2013), Glazer, S. (2006, April 14) http://library.cqpress.com/cqresearcher/. In addition the report indicates that most leave was taken due to the workers' own illness. Some 57 percent of the leave workers took was due to their own illness the report said, while 22 percent took leave in connection with the birth or adoption of a child and 19 percent said they took leave to care for a spouse, child, or parent. (DOL Report 2012-2013) Although the FMLA only mandates that covered employers provide workers with unpaid leave, the survey found that most workers who took leave for FMLA covered reasons received some pay with 48 percent receiving full pay and another 17 percent receiving partial pay. However for leaves of more than 10 days only 40 percent of workers received pay while 60 percent were paid during leaves of 10 days or less. Most of the pay was due to using sick time, vacation time and other compensations.

Gerstel and McGonagle (1999) with their landmark research examined the need for and use of leaves designated by the Family and Medical Leave Act. Using national data, they showed that women, parents, those with little income, and African Americans are particularly likely to perceive a need for job leaves. "However, it is married-not single-women and Whites who are particularly likely to take such leaves." Gerstel and McGonagle, 1999, and Mayer, G 2013. Thus reinforcing inequality based on gender, race, and family status. (Armenia & Gerstel (2006) and Mayer G. 2013).

According to the National Partnership for Women & Families, only 11 percent of American workers have access to paid family leave. Recently, advocacy groups are demanding expansion of the FMLA to include paid leave and pushing the laws scope for those who are eligible. Mayer, G. (2013) writes that supporters of the FMLA have proposed amendments to the act that would expand employee coverage. "Some of these suggestions would make it easier for employees to qualify for leave, allow employees to take leave to care for more members of their family or household, expand the types of leave, or expand employer coverage to include employees of smaller employers. On the other hand, Mayer sites that others have proposed changes in the law that would "narrow the definition of a serious health condition or curtail the use of intermittent leave for a chronic health condition that has been reported.

Employer groups express that FMLA has had some benefits for those who meet the qualifications. However, many of these groups point out that for many, FMLA is problematic, and expansion and change is needed. FMLA is the first step to a family friendly nation and policies. The National Partnership for Women and Families (NPWF) is requesting that Congress expand the law so that more workers can take leave for more reasons and to "adopt a national paid family and medical leave program." NPWF cited that FMLA is not available for workers who need time off to care for, parents-in-law, grandparents, grandchildren, siblings, domestic partners, or some same-sex spouses, nor for domestic violence victims. In addition, NPWF and some law makers cite in a statement that "creating a national paid leave insurance program would ease burdens for both employees who need paid leave and employers who cannot afford the full cost of offering paid leave to their workers."

While much conflict continues to abound regarding the FML, this is the first step towards ethical fairness for employees and employers.

Questions:

Has the Family and Medical Leave Act Achieve Work Place Equality?
Should the Family Medical Leave Act Be expanded to include paid leave?
What are the race and cultural differences with utilizing the FMLA?

References

Amenia A, Gerstel N. (2006). Family Leaves, The FMLA and Gender Neutrality: The Intersection of Race and Gender. Social Science Research, 25, pgs. 871–891.

Gerstel N. and McGonagle K, (1999) "Job Leaves and the Limit of the Family and Medical Leave Act. The effects of Gender, Race and Family. Retrieved July 26, 2014 http://wox.sagepub.com/content/26/4/510.

Johnson, M. CQ Research (2013) http://www.cquesearch.com. Vol. 23, Number 27, pgs. 645–668.

King, N., (1999) "Family Medical Leave Act: An Ethical Model for Human Resource policies: An Ethical Model for Human Resource Policies and Decisions. Marquette Law Review, 83 (2).

Mayer, G. (2013) "The Family and Medical Leave Act (FMLA): Policy Issues. Congressional Research Service. Retrieved July 26, 2014 http://assets.opencrs.com/rpts/R4314_20130904.

US Department of Labor (2013) retrieved July 26, 20014 http://wlow.dol/whd/fmila.

US Department of Labor, (2012) "Family Medical Leave 2012) retrieved July 26, 2014 www.dol.gov/asp/fmla2012.

FURTHER READINGS

Bradford Wilcox, W., and Kathleen Kovner Kline, eds. *Gender and Parenthood: Biological and Social Scientific Perspectives*. New York: Columbia University Press, 2013.

Brighouse, Harry, and Adam Swift. *Family Values: The Ethics of Parent–Child Relationships*. Princeton, NJ: Princeton University Press, 2014.

McClain, Linda C., and Daniel Cere, eds. *What Is Parenthood?: Contemporary Debates about the Family (Families, Law, Society)*. New York: New York University Press, 2013.

Riblett Wilkie, Jane. "The Trend toward Delayed Parenthood." *Journal of Marriage and Family* 43, no. 3 (1981): 583–91.

Richards, Norvin. *The Ethics of Parenthood*. New York: Oxford University Press, 2010.

Ruddick, William. "Children's Rights and Parents' Virtue." In *Philosophy, Children, and the Family (Child Nurturance)*, edited by Albert C. Cafagna, Richard T. Peterson, and Craig A. Staudenbaur, 165–73. New York: Springer USA, 1982.

Westman, Jack C. *Parenthood in America: Undervalued, Underpaid, Under Siege*. Madison: University of Wisconsin Press, 2001.

Chapter 22

Utilitarianism and Drugs: The Problem and the Solution

By wetpig.com

One way to approach the moral issue of drug use and legalization (as much as drugs themselves could be seen as a moral issue), is the application of utilitarianism in trying to resolve this problem. If in fact drug use is a moral problem, then first we need to explain how it is a moral problem and the possible morally apt solution.

In assessing whether or not something is ever a moral problem, it's important to distinguish the overlying assumptions that presuppose such a claim. For our case, we'll be examining utilitarianism and how it would view the moral problem of drugs. In our analysis I would like to propose then a utilitarian identification of the problem of drug use, as well as a reciprocating utilitarian solution to the problem as well. The presuppositions that follow from this utilitarian approach is rather simple: the good is that which maximizes utility for the most amount of people on average (average utility); and its opposite, that which hinders or leads to less average utility is morally bad—even if unintentional. That being said, what is utility? Utility is a rather difficult concept to define, but for this purpose we shall avoid the classical definition understood by Bentham as merely pleasure and the absent of pain, and propose a more complex and applicable definition. For our purposes here, let's define utility as happiness as a necessary component for well-being, and in this it follows that the rules dictating those behaviors or policies that increase the maximum utility will be on par with the increase of happiness as it relates to well-being on a morally relevant (rather than prudential) basis.

Now that the presuppositions have been taken care of, we should look further into the problem of drug-use as a moral issue. Note, by drugs I'm referring to illicit narcotic chemicals used for the purpose of artificial performance enhancement, artificial chemical stimulus of the central nervous system, and those recreational substances used for the purpose of attaining extreme mental states of pleasure and/or euphoria. At this point in time, our clarification distinguishing utility from hedonism becomes important. For, the hedonist might say that the overall pleasure experienced

Copyright © 2007 by wetpig.com.

from taking an intoxicating chemical that stimulates one's mind into a state of euphoria might be aggregately more intense and pleasurable than any negative side-effects this behavior might incur. Naturally, it follows then that drug use wouldn't be a moral problem at all, and if one is willing to try the experience and finds it more pleasurable, then this is perhaps morally good. However, this definition rests on two assumptions of the problem that we no longer need to worry about: first, we have distinguished overall average utility as the main component of our moral assessment (rather than overall), and we have defined it not merely on increasing pleasure and avoiding pain, which deals with simply mental states at the subjective level. It should also be noted now that pleasures may in fact be ranked accordingly to a hierarchy, such as John Stuart Mill devised.

Now, the problem of drug use as a moral issue from the perspective of the utilitarian must rest on consequentialist grounds. Also, we will compose our dissection of this problem both from the perspective of the individual and society at large while still relating to average utility; secondly, our solution will follow suit. The problem for the individual can be difficult to identify beyond mere physical effects of narcotics on his body, which is not solely grounds enough for us terming it a moral problem (at least in the tradition of utilitarianism). We have to identify that the consequences (as they relate to maximizing utility) are both for the individual (and society) bad, and that the solution is good. In identifying such a problem, we need to look at the problems faced by the drug user himself and the use of drugs on society at large.

For the drug user himself, narcotics as they exist as illegal substances, creates a myriad of problems—ultimately dependent on the type and degree of his addiction. If one finds himself addicted to a very potent opiate, such as heroine, we need not examine further the moral decay of his character and the consequences this may have for his individual utility or for that of society. But what about less obviously dangerous substances, like alcohol, nicotine, and THC (marijuana)? The effects of these drugs certainly don't necessarily result in one finding himself desperately searching for his next fix in some dark alley ... so how might the utilitarian address this as a moral problem?

The utilitarian might say that the person who uses these substances is forcing himself to accept negative consequences of his behavior that are undoubtedly infringing upon the maximization of his own utility by diverting his attention from other more important paths in his life. It is not too hard to imagine someone who chooses to drink instead of paint masterpieces, write deeply profound political tracts, or pursue some other end that indeed makes his life go better and better for society as well. The utilitarian might say that, while the drug user is pursuing his own pleasure (and even if it is not at odds with societal utility) he is nonetheless neglecting his other interests and pursuits that are fundamentally (and hierarchically) more important to the development and growth of his individual person for which his attainment is dependent upon the consequences of his own actions.

Likewise, it need not be said that he may ignore his own responsibilities by diverting financial resources towards his habit, which could have gone elsewhere. Imagine a man using the rest of his paycheck (assuming he works) to purchase a minimal quantity of marijuana, a carton of cigarettes, or a 1 liter bottle of Vodka instead of spending time with his kids. Now more than just the individual have been affected by the consequences of his choice, but those whose growth and development are dependent upon his choices are harmed as well. And so it goes. The toll on the community and the immediate family members of the user must be taken into an overall account of utility as well, for which much stress may be attributed.

Now we can imagine such behavior extending well beyond the realm of the individual and we have a societal problem. The use of drugs is inextricable accompanied by the traffic and dealing of drugs in communities, cities, towns, etc. which has a direct relationship to assorted crimes, from money laundering, robbery, theft, violence, etc. (not to mention the fact that trafficking and dealing are both in themselves crimes to begin with). A society of drug users (even if not the majority) will either have to place them in jail, rehab centers, or both—depending on how society decides to deal with these problems. What we have here now is a collective problem that drains resources, promotes crime (often times violent), and must now utilize resources from other areas of possible development to deal retroactively with a multitude of problems.

These problems have dealt only with the treatment of drug use as it remains illegal to consume, possess, or traffic. The situation would change drastically if currently illegal substances were decriminalized or even more so, if they were legalized and treated as a legitimate industry. The problem for the utilitarian is one dependent upon empirical data and historical evidence. Speculation into how drug use would reflect upon the maximization of utility once legal would present another problem, one of research and data collecting to see if this would be an appropriate solution that whose consequences wouldn't burden utility, and in fact, would promote it. How this is to be resolved is another matter altogether; however, the problem with legalization is that it assumes that the use of drugs in and of itself is not a morally bad thing, or that at best it is neutral without serious consequences for the rest of the society. This is an individualistic view (although a utilitarian position could quite easily be drafted for this line of reasoning as well), and is not attempting to resolve the problems I have set forth here in this article.

So, if we may move forward with the idea that drug use itself—whether illegal or legal, is bad for the maximization of utility then we have to come to a resolution that addresses the problem with means that follow accordingly towards our proposed ends. What the utilitarian must consider before making any propositions is the historical precedents surrounding the drug problem and how it is being dealt with today. Clearly, there exists some problems that have yet to be address, otherwise such a problem wouldn't exist at all. Secondly, we can accept that our current treatment of both users, possessors, and dealers is inadequate as the problem continues to progressively get worse.

A utilitarian solution which might resolve this problem then should look something like a combination solution involving both physical rehabilitation as well as retributive justice that aims at assisting the recovery over addiction for the addict, removes him wholly from society while undergoing this process, removing him from sources that may inhibit his recovery, and make productive, useful members of society out of these people to the maximum levels of their capacity and potential. Such a system would incorporate the medical and psychological aspect of their physical additions, and provide a set number of hours for counseling and treatment. The rest of the time should be devoted to hard labor for constructive purposes, as well as accompanied by educational seminars for helping them to learn trades, skills, and valuable knowledge in transforming them into productive citizens. The labor oriented aspect serves both as punishment and maximization of utility. These laborers could perform the more mundane tasks for important projects without having to risk sabotage to the overall project. This will provide society with a new source of labor to improve infrastructure and pursue other projects, with a possibility of returning citizens back into the general population free of their addiction and with the hope of using their newfound skills for the greater good of society.

The program should be extremely intensive and laborious; but rather than having drug users, traffickers, and possessors sit in prison cells where their behaviors are made worse by their surroundings, the atmosphere should be one that is entirely sterile and under complete surveillance using the latest in such technology, so that their every movement is recorded and observed in real time. Likewise, all facilities should remain 100% sterile from the presence of narcotics or other abused substances so that their is no underground dealing or using within. All occupants should be subject to hair tests on a weekly basis to ensure that they are not obtaining substances to ensure the success of the program. The duration of their stay should be mandated at a minimum sentence whereas afterwards their success through the program should be determined by a competent board of law enforcement, medical, and psychological officials to determine if the individual is thoroughly capable of being reintroduced to society. The costs of such a project are likely to be relatively high, but the outcomes should provide far superior results than that of which we have now, and statistics will be able to verify upon the application of such a program how successful they are through the monitoring and upkeep of databases on individuals as they re-enter the general population.

This is perhaps only one solution to the drug problem, which depends on a number of presuppositions I discussed previously. This is just to show how philosophy can be utilized to generate rationales behind different resolutions to real-world problems. Of course, much more research and thought would have to go into a potential alternative to dealing with the problem of drugs than I have outlined here, but it is merely a demonstration of one philosophical model in its pragmatic use.

FURTHER READINGS

Cook, Christopher C. H. *Alcohol, Addiction, and Christian Ethics*. New York: Cambridge University Press, 2006.

Levy, Neil. *Addiction and Self-Control: Perspectives from Philosophy, Psychology, and Neuroscience.* New York: Oxford University Press, 2014.

Poland, Jeffrey, and George Graham, eds. *Addiction and Responsibility*. Boston: The MIT Press, 2011.

Szasz, Thomas S. "The Ethics of Addiction." *The American Journal of Psychiatry* 128, no. 5 (1971): 541–46.

Modern Trends in Family: Violence

Chapter 23

Intimate Partner Violence: Causes and Prevention

By Rachel Jewkes

Unlike many health problems, there are few social and demographic characteristics that define risk groups for intimate partner violence. Poverty is the exception and increases risk through effects on conflict, women's power, and male identity. Violence is used as a strategy in conflict. Relationships full of conflict, and especially those in which conflicts occur about finances, jealousy, and women's gender role transgressions are more violent than peaceful relationships. Heavy alcohol consumption also increases risk of violence. Women who are more empowered educationally, economically, and socially are most protected, but below this high level the relation between empowerment and risk of violence is non-linear. Violence is frequently used to resolve a crisis of male identity, at times caused by poverty or an inability to control women. Risk of violence is greatest in societies where the use of violence in many situations is a socially-accepted norm. Primary preventive interventions should focus on improving the status of women and reducing norms of violence, poverty, and alcohol consumption.

Poverty or patriarchy, alcohol or aggression; the causes of intimate partner violence have been contested by social scientists for decades. Underlying the controversy is an inescapable problem: evidence for causation of intimate partner violence is weak when assessed with epidemiological criteria.[1] Most research has been from North America and, with some exceptions, has been based on women accessing sources of help, with data obtained from shelters, official records, or clinic samples.[4-6] However, during the past decade, the research base has been expanded substantially by several well designed cross-sectional studies of violence against women from developing countries, which focus on both women[7-9] and men,[6,10,11] and by ethnographic studies.[12,13] This increase in data has enabled researchers to identify associations that pertain to more than one setting, explore hypotheses critically, and understand the plausibility of associations when considered in the light of what else is known about a society. Furthermore, understanding of the mechanisms through which many associated factors contribute to intimate partner violence has been greatly advanced, helping clarify interventions needed for primary prevention.

Rachel Jewkes, "Intimate Partner Violence: Causes and Prevention," *The Lancet, vol. 359, no. 9315,* pp. 1423–1429. Copyright © 2002 by Elsevier B.V. Reprinted with permission.

Understanding the causes of intimate partner violence is substantially more difficult than studying a disease. For example, diseases usually have a biological basis and occur within a social context, but intimate partner violence is entirely a product of its social context. Consequently, understanding the causes of such violence requires research in many social contexts. Most diseases can be investigated with various objective measures, but measurement of intimate partner violence has posed a challenge. Furthermore, measurement of social conditions thought to be risk factors, such as the status of women, gender norms, and socioeconomic status poses difficulties, especially across cultures. Although a consensus has emerged on the need to explore male and female factors and aspects of the dynamics of relationships, this has been done in very few studies. Additionally, the validity of research on sensitive topics is dependent on the context of the interview and good interviewer training. Interviewer effects can be substantial.[14–16] Researchers have only recently begun to use a multilevel approach in analyses that allows for interviewer effects.[17]

In this paper, intimate partner violence describes physical violence directed against a woman by a current or ex-husband or boyfriend. The term "intimate partner violence" often includes sexual violence and can also include psychological abuse; both these forms of abuse often, but not always, accompany physical violence. However, inconsistencies in the definitions used in research, particularly with regard to inclusion or exclusion of sexual and psychological abuse by male intimate partners, has resulted in most global quantitative studies on the causes of intimate partner violence focusing solely on physical violence.

SOCIAL AND DEMOGRAPHIC CHARACTERISTICS

With the exception of poverty, most demographic and social characteristics of men and women documented in survey research are not associated with increased risk of intimate partner violence. Age, for example, has occasionally been noted to be a risk factor for such violence, with a greater risk attached to youth,[18,19] but in most research a relation with age of either partner has not been seen.[7,9,11,20] Similarly, age at marriage is not an associated factor.[11]

Intimate partner violence is mainly a feature of sexual relationships or thwarted sexual relationships in the case of stalking violence. Its relation with marital status varies between settings and is at least partly dependent on the extent to which women have premarital and extramarital sexual relationships. In countries such as Nicaragua where such sexual relationships are rare, intimate partner violence is closely linked to marriage.[8] Where premarital sex is the norm, marital status is not associated with violence.[7] In North America there is a high prevalence of violent experiences in separated or divorced women,[18] but this has not been noted in other countries.[7,8]

Most household characteristics are not associated with intimate partner violence. These characteristics include living in large[11] or crowded homes[7] and living with in-laws.[11] Similarly, urban or rural residence are not factors.[7,11] The exception is number of children, which is frequently associated with intimate partner violence.[21] However, in a study in Nicaragua, the first incident in almost all violent relationships occurred within a couple of years of marriage. Thus, rather than a large family causing intimate partner violence, the causation was in the reverse direction.[8]

In North America, belonging to a minority ethnic group has been thought to be associated with intimate partner violence, but associations have been largely explained by differences in education and income.[22,23] Risk of intimate partner violence varies between countries and between otherwise similar settings within countries. These differences persist after adjustment for social and demographic factors, relationship characteristics, and other risk factors.[7,9,11] Some of the difference may be explained by factors such as study design and willingness to disclose violent experience in interview settings. However, other factors also seem to be involved. Research has not been undertaken to identify exactly what these factors are. Possibly they relate to cultural differences in the status of women or acceptability of interpersonal violence. Research aimed at understanding the roots of substantial differences in prevalence between otherwise similar social settings is likely to provide important insights into the causes of violence.

POVERTY

Poverty and associated stress are key contributors to intimate partner violence. Although violence occurs in all socioeconomic groups, it is more frequent and severe in lower groups across such diverse settings as the USA, Nicaragua, and India.[8,11,18–20,24] An influential theory explaining the relation between poverty and intimate partner violence is that it is mediated through stress. Since poverty is inherently stressful, it has been argued that intimate partner violence may result from stress,[25,26] and that poorer men have fewer resources to reduce stress.[5,21] However, this finding has not been supported by results from a large study of intimate partner violence in Thailand in which several sources of stress reported by men and their relation with intimate partner violence were analysed.[6]

Research has shown the importance of levels of conflict in mediating the relation between poverty and abuse.[6,7] In a study in South Africa, physical violence was not associated in the expected way with indicators of socioeconomic status including ownership of household goods, male and female occupations, and unemployment. Intriguingly, women are protected from intimate partner violence in some of the poorest households, which are those that are mainly supported by someone other than the woman or her partner (43% of all women in the study). Further analysis indicated that this form of extreme poverty reduced the scope for conflicts about household finance.[7]

Financial independence of women is protective in some settings,[27,28] but not all.[7,8] Circumstances in which the woman, but not her partner, is working convey additional risk.[9] This finding suggests that economic inequality within a context of poverty is more important than the absolute level of income or empowerment of a man or woman in a relationship. Violence is associated with the product of inequality, whether in the form of advantage to either party. Because socioeconomic injustice at a community or societal level is increasingly being shown to be important in other forms of violence,[29] it might be important in explaining differences in prevalence of intimate partner violence, but there are no data on this factor.

POVERTY, POWER, AND SEX IDENTITY

Within any setting ideas vary on what it means to be a man and what constitutes successful manhood.[30] Gelles[25] first postulated that the link between violence and poverty could be mediated through masculine identity. He argued that men living in poverty were unable to live up to their ideas of "successful" manhood and that, in the resulting climate of stress, they would hit women. Some social scientists have become especially interested in the effect of poverty on male identity and relations between male vulnerability and violence against women. They have argued that such relations are mediated through forms of crisis of masculine identity,[31–35] which are often infused with ideas about honour and respect.[31,34,35]

Bourgois[31,32] described how Puerto Rican men growing up in New York slums feel pressurised by models of masculinity and family of their parents' and grandparents' generations, and present-day ideals of successful manhood that emphasise consumerism. Trapped in urban slums, with little or no employment, neither model of masculine success is attainable. In these circumstances, ideals of masculinity are reshaped to emphasise misogyny, substance use, and participation in crime.[31,32] Violence against women becomes a social norm in which men are violent towards women they can no longer control or economically support. Violence against women is thus seen not just as an expression of male powerfulness and dominance over women, but also as being rooted in male vulnerability stemming from social expectations of manhood that are unattainable because of factors such as poverty experienced by men. Male identity is associated with experiences of power.[34] Challenges to the exercise of power by men can be perceived by them as threats to their masculine identity. An inability to meet social expectations of successful manhood can trigger a crisis of male identity. Violence against women is a means of resolving this crisis because it allows expression of power that is otherwise denied.

Associations between intimate partner violence and situations in which husbands have lower status or fewer resources than their wives[25,36,37] may also be substantially mediated through ideas of successful manhood and crises of male identity. The salient forms of inequality vary between settings. For example, in North America differences in education and occupational prestige convey risk,[25,38] whereas in India employment differences are more important.[9] These crossnational variations probably result from differences in cultural ideas of successful manhood. This finding shows the need for renegotiation of ideas of masculinity, and recognition of the effects of poverty and unemployment on men in prevention of intimate partner violence.

WOMEN AND POWER

High levels of female empowerment seem to be protective against intimate partner violence, but power can be derived from many sources such as education, income, and community roles and not all of these convey equal protection or do so in a direct manner. In many studies, high educational attainment of women was associated with low levels of violence.[5,7,11,21,39,40] The same finding has been noted for men. Education confers social empowerment via social networks, self-confidence, and an ability to use information and resources available in society, and may also translate into wealth. The relation between intimate partner violence and female education, however, is complex. In the USA and South Africa the relation has an inverted U-shape, with protection at lowest and highest educational levels.[21,41]

Crosscultural research suggests that societies with stronger ideologies of male dominance have more intimate partner violence.[42] These ideologies usually have effects at many levels within a society. At a societal level they affect, for example, female autonomy, access to political systems, influence in the economy, and participation in academic life and the arts. Such ideologies also affect laws, police, criminal justice systems, whether violence against women is criminalised, and the seriousness with which complaints from women about abuse are treated by law enforcers. At an individual level, men who hold conservative ideas about the social status of women are more likely to abuse them.[7,43] Women who hold more liberal ideas are at greater risk of violence.[7,43] The degree of liberality of women's ideas on their role and position is closely and positively associated with education—ie, more educated women are more liberal in these respects.[7] The most likely explanation for the inverted U-shaped relation with education is that having some education empowers women enough to challenge certain aspects of traditional sex roles, but that such empowerment carries an increased risk of violence until a high enough level is reached for protective effects to predominate. Thus, during periods of transition in gender relations women may be at increased risk of violence.[12]

Social support is another source of power for women. In studies from several countries, good social support was shown possibly to be protective against intimate partner violence.[9,12] Temporal issues need clarification as abusive men often restrict their partner's movement and contact with others, and so abused women become isolated. This isolation is compounded by the effects of abuse on women's mental state, which can result in them withdrawing into themselves, and also by problems of compassion fatigue in those who are asked to play a supportive part.[44] Social support during relationship problems has also been associated with increased risk of violence, but it seems likely that the explanation is that some women are more likely to discuss relationship problems when these become more severe.[7] Not withstanding this factor, social support, especially from a woman's family, may indicate that she is valued, enhance her self-esteem, and be a source of practical assistance during violent experiences or afterwards.[12] Anthropological research indicates that in settings where women are valued in their own right,[42] and the social position of single women is sufficiently high to make being unmarried or unattached a realistic option,[45] divorce is relatively easy to obtain and women are less likely to be abused.

Ethnographic research suggests that protective effects of social empowerment extend outside the home. Women who have respect and power outside the home through community activities, including participation in microcredit schemes, are less likely to be abused than those who do not.[12,27,42]

RELATIONSHIP CONFLICT

The frequency of verbal disagreements and of high levels of conflict in relationships are strongly associated with physical violence.[6,7,21,46] Violence is often deployed as a tactic in relationship conflict[21] as well as being an expression of frustration or anger.[35] Not surprisingly, marital instability—ie, a partner considering leaving the marriage—is a time of especial risk of violence.[47,48] Women who leave relationships are afterwards more at risk of stalking,[2,49] murder, and attempted murder.[50]

Forms of conflict especially likely to be associated with violence centre on women's transgression of conservative gender roles or challenges to male privilege, as well as matters of finance. If many sources of conflict are analysed with multiple logistic regression analysis, conflicts about transgressions of gender norms and failure to fulfil cultural stereotypes of good womanhood are among the most important variables for risk of intimate partner violence.[7,26] In South India, pertinent factors include dowry disputes, female sterilisation, and not having sons,[28] whereas factors in South Africa include women having other partners, drinking alcohol, and arguing about their partner's drinking.[7] The differences between the variables identified reflect crosscultural differences in expected gender roles or manifestations of male privilege.

ALCOHOL

Alcohol consumption is associated with increased risk of all forms of interpersonal violence.[51,52] Heavy alcohol consumption by men (and often women)[7] is associated with intimate partner violence,[6,9,53] if not consistently.[6] Alcohol is thought to reduce inhibitions, cloud judgment, and impair ability to interpret social cues.[54] However, biological links between alcohol and violence are complex.[55] Research on the social anthropology of alcohol drinking suggests that connections between violence and drinking and drunkenness are socially learnt and not universal.[56] Some researchers have noted that alcohol may act as a cultural "time out" for antisocial behaviour. Thus, men are more likely to act violently when drunk because they do not feel they will be held accountable for their behaviour.[25] In some settings, men have described using alcohol in a premeditated manner to enable them to beat their partner because they feel that this is socially expected of them.[10,57] It seems likely that drugs that reduce inhibition, such as cocaine, will have similar relations to those of alcohol with intimate partner violence, but there has been little population-based research on this subject.

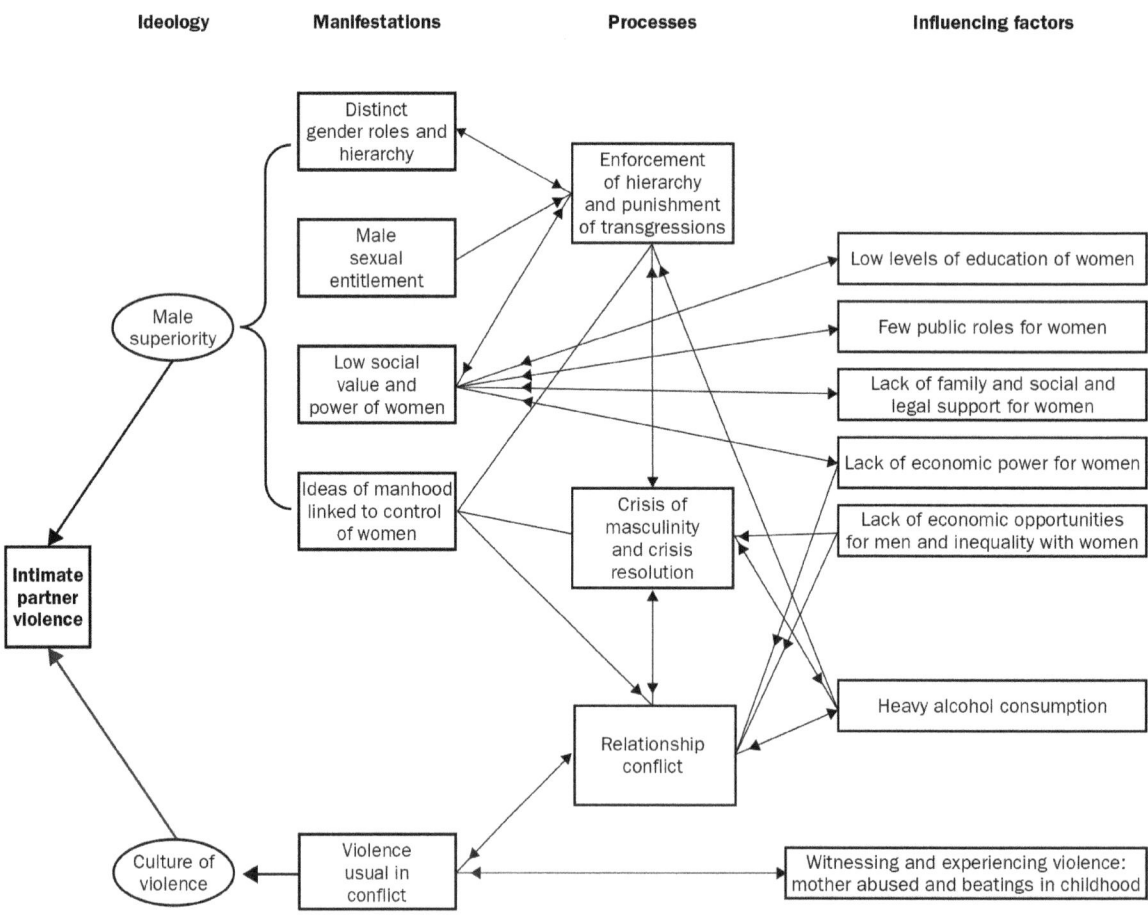

Figure 23.1. Causes of intimate partner violence

SOCIAL NORMS

Many researchers have discussed intimate partner violence as a learned social behaviour for both men and women. The intergenerational cycling of violence has been documented in many settings. The sons of women who are beaten are more likely to beat their intimate partners[8,10] and, in some settings, to have been beaten themselves as children. The daughters of women who are beaten are more likely to be beaten as adults.[7,20] Women who are beaten in childhood by parents are also more likely to be abused by intimate partners as adults.[7] Experiences of violence in the home in childhood teach children that violence is normal in certain settings. In this way, men learn to use violence and women learn to tolerate it or at least tolerate aggressive behaviour.

Crosscultural studies of intimate partner violence suggest that it is much more frequent in societies where violence is usual in conflict situations and political struggles.[42] An example of this relation is South Africa, where not only is there a history of violent state repression and community insurrection, but also violence is deployed frequently in many situations including disputes between neighbours[41] and colleagues at work.[10] Verbal and physical violence between staff and patients in health settings is also very common and contributes to violence being accepted as a social norm.[58] Many cultures condone the use of physical violence by men against women in certain circumstances and within certain boundaries of severity. In these settings, so long as boundaries are not crossed, the social cost of physical violence is low. This tolerance may result from families or communities emphasising the importance of maintenance of the male-female union at all costs, police trivialising reports of domestic strife, or lack of legislation to protect women.

CONCLUSIONS AND IMPLICATIONS FOR PREVENTION

The causes of intimate partner violence are complex. However, two factors seem to be necessary in an epidemiological sense: the unequal position of women in a particular relationship (and in society) and the normative use of violence in conflict. Without either of these factors, intimate partner violence would not occur. These factors interact with a web of complementary factors to produce intimate partner violence (figure 23.1). The figure shows how ideologies of male superiority legitimise disciplining of women by men, often for transgressions of conservative female gender roles, and the use of force in this process. Within such ideologies, women are also defined as appropriate vehicles for reconfirmation of male power. Violence against women is a demonstration of male power juxtaposed against the lesser power of women. Where women have low status they often lack the necessary perceptions of self-efficacy and the social and economic ability to leave a relationship and return to their family or live alone, and thus are severely curtailed in their ability to act against an abuser. Women might also have no legal access to divorce or redress for abuse. Conversely, at higher levels, empowerment of women protects against violence. Intimate partner violence is increased in settings where the use of violence is normal, and in these settings, sanctions against abusers are often also low. Childhood experiences of violence in the home reinforce for both men and women the normative nature of violence, thus increasing the likelihood of male perpetration and women's acceptance of abuse. Alcohol contributes to intimate partner violence by reducing inhibitions and providing social space for punishment. Similarly, the effects of poverty and economic inequality are mediated through

Primary Prevention of Intimate Partner Violence

Prevention Strategy	Interventions by the Health Sector	Interventions by other Sectors for which the Health Sector should Advocate
Creating a climate of non-tolerance of intimate partner violence	Health-information campaigns to inform women of their rights, the law, and how health services can help Training health-sector staff about intimate partner violence and equipping them to help abused women and address abuse in their own lives	Comprehensive legislation on sex equality, intimate partner violence, sexual violence, and sexual harassment Training and monitoring the police and criminal justice system to ensure Raising awareness through the media, especially use of educational dramas such as *Soul City* in South Africa or *The Archers* in the UK Support for community action and supporting non-governmental organisations assisting abused women Public-information campaigns based around basic messages—eg, "No woman deserves to be beaten"
Empowering women and improving their status in society	Empowering women to control their fertility through accessible contraceptive and abortion services Promoting sexual equality in employment and empowering female employees within health services Promoting sexual equality in clinical practice and training	Improving opportunities for women's employment and access to credit Improving levels of female education Improving levels of female involvement in political activities locally and nationally—eg, through quota systems Positive role modelling of women in the media Measures to reduce the objectification of women in society—eg, by pornography and beauty contests Promotion of sexual equality in schools by appropriate training of teachers Legislation to facilitate women's access to divorce and maintenance
Reducing use of violence	Improving staff-patient relationships in the health sector with firm action against verbal and physical abuse of patients	Parenting programmes and measures to reduce physical punishment in child rearing Legislation banning corporal punishment Reducing portrayal of violence in the media Gun-control activities
Changing community norms	Addressing issues of gender and violence in community-based sexual and reproductive health and HIV-prevention education and training programmes	Addressing gender issues, violence, and non-violent conflict resolution in school life-skills programmes Supporting community theatre, action, and campaigns in the media on violence against women Promotion of men's groups addressing issues of male violence against women
Research and monitoring	Collection of data on violence against women including fatal and non-fatal injuries, information on perpetrators, and support for research Allocation of funds to support medical research into the epidemiology of violence against women and development and assessment of interventions	Allocation of funds to support research into development and assessment of interventions in all sectors
Risk factor		
Poverty		Measures to reduce poverty for women and men Employment creation for women and men
Alcohol	Health-promotion activities to reduce alcohol consumption	Legislative and fiscal-policy measures aimed at reducing alcohol consumption

their effect on levels of conflict over resources, women's ability to leave relationships, and men's ability to perceive themselves as successful men.

Figure 23.1 shows that many of the complementary factors are inter-related; however, the effects are not unidirectional. The many interconnections between factors can mean that a change in one factor in what seems to be the right direction, for example, a small increase in women's education, can have a net result of added risk of interpersonal violence. The implication of this finding is that prevention of intimate partner violence must involve engagement with both sides of a relationship. Coordinated action seems to be needed at many levels to ensure that material efforts to improve the status of women are coupled with a focus on men to promote acceptance of the need for change, whether at an individual level, for example, redefinition of successful masculinity in the classroom, or through interventions focusing on men with low socioeconomic status.

The panel shows activities to address risk factors that could form an intervention strategy for primary prevention, although priorities for a particular country will depend on national circumstances. Clearly this approach encompasses, but extends beyond, the health sector, including many other sectors of society and government. Inputs are needed from individuals, families, governments, and societies. There is very little evidence of the effectiveness of primary prevention interventions in this area or the relative importance of the suggested interventions. Given the urgency of the problem of intimate partner violence, development of such an evidence base is a priority, but one that should be undertaken in parallel with development of policies and programmes. The challenges for the health sector are to recognise that addressing intimate partner violence should be part of a public-health agenda, develop meaningful intersectoral partnerships to further this work, and ensure that measures are put in place for a competent and appropriate response to violence against women. There is an enormous potential for detailed assessments of intervention strategies, not only to guide future policy, but also to provide insights into inter-relations between causal factors and develop knowledge of the causes of intimate partner violence.

REFERENCES

1. Hill AB. The environment and disease: association or causation? *Proc R Soc Med* 1965: **58**: 295–300.
2. Tjaden P, Thoennes N. Prevalence and consequences of male-to-female and female-to-male intimate partner violence as measured by the national violence against women survey. *Violence Against Women* 2000; **6**: 142–61.
3. Johnson H. Dangerous domains: violence against women in Canada. Ontario: Nelson Canada Publishing, 1996: 252.
4. Gelles RJ. Family violence. Beverley Hills: Sage, 1987.
5. Steinmetz SK. Family violence: past, present and future. In: Sussman MB, Steinmetz SK, eds. Handbook of marriage and the family. New York: Plenum Press, 1987: 725–65.
6. Hoffman KL, Demo DH, Edwards JN. Physical wife abuse in a non-Western society: an integrated theoretical approach. *J Marriage Fam* 1994; **56**: 131–46.
7. Jewkes R, Penn-Kekana L, Levin J. Risk factors for domestic violence: findings from a South African cross-sectional study. *Soc Sci Med* (in press).

8. Ellsberg MC, Pena R, Herrera A, Liljestrand J, Winkvist A. Wife abuse among women of childbearing age in Nicaragua. *Am J Public Health* 1999; **89**: 241–44.
9. International Clinical Epidemiologists Network. Domestic violence in India. a summary report of a multi-site household survey. Washington: International Centre for Research on Women, 2000.
10. Abrahams N, Jewkes R, Laubscher R. "I don't believe in democracy in the home": men's relationships with and abuse of women. Cape Town: MRC Technical Report, 1999.
11. Martin SL, Tsui AO, Maitra K, Marinshaw R. Domestic violence in Northern India. *Am J Epidemiol* 1999; **150**: 417–26.
12. Counts D, Brown J, Campbell J. Sanctions and sanctuary. Boulder: Westview Press, 1992.
13. Harvey P, Gow P, eds. Sex and violence: issues in representation and experience. London: Routledge, 1994.
14. Ellsberg M, Heise L, Pena R, Agurto S, Winkvist A. Researching violence against women, methodological considerations from three Nicaraguan Studies. *Stud Fam Plann* 2001; **32**: 1–16.
15. Jewkes R, Watts C, Abrahams A, Penn-Kekana L, Garcia-Moreno C. Conducting ethical research on sensitive topics: lessons from gender-based violence research in Southern Africa. *R Health Matters* 2000; **8**: 93–103.
16. O'Muircheartaigh C, Campanelli P. The relative impact of interviewer effects and sample design on survey precision. *J R Stat Soc A* 1998; **161**: 63–77.
17. Skinner CJ. Introduction to part A. In: Skinner CJ, Holt D, Smith TMF, eds. Analysis of complex surveys. Chichester: Wiley, 1989.
18. Bachman R, Saltzman LE. Violence against women: estimates from the redesigned survey. Washington: Bureau of Justice Statistics, National Institute of Justice, 1995.
19. Ratner PA. The incidence of wife abuse and mental health status in abused wives in Edmonton, Alberta. *Can J Public Health* 1993; **83**: 246–49.
20. Hotaling GT, Sugarman DB. An analysis of risk markers in husband to wife violence: the current state of knowledge. *Violence Vict* 1986; **1**: 101–24.
21. Straus MA, Gelles RJ, Steinmetz SK. Behind closed doors: violence in the American family. New York: Anchor Press, 1980.
22. Dearwater SR, Coben JH, Nah G, et al. Prevalence of domestic violence in women treated at community hospital emergency department. *JAMA* 1998; **480**: 433–38.
23. Jones AS, Campbell JC, Schollenberger J, et al. Annual and lifetime prevalence of partner abuse in a sample of female HMO enrollees. *Womens Health Issues* 1999; 9: 295–305.
24. Gelles RJ, Straus MA. Intimate violence: the causes and consequences of abuse in the American family. New York: Simon and Schuster, 1998.
25. Gelles RJ. The violent home. Beverley Hills: Sage, 1974.
26. Cosner LA. Continuities in the study of social conflict. New York: Free Press, 1967.
27. Schuler SR, Hashemi SM, Riley AP, Akhter S. Credit programmes, patriarchy and men's violence against women in rural Bangladesh. *Soc Sci Med* 1996; **43**: 1729–42.
28. Rao V. Wife-beating in rural south India: a qualitative and econometric analysis. *Soc Sci Med* 1997; **44**: 1169–80.
29. Kawachi I, Kennedy BP. Health and social cohesion: why care about income inequality? *BMJ* 1997; **314**: 1037–40.
30. Cornwall A, Lindisfarne N. Dislocating masculinities. London: Routledge, 1994.

31. Bourgois P. In search of masculinity—violence, respect and sexuality among Puerto Rican crack dealers. *B J Criminol* 1996; **36:** 412–27.
32. Bourgois P. In search of respect: selling crack in El Barrio. Cambridge: Cambridge University Press, 1996.
33. Morrell R, ed. Changing men in Southern Africa. Pietermaritzburg: University of Natal Press, 2001.
34. Moore H A passion for difference: essays in anthropology and gender. London: Polity Press, 1994.
35. Wood K, Jewkes R. "Dangerous" love: reflections on violence among Xhosa township youth. In: Morrell R, ed. Changing men in Southern Africa. Pietermaritzburg: University of Natal Press, 2001.
36. O'Brien JE. Violence in divorce prone families. *J Marriage Fam* 1971; **33:** 692–98.
37. Rodman H. Marital power and the theory of resources in cultural context. *J Comp Fam Stud* 1972; **3:** 50–69.
38. Yllo K, Bogard M, eds. Feminist perspectives on wife abuse. Newbury Park: Sage, 1998.
39. McCall GJ, Shields NM. Social and structural factors in family violence. In: Lystad M, ed. Violence in the home: interdiscipinary perspectives. New York: Brunner/Mazel, 1986.
40. Okun L. Women abuse: facts replacing myths. Albany: State University of New York, 1986.
41. Department of Health. South Africa demographic and health survey 1998: final report. Pretoria: Department of Health (in press).
42. Levinson D. Violence in cross-cultural perspective. Newbury Park: Sage Publications, 1989.
43. Sugarman D, Frankel SL. Patriarchal ideology and wife-assault: a meta-analytic review. *J Fam Viol* 1996; **11:** 13–40.
44. Heise L, Ellsberg M, Gottemoeller M. Ending violence against women: population reports volume 27, number 4. Baltimore: Johns Hopkins University, 1999.
45. Mager AK. Gender and the making of a South African Bantustan: a social history of the Ciskei, 1945–1959. Cape Town: David Philip, 1999.
46. Stets JE. Verbal and physical aggression in marriage. *J Marriage Fam* 1990; **52:** 501–14.
47. Edwards JN, Fuller TD, Vorakitphokatorn S, Sermsri S. Female employment and marital instability: evidence from Thailand. *J Marriage Fam* 1992; 54: 59–68.
48. Pagelow MD. Family violence. New York: Praeger, 1984.
49. Mechanic MB, Uhlmansiek MH, Weaver TL, Resick PA. Impact of severe stalking experienced by acutely battered women: an examination of violence, psychological symptoms and strategic responding. *Violence Victim* 2000; **15:** 443–58.
50. McFarlane J, Campbell J, Watson K. Intimate partner stalking and femicide: urgent implications for women's safety. *Am J Public Health* (in press).
51. Farrington DP. Predictors, causes and correlates of male youth violence. In: Tonry M, Moore MH, eds. Youth violence. Chicago: University of Chicago Press, 1998: 421–75.
52. Wikström P-O H. Everyday violence in contempory Sweden. Stockholm: National Council for Crime Prevention, 1985.
53. Kantor GK. Refining the brushstrokes in portraits on alcohol and wife assaults. In: Martin S, ed. Alcohol and interpersonal violence: fostering multidisciplinary perspectives. Rockville: National Institute on Alcohol Abuse and Alcoholism, 1993: 281–90.

54. Abby A, Ross LT, McDuffie D. Alcohol's role in sexual assault. In: Watson RR, ed. Drug and alcohol reviews, volume 5: addictive behaviours in women. Totowa: Humana Press, 1995.
55. Miczek KA, BeBold JF, Haney M, Tidey J, Vivian J, Weerts EM. Alcohol, drugs of abuse, aggression and violence. In: Reiss AJ, Roth JA, eds. Understanding and preventing violence, volume 3: social influences. Washington: National Academy Press, 1994: 377–570.
56. McDonald M, ed. Gender, drink and drugs. Oxford: Berg Publishers, 1994: 14.
57. Anon. Soul City 1997, violence against women: a report—social surveys. Johannesburg: Braamfontein, 1997.
58. Jewkes R, Abrahams N, Mvo Z. Why do nurses abuse patients?: reflections from South African obstetric services. *Soc Sci Med* 1998; 47: 1781–95.

Chapter 24

The Basics of Domestic Violence

By H. Lien Bragg

CHAPTER 3: THE BASICS OF DOMESTIC VIOLENCE

To establish a foundation for understanding child protection in families experiencing domestic violence, this chapter provides an overview of the definition, scope, and causes of domestic violence, along with the evolving societal responses. The chapter also provides a description of victims and perpetrators of domestic violence, highlighting prevalent misconceptions, common behaviors, and parenting issues.

What is Domestic Violence?

Historically, domestic violence has been framed and understood exclusively as a women's issue. Domestic abuse affects women, but also has devastating consequences for other populations and societal institutions. Men also can be victims of abuse, children are affected by exposure to domestic violence, and formal institutions face enormous challenges responding to domestic violence in their communities. The effects of domestic violence on victims are more typically recognized, but perpetrators also are impacted by their abusive behavior as they stand to lose children, damage relationships, and face legal consequences. Domestic violence cuts across every segment of society and occurs in all age, racial, ethnic, socio-economic, sexual orientation, and religious groups. Domestic violence is a social, economic, and health concern that does not discriminate. As a result, communities across the country are developing strategies to stop the violence and provide safe solutions for victims of domestic violence.

H. Lien Bragg, from *Child Protection in Families Experiencing Domestic Violence,* pp. 15–33. Copyright in the Public Domain.

Defining Domestic Violence

Domestic violence is a "pattern of coercive and assaultive behaviors that include physical, sexual, verbal, and psychological attacks and economic coercion that adults or adolescents use against their intimate partner." Domestic violence is not typically a singular event and is not limited to only physical aggression. Rather, it is the pervasive and methodical use of threats, intimidation, manipulation, and physical violence by someone who seeks power and control over their intimate partner. Abusers use a specific tactic or a combination of tactics to instill fear in and dominance over their partners. The strategies used by abusers are intended to establish a pattern of desired behaviors from their victims. Certain behaviors often are cited by the perpetrator as the reason or cause of the abusive behavior, therefore, abusive verbal and physical actions are often intended to alter or control that behavior.

Scope of the Problem

Currently, national crime victimization surveys, crime reports, and research studies indicate:

- An estimated 85 to 90 percent of domestic violence victims are female.
- Females are victims of intimate partner violence at a rate about five times that of males.
- Females between the ages of 16 and 24 are most vulnerable to domestic violence.
- Females account for 39 percent of hospital emergency department visits for violence-related injuries, and 84 percent of persons treated for intentional injuries caused by an intimate partner. As many as 324,000 females each year experience intimate partner violence during their pregnancy, and pregnant and recently pregnant women are more likely to be victims of homicide than to die of any other cause.
- Females experience the greatest assault rate (21.3 per 1000 females) between the ages of 20 and 24. This is eight times the peak rate for males (3 per 1000 males ages 25 to 34).
- Domestic violence constitutes 22 percent of violent crime against females and 3 percent of violent crime against males.
- Eight percent of females and 0.3 percent of males report intimate partner rape.
- Approximately 33 percent of gays and lesbians are victims of domestic violence at some time in their lives.
- Twenty-eight percent of high school and college students experience dating violence and 26 percent of pregnant teenage girls report being physically abused.
- Seventy percent of intimate homicide victims are female, and females are twice as likely to be killed by their husbands or boyfriends than murdered by strangers.
- On average, more than three women are murdered by their husbands or boyfriends in the United States every day. In 2000, 1,247 women were killed by an intimate partner. The same year, 440 men were killed by an intimate partner.
- An estimated 5 percent of domestic violence cases are males who are physically assaulted, stalked, and killed by a current or former wife, girlfriend, or partner.
- Domestic violence victims lose a total of nearly 8.0 million days of paid work—the equivalent of more than 32,000 full-time jobs—and nearly 5.6 million days of household productivity as a result of the violence.
- The costs of intimate partner rape, physical assault, and stalking exceed $5.8 billion each year, nearly $4.1 billion of which is for direct medical and mental health care services.

- Males are significantly more likely to be victimized by acquaintances (50 percent) or strangers (44 percent) than by intimates or other relatives.
- Females experience over 5 to 10 times as many incidents of domestic violence than males. In comparison to men, women have a significantly greater risk for being a victim of domestic violence and suffering chronic and severe forms of physical assaults.

Domestic Violence Tactics

The types of domestic violence actions perpetrated by abusers include physical, sexual, verbal, emotional, and psychological tactics; threats and intimidation; economic coercion; and entitlement behaviors. Examples of each are provided below. Some of the behaviors identified [as domestic violence] do not constitute abuse in and of themselves, but frequently are tactics used in a larger pattern of abusive and controlling behavior. (…)

Root Causes of Domestic Violence

Some people believe domestic violence occurs because the victim provokes the abuser to violent action, while others believe the abuser simply has a problem managing anger. In fact, the roots of domestic violence can be attributed to a variety of cultural, social, economic, and psychological factors. As a learned behavior, domestic violence is modeled by individuals, institutions, and society, which may influence the perspectives of children and adults regarding its acceptability. (…)

Domestic violence is reinforced by cultural values and beliefs that are repeatedly communicated through the media and other societal institutions that tolerate it. The perpetrator's violence is further supported when peers, family members, or others in the community (e.g., coworkers, social service providers, police, or clergy) minimize or ignore the abuse and fail to provide consequences. As a result, the abuser learns that not only is the behavior justified, but also it is acceptable.

Psychopathology, substance abuse, poverty, cultural factors, anger, stress, and depression often are thought to cause domestic violence. While there is little empirical evidence that these factors are *direct* causes of domestic violence, research suggests that they can affect its severity, frequency, and the nature of the perpetrator's abusive behavior. Although there is debate among researchers regarding a definitive theory to explain domestic violence, there is little disagreement that it is an insidious problem requiring a complex solution.

Evolving Societal Responses to Domestic Violence

Many believe the historical inequality of women and gender socialization of females and males contribute to the root causes of domestic violence. Until the 1970's, women who were raped or suffered violence in their homes had no formal place to go for help or support. Shelters and services for victims of domestic violence did not exist and there was little, if any, response from criminal or civil courts, law enforcement, hospitals, and social service agencies. Society and its formal institutions viewed domestic violence as a "private matter." As awareness and recognition of this problem grew, groups of women organized an advocacy movement that focused on addressing the safety needs of victims and the systemic barriers and social attitudes that contributed to domestic violence. Volunteers established safe havens and crisis services for victims of domestic violence in their homes and held meetings where they began to define violence against women as a political issue. This grass roots effort, commonly referred to as the "Battered Women's Movement," revolutionized the responses to injustices against women into a social movement that forms the foundation of existing domestic violence advocacy and community-based programs throughout the country. (…)

Domestic violence programs also engage in continuous advocacy efforts that include developing public awareness campaigns, collaborating with community service providers, and being active in political lobbying efforts aimed at improving safety for victims and their children. One of the benefits of the increased awareness of the problem garnered by these activities is the greater recognition that many sectors of society—beyond shelters, law enforcement, and the judicial system—have important roles to play in identifying and addressing this problem. These sectors include child welfare, health care, mental health, substance abuse treatment, business, and faith communities. Along with the recognition that legal sanctions are not always the best response, there is a growing awareness that communities themselves must take responsibility for preventing and aiding victims of domestic violence by establishing programs and services that meet the needs of their citizens. One example is a community based approach that involves combining the efforts of law enforcement, domestic violence victim advocates, social service providers, faith-based communities, and community members.

Society's recognition that domestic violence is no longer a private matter, but a widespread social problem, is evidenced in the establishment of approximately 2,000 shelters and domestic violence programs, legislation in every State identifying domestic violence as a criminal act, legal rights to civil protection orders, and Federal legislation that provides funding and national recognition regarding its seriousness. Exhibits 3-1 and 3-2 outline Federal legislation that addresses domestic violence and child maltreatment and provides a legal framework and guidance for providing services and intervention.

Victims of Domestic Violence

This section describes some common characteristics of victims of domestic violence, dynamics of the victimization (e.g., common barriers to leaving an abusive relationship, protective strategies), and the impact that domestic violence has on the individual and on parenting behaviors.

Who Is the Victim?

Victims of domestic violence do not possess a set of universal characteristics or personality traits, but they do share the common experience of being abused by someone close to them. Anyone can become a victim of domestic violence. Victims of domestic violence can be women, men, adolescents, disabled persons, gays, or lesbians. They can be of any age and work in any profession. Normally, victims of domestic violence are not easily recognized because they are not usually covered in marks or bruises. If there are injuries, victims have often learned to conceal them to avoid detection, suspicion, and shame.

Unfortunately, an array of misconceptions about victims of domestic violence has led to harmful stereotypes and myths about who they are and the realities of their abuse. Consequently, victims of domestic violence often feel stigmatized and misunderstood by the people in their lives. These people may be well-intended family members and friends or persons trained to help them, such as social workers, police officers, or doctors. Exhibit 3-3 presents common myths about victims of domestic violence.

Case Example

Myth One: Only Poor, Uneducated Women are Victims of Domestic Violence.

Victims of abuse can be found in all social and economic classes and can be of either sex. They can be wealthy, educated, and prominent as well as undereducated and financially destitute. Victims of domestic violence live in rural towns, urban cities, subsidized housing projects, and in gated communities. The overrepresentation of underprivileged women in domestic violence crime reports may be due to several factors, including the fact that those seeking public assistance or services are subject to data tracking trends that often capture this information. Victims of domestic violence who have higher incomes are more likely to seek help from private therapists or service providers who can protect their identity through confidentiality agreements.

Myth Two: Victims Provoke and Deserve the Violence they Experience.

An abusive tactic used by perpetrators is to accuse their partners of "making" them violent. This accusation is even more effective when the perpetrator and other people tell the victim that he or she deserved the abuse. As a result, many victims remain in the abusive relationship because they believe that the violence is their fault. Many victims make repeated attempts to change their behavior in order to avoid the next assault. Unfortunately, no one, including the victim, can change the behavior except for the perpetrator. The perpetrator is accountable for the behavior and responsible for ending the violence.

Myth Three: Victims of Domestic Violence move from One Abusive Relationship to Another.

Although approximately one-third of victims of domestic violence experience more than one abusive relationship, most victims do not seek or have multiple abusive partners. Victims of domestic violence who have a childhood history of physical or sexual victimization may be at greater risk of being harmed by multiple partners.[58]

Myth Four: Victims of Domestic Violence Suffer from low Self-esteem and Psychological Disorders.

Some people believe that victims of domestic violence are mentally ill or suffer from low self-esteem. Otherwise, it is thought, they would not endure the abuse. In fact, a majority of victims does not have mental disorders, but may suffer from the psychological effects of domestic violence, such as posttraumatic stress disorder or depression.[59] Furthermore, there is little evidence that low selfesteem is a factor for initially becoming involved in an abusive relationship.[60] In reality, some victims of domestic violence experience a decrease in self-esteem because their abusers are constantly degrading, humiliating, and criticizing them, which also makes them more vulnerable to staying in the relationship.

Myth Five: Victims of Domestic Violence are Weak and Always Want Help.

Some victims of domestic violence are passive while others are assertive. Some victims actively seek help, while others may refuse assistance. Again, victims are a diverse group of individuals who possess unique qualities and different life situations. Victims of domestic violence may not always want help and their reasons vary. They may not be prepared to leave the relationship, they may be scared their partners will harm them, or they may not trust people if past efforts to seek help have failed.

Barriers to Leaving an Abusive Relationship

The most commonly asked question about victims of domestic violence is "Why do they stay?" Family, friends, coworkers, and community professionals who try to understand the reasons why a victim of domestic violence has not left the abusive partner often feel perplexed and frustrated. Some victims of domestic violence do leave their violent partners while others may leave and return at different points throughout the abusive relationship.[61] Leaving a violent relationship is a process, not an event, for many victims, who cannot simply "pick up and go" because they have many factors to consider. To understand the complex nature of terminating a violent relationship, it is essential to look at the barriers and risks faced by victims when they consider or attempt to leave. Individual, systemic, and societal barriers faced by victims of domestic violence include:

- **Fear.** Perpetrators commonly make threats to find victims, inflict harm, or kill them if they end the relationship. This fear becomes a reality for many victims who are stalked by their partner after leaving. It also is common for abusers to seek or threaten to seek sole custody, make child abuse allegations, or kidnap the children. Historically, there has been a lack of protection and assistance from law enforcement, the judicial system, and social service agencies charged with responding to domestic violence. Inadequacies in the system and the failure of past efforts by victims of domestic violence seeking help have led many to believe that they will not be protected from the abuser and are safer at home. While much remains to be done, there is a growing trend of increased legal protection and community support for these victims.
- **Isolation.** One effective tactic abusers use to establish control over victims is to isolate them from any support system other than the primary intimate relationship. As a result, some victims are unaware of services or people that can help. Many believe they are alone in dealing with the abuse. This isolation deepens when society labels them as "masochistic" or "weak" for enduring the abuse. Victims often separate themselves from friends and family because they are ashamed of the abuse or want to protect others from the abuser's violence.
- **Financial dependence.** Some victims do not have access to any income and have been prevented from obtaining an education or employment. Victims who lack viable job skills or education, transportation, affordable daycare, safe housing, and health benefits face very limited options. Poverty and marginal economic support services can present enormous challenges to victims who seek safety and stability. Often, victims find themselves choosing between homelessness, living in impoverished and unsafe communities, or returning to their abusive partner.
- **Guilt and shame.** Many victims believe the abuse is their fault. The perpetrator, family, friends, and society sometimes deepen this belief by accusing the victim of provoking the violence and casting blame for not preventing it. Victims of violence rarely want their family and friends to know they are abused by their partner and are fearful that people will criticize them for not leaving the relationship. Victims often feel responsible for changing their partner's abusive behavior or changing themselves in order for the abuse to stop. Guilt and shame may be felt especially by those who are not commonly recognized as victims of domestic violence. This may include men, gays, lesbians, and partners of individuals in visible or respected professions, such as the clergy and law enforcement.
- **Emotional and physical impairment.** Abusers often use a series of psychological strategies to break down the victim's self-esteem and emotional strength. In order to survive, some victims begin to perceive reality through the abuser's paradigm, become emotionally dependent, and

believe they are unable to function without their partner. The psychological and physical effects of domestic violence also can affect a victim's daily functioning and mental stability. This can make the process of leaving and planning for safety challenging for victims who may be depressed, physically injured, or suicidal. Victims who have a physical or developmental disability are extremely vulnerable because the disability can compound their emotional, financial, and physical dependence on their abusive partner.

- **Individual belief system.** The personal, familial, religious, and cultural values of victims of domestic violence are frequently interwoven in their decisions to leave or remain in abusive relationships. For example, victims who hold strong convictions regarding the sanctity of marriage may not view divorce or separation as an option. Their religious beliefs may tell them divorce is "wrong." Some victims of domestic violence believe that their children still need to be with the offender and that divorce will be emotionally damaging to them.
- **Hope.** Like most people, victims of domestic violence are invested in their intimate relationships and frequently strive to make them healthy and loving. Some victims hope the violence will end if they become the person their partner wants them to be. Others believe and have faith in their partner's promises to change. Perpetrators are not "all bad" and have positive, as well as, negative qualities. The abuser's "good side" can give victims reason to think their partner is capable of being nurturing, kind, and nonviolent.
- **Community services and societal values.** For victims who are prepared to leave and want protection, there are a variety of institutional barriers that make escaping abuse difficult and frustrating. Communities that have inadequate resources and limited victim advocacy services and whose response to domestic abuse is fragmented, punitive, or ineffective can not provide realistic or safe solutions for victims and their children.
- **Cultural hurdles.** The lack of culturally sensitive and appropriate services for victims of color and those who are non-English speaking pose additional barriers to leaving violent relationships. Minority populations include African-Americans, Hispanics, Asians, and other ethnic groups whose cultural values and customs can influence their beliefs about the role of men and women, interpersonal relationships, and intimate partner violence. For example, the Hispanic cultural value of "machismo" supports some Latino men's belief that they are superior to women and the "head of their household" in determining familial decisions. "Machismo" may cause some Hispanic men to believe that they have the right to use violent or abusive behavior to control their partners or children. In turn, Latina women and other family or community members may excuse violent or controlling behavior because they believe that husbands have ultimate authority over them and their children.

Examples of culturally competent services include offering written translation of domestic violence materials, providing translators in domestic violence programs, and implementing intervention strategies that incorporate cultural values, norms, and practices to effectively address the needs of victims and abusers. The lack of culturally competent services that fail to incorporate issues of culture and language can present obstacles for victims who want to escape abuse and for effective interventions with domestic violence perpetrators. Well-intended family, friends, and community members also can create additional pressures for the victim to "make things work."

The Impact of Domestic Violence on Victims

As with anyone who has been traumatized, victims demonstrate a wide range of effects from domestic violence. The perpetrator's abusive behavior can cause an array of health problems and physical injuries. Victims may require medical attention for immediate injuries, hospitalization for severe assaults, or chronic care for debilitating health problems resulting from the perpetrator's physical attacks. The direct physical effects of domestic violence can range from minor scratches or bruises to fractured bones or sexually transmitted diseases resulting from forced sexual activity and other practices. The indirect physical effects of domestic violence can range from recurring headaches or stomachaches to severe health problems due to withheld medical attention or medications.

Many victims of abuse make frequent visits to their physicians for health problems and for domestic violence-related injuries. Unfortunately, research shows that many victims will not disclose the abuse unless they are directly asked or screened for domestic violence by the physician. It is imperative, therefore, that health care providers directly inquire about possible domestic violence so victims receive proper treatment for injuries or illnesses and are offered further assistance for addressing the abuse.

The impact of domestic violence on victims can result in acute and chronic mental health problems. Some victims, however, have histories of psychiatric illnesses that may be exacerbated by the abuse; others may develop psychological problems as a direct result of the abuse. Examples of emotional and behavioral effects of domestic violence include many common coping responses to trauma, such as:

- Emotional withdrawal
- Denial or minimization of the abuse
- Impulsivity or aggressiveness
- Apprehension or fear
- Helplessness
- Anger
- Anxiety or hypervigilance
- Disturbance of eating or sleeping patterns
- Substance abuse
- Depression
- Suicide
- Post-traumatic stress disorder.

Some of these effects also serve as coping mechanisms for victims. For example, some victims turn to alcohol to lessen the physical and emotional pain of the abuse. Unfortunately, these coping mechanisms can serve as barriers for victims who want help or want to leave their abusive relationships. Psychiatrists, psychologists, therapists, and counselors who provide screening, comprehensive assessment, and treatment for victims can serve as the catalyst that helps them address or escape the abuse.

Parenting and the Victim

Emerging research indicates that the harmful effects of domestic violence can negatively influence parenting behaviors. Parents who are suffering from abuse may experience higher stress levels, which in turn, can influence the nature of their relationship with and responses to their children. Victims who are preoccupied with avoiding physical attacks and coping with the violence confront additional challenges in their efforts to provide safety, support, and nurturance to their children. Unfortunately, some victims of domestic violence are emotionally or physically unavailable to their children due to injuries, emotional exhaustion, or depression.

Studies have found that victims of domestic violence are more likely to maltreat their children than those who are not abused by their partners. In some cases, victims who use physical force or inappropriate discipline techniques are trying to protect their children from potentially more severe forms of violence or discipline by the abuser. For example, a victim of domestic violence might slap the child when the abuser threatens harm if the child is not quiet. Seemingly, neglectful behaviors by the victim also may be a direct result of the domestic violence. This is illustrated when the abuser prevents the victim from taking the child to the doctor or to school because the adult victim's injuries would reveal the abusiveness.

The majority of victims of domestic violence are not bad, ineffective, or abusive parents, but researchers note that domestic violence is one of a multitude of stressors that can negatively influence parenting. However, many victims, despite ongoing abuse, are supportive, nurturing parents who mediate the impact of their children's exposure to domestic violence. Given the impact of violence on parenting behaviors, it is beneficial that victims receive services that alleviate their distress so they can support and benefit the children.

Strategies Victims Use to Protect Themselves and Their Children

Protective strategies that frequently are recommended by family, friends, and social services providers include contacting the police, obtaining a restraining order, or seeking refuge at a friend or relative's home or at a domestic violence shelter. It is ordinarily assumed that these suggestions are successful at keeping victims and their children safe from violence. It is crucial to remember, however, that while these strategies can be effective for some victims of domestic violence, they can be unrealistic and even *dangerous* options for other victims. For example, obtaining a restraining order can be useful in deterring some perpetrators, but it can cause other perpetrators to become increasingly abusive and threatening. Since these recommendations are concrete and observable, they tend to reassure people that the victim of domestic violence is actively taking steps to address the abuse and to be safe, even if they create additional risks. Furthermore, these options only address the physical violence in a victim's life. They do not address the economic or housing challenges the victim must overcome to survive, nor do they provide the emotional and psychological safety the victims need. Therefore, victims often weigh "perpetrator-generated" risks versus "life-generated" risks as they try to make decisions and find safety.

Typically, victims do not passively tolerate the violence in their lives. They often use very creative methods to avoid and deescalate their partner's abusive behavior. Some of these are successful and others are not. Victims develop their own unique set of protective strategies based on their past experience of what is effective at keeping them emotionally and physically protected from their partner's violence. In deciding which survival mechanism to use, victims engage in a methodical problem-solving process that involves analyzing: available and realistic safety options; the level of danger created by the abuser's violence; and the prior effectiveness and consequences of previously used strategies. After careful consideration, victims of domestic violence decide whether to use, adapt, replace, or discard certain approaches given the risks they believe it will pose to them and their children. (…)

Perpetrators of Domestic Violence

This section presents common characteristics and behavioral tactics of perpetrators, indicators of dangerousness, and relevant parenting issues.

Who Is a Perpetrator of Domestic Violence?

As is the case with victims of domestic violence, abusers can be anyone and come from every age, sex, socioeconomic, racial, ethnic, occupational, educational, and religious group. They can be teenagers, college professors, farmers, counselors, electricians, police officers, doctors, clergy, judges, and popular celebrities. Perpetrators are not always angry and hostile, but can be charming, agreeable, and kind. Abusers differ in patterns of abuse and levels of dangerousness. While there is not an agreed upon universal psychological profile, perpetrators do share a behavioral profile that is described as "an ongoing pattern of coercive control involving various forms of intimidation, and psychological and physical abuse."

While many people think violent and abusive people are mentally ill, research shows that perpetrators do not share a set of personality characteristics or a psychiatric diagnosis that distinguishes them from people who are not abusive. There are some perpetrators who suffer from psychiatric problems, such as depression, post-traumatic stress disorder, or psychopathology. Yet, most do not have psychiatric illnesses, and caution is advised in attributing mental illness as a root cause of domestic violence. The Diagnostic and Statistical Manual of the American Psychological Association (DSM-IV) does not have a diagnostic category for perpetrators, but mental illness should be viewed as a factor that can influence the severity and nature of the abuse.

Examples of the most prevalent behavioral tactics by perpetrators include:

- **Abusing power and control.** The perpetrator's primary goal is to achieve power and control over their intimate partner. In order to do so, perpetrators often plan and utilize a pattern of coercive tactics aimed at instilling fear, shame, and helplessness in the victim. Another part of this strategy is to change randomly the list of "rules" or expectations the victim must meet to avoid abuse. The abuser's incessant degradation, intimidation, and demands on their partner are effective in establishing fear and dependence. It is important to note that perpetrators may also engage in impulsive acts of domestic violence and that not all perpetrators act in such a planned or systematic way.
- **Having different public and private behavior.** Usually, people outside the immediate family are not aware of and do not witness the perpetrator's abusive behavior. Abusers who maintain an amiable public image accomplish the important task of deceiving others into thinking they are loving, "normal," and incapable of domestic violence. This allows perpetrators to escape accountability for their violence and reinforces the victims' fears that no one will believe them.
- **Projecting blame.** Abusers often engage in an insidious type of manipulation that involves blaming the victim for the violent behavior. Such perpetrators may accuse the victim of "pushing buttons" or "provoking" the abuse. By diverting attention to the victim's actions, the perpetrator avoids taking responsibility for the abusive behavior. In addition to projecting blame on the victim, abusers also may project blame on circumstances, such as making the excuse that alcohol or stress caused the violence.

- **Claiming loss of control or anger problems.** There is a common belief that domestic violence is a result of poor impulse control or anger management problems. Abusers routinely claim that they "just lost it," suggesting that the violence was an impulsive and rare event beyond control. Domestic violence is not typically a singular incident nor does it simply involve physical attacks. It is a deliberate set of tactics where physical violence is used to solidify the abuser's power in the relationship. In reality, only an estimated 5 to 10 percent of perpetrators have difficulty with controlling their aggression. Most abusers do not assault others outside the family, such as police officers, coworkers, or neighbors, but direct their abuse toward the victim or children. This distinction challenges claims that they cannot manage their anger.
- **Minimizing and denying the abuse.** Perpetrators rarely view themselves or their actions as violent or abusive. As a result, they often deny, justify, and minimize their behavior. For example, an abuser might forcibly push the victim down a flight of stairs, then tell others that the victim tripped. Abusers also rationalize serious physical assaults, such as punching or choking, as "self-defense." Abusers who refuse to admit they are harming their partner present enormous challenges to persons who are trying to intervene. Some perpetrators do acknowledge to the victim that the abusive behavior is wrong, but then plead for forgiveness or make promises of refraining from any future abuse. Even in situations such as this, the perpetrator commonly minimizes the severity or impact of the abuse.

It is equally important to acknowledge that abusers also possess positive qualities. There are abusers who are remorseful, accept responsibility for their violence, and eventually stop their abusive behavior. Perpetrators are not necessarily "bad" people, but their abusive behavior is unacceptable. Some perpetrators have childhood histories where they were physically or sexually abused, neglected, or exposed to domestic abuse. Some suffer from substance abuse and mental health problems. All of these factors can influence their psychological functioning and contribute to the complexity and severity of the abusive behavior. Perpetrators need support and intervention to end their violent behavior and any additional problems that compound their abusive behavior. Through specialized interventions, community services, and sanctions, some abusers can change and become nonviolent.

Indicators of Dangerousness

Different levels of violence and types of abuse are perpetrated by domestic violence offenders. Some abusers rarely use physical violence, while others assault their partners daily. There are perpetrators who are only abusive towards family members and others who are violent toward a variety of people. There are abusers who are more likely to inflict serious injury or become homicidal. Some frequently degrade the victim, while some rarely, if ever, implement that particular tactic.

It is critical that professionals and community service providers who intervene in domestic violence cases engage in thorough and continuous assessment of the perpetrator's level of dangerousness. Evaluating this dangerousness involves identifying risk indicators that reflect the capacity to continue perpetrating severe violence. Although domestic violence homicides or severe assaults cannot be predicted, there are several risk factors that help determine the likelihood that severe forms of violence may be imminent. (…)

Parenting and the Perpetrator

Can perpetrators be supportive parents when they are abusive towards the other parent? An emerging issue facing victims of domestic violence and child advocacy groups is the role and impact that perpetrators have in their children's lives. There are perpetrators who have positive interactions with their children, provide for their physical and financial needs, and are not abusive towards them. There also are perpetrators who neglect or physically harm their children. Although abusers vary tremendously in parenting styles, there are some behaviors common among perpetrators that can have harmful effects on children:

- **Authoritarianism.** Perpetrators can be rigid and demanding with their children. They often have high and unrealistic expectations and expect children to obey without question or resistance. This parenting style is intimidating for children and alters their sense of safety around the abuser. These perpetrators are more likely to use harsher forms of physical discipline, which can make the children increasingly vulnerable to becoming direct targets of violence.
- **Neglect, irresponsibility, and lack of involvement.** Some abusers are infrequently involved in the daily parenting activities of their children. They may view their children as hindrances and become easily annoyed with them. Furthermore, the perpetrator's preoccupation with controlling the partner and meeting his or her own emotional needs leaves little time to engage the children. Unfortunately, the perpetrator's physical and emotional unavailability can produce unrequited feelings of anticipation and fondness in the children who eagerly await attention.
- **Undermining the victim.** The perpetrator's coercive and violent behavior towards the victim sometimes sends children a message that it is acceptable for them to treat that parent in the same manner. More overt tactics that weaken the victim's influence over the children include the perpetrator disregarding the victim's parenting decisions, telling the children that the victim is an inadequate parent, and belittling the victim in the presence of the children. Being victimized by abuse can lead children to perceive the parent in a weaker, passive role with no real authority over their lives.
- **Self-centeredness.** Some perpetrators use their children to meet their own emotional needs. Perpetrators may expect their children to be immediately available only when they are interested and often overwhelm them with their problems. This can result in children feeling burdened and responsible for helping their parent while their own needs are neglected.
- **Manipulation.** To gain power in the home, perpetrators may manipulate their children into aligning against the victim. Abusers may make statements or exhibit behaviors that confuse the children regarding who is responsible for the violence and coerce them into believing that they are the preferable parent. Abusers also may directly or indirectly use their children to control and intimidate the victim. Perpetrators sometimes may threaten to abduct, seek sole custody of, or physically harm the children if the victim is not compliant. Sometimes these are threats exclusively and the abuser does not intend or really want to carry out the action, but the threats are typically perceived as being very real.

Children's perception of the perpetrator's violence can play a significant role in the nature of their relationship. Children often feel anxious, scared, and angry when they witness abuse. At the same time, many children also feel affection, loyalty, and love for the abuser. It is common for children to experience ambivalent feelings towards the abuser and this can be difficult for them to resolve.

Domestic violence can influence the children's feelings toward the victim. Many children know the abuse is wrong and may even feel responsible for protecting the battered parent. Yet, they also experience confusion and resentment towards the victim for "putting up" with the abuse and are more likely to express their anger towards the victim rather than directly at the perpetrator.

Children need additional support as they struggle with their conflicting feelings towards the perpetrator. The responsibility of perpetrators as parents primarily focuses on preventing the recurrence of the violence. Some victims want their children to have a safe and positive relationship with the perpetrator, and some children crave that connection. Consequently, community service providers are confronted with the challenge of developing resources and strategies to help perpetrators become supportive and safe parents. (…)

Chapter 25

Domestic Violence: Facts Sheet

By National Coalition Against Domestic Violence

WHAT IS DOMESTIC VIOLENCE?

Domestic violence is the willful intimidation, physical assault, battery, sexual assault, and/or other abusive behavior as part of a systematic pattern of power and control perpetrated by one intimate partner against another. It includes physical violence, sexual violence, threats, and emotional abuse. The frequency and severity of domestic violence can vary dramatically.

WHY IT MATTERS

Domestic violence is an epidemic affecting individuals in every community, regardless of age, economic status, sexual orientation, gender, race, religion, or nationality. Intimate partner violence is often accompanied by emotionally abusive and controlling behavior which is only a fraction of a systematic pattern of dominance and control. Domestic violence can result in physical injury, psychological trauma, and in severe cases, even death. The devastating consequences of domestic violence can cross generations and last a lifetime.

DID YOU KNOW?

- On average, nearly 20 people per minute are victims of physical violence by an intimate partner in the United States. During one year, this equates to more than 10 million women and men.[1]

Copyright © 2014 by National Coalition Against Domestic Violence. Reprinted with permission.

- 1 in 3 women and 1 in 4 men have experienced [some form of] physical violence by an intimate partner within their lifetime.[1]
- 1 in 5 women and 1 in 7 men have experienced <u>severe</u> physical violence by an intimate partner in their lifetime.[1]
- 1 in 7 women and 1 in 18 men have experienced stalking victimization during their lifetime in which they felt very fearful or believed that they or someone close to them would be harmed or killed.[1]
- On a typical day, there are more than 20,000 phone calls placed to domestic violence hotlines nationwide.[9]
- In domestic violence homicides, women are six times more likely to be killed when there is a gun in the house.[10]
- Intimate partner violence accounts for 15% of all violent crime.[2]
- Only approximately one-quarter of all physical assaults, one-fifth of all rapes, and one-half of all stalkings perpetuated against females by intimate partners are reported to the police.[1]

SEXUAL ASSAULT

- 1 in 5 women and 1 in 59 men in the United States has experienced rape in her lifetime.[1]
- 9.4% of women in the United States have been raped by an intimate partner in their lifetime.[1]

STALKING

- 19.3 million women and 5.1 million men in the United States have experienced stalking in their lifetime. 66.2% of these female stalking victims reported stalking by a current or former intimate partner.[1]

HOMICIDE

- A study of intimate partner homicides found that 20% of victims were not the intimate partners themselves, but family members, friends, neighbors, persons who intervened, law enforcement responders, or bystanders.[3]
- 72% of all murder-suicides involve an intimate partner and 94% of the victims of these murder-suicides are female.[8]

PHYSICAL/MENTAL EFFECTS

- Women who suffer from intimate partner violence are at an increased vulnerability of contracting HIV or other STI's due to forced intercourse or prolonged exposure to stress.[7]
- Studies suggest that there is a relationship between intimate partner violence and depression and suicidal behavior.[7]

- It is estimated that half of the women in abusive relationships in the United States are physically injured by their partners.[7]

ECONOMIC EFFECTS

- Victims of intimate partner violence lose a total of 8.0 million days of paid work each year.[6]
- The cost of intimate partner violence exceeds $8.3 billion per year.[6]
- Between 21-60% of victims of intimate partner violence lose their jobs due to reasons stemming from the abuse.[6]
- Between 2003 and 2008, 142 women were murdered in their workplace as a result of intimate partner violence. This amounts to 22% of workplace homicides

REFERENCES

1. Black, M.C., Basile, K.C., Breiding, M.J., Smith, S.G., Walters, M.L., Merrick, M.T., Chen, J., & Stevens, M. (2011). The National Intimate Partner and Sexual Violence Survey: 2010 Summary Report. National Center for Injury Prevention and Control, Centers for Disease Control and Prevention. Retrieved from: http://www.cdc.gov/violenceprevention/pdf/nisvs_report2010-a.pdf
2. Truman, J. & Morgan, R. (2014). Nonfatal Domestic Violence, 2003-2012. U.S. Department of Justice, Office of Justice Programs, Bureau of Justice Statistics. Retrieved from: http://www.bjs.gov/content/pub/pdf/ndv0312.pdf
3. Smith, S., Fowler, K., & Niolon, P. (2014). Intimate Partner Homicide and Corollary Victims in 16 States: National Violent Death Reporting System, 2003¬2009. American Journal of Public Health, 104(3). DOI: 10.2105/AJPH.2013.301582
4. Tiesman, H., Gurka, K., Konda, S., Coben, J., Amandus, H. (2012). Workplace Homicides Among U.S. Women: The Role of Intimate Partner Violence. Annals of Epidemiology, 22(4). DOI: 10.1016/j.annepidem.2012.02.009
5. Finkelhor, D., Turner, H., Ormrod, R., & Hamby, S. (2011). Children's Exposure to Intimate Partner Violence and Other Family Violence. U.S. Department of Justice, Office of Juvenile Justice and Delinquency Prevention. Retrieved on August 15, 2014 from: https://www.ncjrs.gov/pdffiles1/ojjdp/232272.pdf
6. Rothman, E., Hathaway, J., Stidsen, A., & de Vries, H. (2007). How Employment Helps Female Victims of Intimate Partner Abuse: A Qualitative Study. Journal of Occupational Health Psychology, 12(2). DOI: 10.1037/1076-8998.12.2.136
7. World Health Organization. (2013). Global and Regional Estimates of Violence against Women: Prevalence and Health Effects of Intimate Partner Violence and Non-partner Sexual Violence. Retrieved from: http://apps.who.int/iris/bitstream/10665/85239/1/9789241564625_eng.pdf?ua=1
8. Violence Policy Center. (2012). American Roulette: Murder-Suicide in the United States. Retrieved from: www.vpc.org/studies/amroul2012.pdf

9. 2013 Domestic Violence Counts: A 24-Hour Census of Domestic Violence Shelters and Services. (n.d.). Retrieved September 4, 2014, from http://nnedv.org/downloads/Census/DVCounts2013/DVCounts13_NatlSummary.pdf
10. Supreme Court Decision Limits Batterers' Access to Guns. (2014, April 11). Retrieved from http://www.justice.gov/ovw/blog/supreme-court-decision-limits-batterers-access-guns

IF YOU NEED HELP, DIAL THE NATIONAL DOMESTIC VIOLENCE HOTLINE AT: 1-800-799-SAFE (7233)

FURTHER READINGS

Anderson, Kristin L. "Gender, Status, and Domestic Violence: An Integration of Feminist and Family Violence Approaches." *Journal of Marriage and Family* 59, no. 3 (1997): 655–69.

Arthur, Christine, and Roger Clark. "Determinants of Domestic Violence: A Cross-National Study." *International Journal of Sociology of the Family* 35, no. 2 (2009): 147–67.

Bell, Linda A. *Rethinking Ethics in the Midst of Violence: A Feminist Approach to Freedom*. New York: Rowman & Littlefield Publishers, 1993.

Fontes, Lisa Aronson. "Ethics in Family Violence Research: Cross-Cultural Issues." *Family Relations* 47, no. 1 (1998): 53–61.

Frenche, Stanley G., Wanda Teays, and Laura M. Purdy, eds. *Violence Against Women: Philosophical Perspectives*. Ithaca: Cornell University Press, 1998.

Straus, Murray A., and Richard J. Gelles. "Societal Change and Change in Family Violence from 1975 to 1985 as revealed by Two National Surveys." *Journal of Marriage and the Family* 48 (1986): 465–79.

Modern Trends in Family: Aging

Chapter 26

Family Relationships in an Aging Society[1]

By Martie Gillen, Terry Mills, and Jenny Jump[2]

AGING IN THE 21ST CENTURY

According to the U.S. Census Bureau, by the year 2050 the nation's elderly population will more than double to 88 million, and the more frail, over-85 population will quadruple to 19 million.

Currently, Florida ranks first in the United States in the percent of the population who are full-time and seasonal residents over the age of 65. Older Floridians, their families, and communities face many issues related to aging.

Aging in the 21st Century is an eight-topic program that addresses issues such as:

- Health and medical care
- Family relationships
- Economic concerns
- Caregiving
- Home modifications
- Retirement
- Nutrition and diet

---

1 This document is FCS2210, one of a series of publications from the distance education in-service *Aging in the 21st Century*, coordinated by Carolyn Wilken, PhD, MPH, Department of Family, Youth and Community Sciences, Florida Cooperative Extension Service, Institute of Food and Agricultural Sciences, University of Florida. First published: May 2003. Revised: November 2012. Please visit the EDIS website at http://edis.ifas.ufl.edu.

2 Martie Gillen, assistant professor and Family and Consumer Economics for Older Adults specialist; Terry Mills, professor of Sociology and dean of the Division of Humanities & Social Sciences at Morehouse College; and Jenny Jump, Extension agent I, Columbia County Extension Office, Lake City, FL; Florida Cooperative Extension Service, Institute of Food and Agricultural Sciences, University of Florida, Gainesville, FL 32611.

Martie Gillen, Terry Mills, and Jenny Jump, "Family Relationships in an Aging Society," *Family Relationships in an Aging Society,* pp. 1–4. Copyright © 2012 by University of Florida, Institute of Food and Agricultural Sciences. Reprinted with permission.

WHAT YOU WILL LEARN

- **Generation vs. Cohort:** Definitions and differences between these two terms
- **Family Structures:** How the family structure is changing through the years
- **Intergenerational Relations:** What the major types of intergenerational relations are and support for the elderly within the family

INTRODUCTION

We will face many new issues as our society ages. Never in the history of America or the world has the population had more older adults than children.

This publication discusses some issues that happen as a result of having a greater number of older adults than children. It also looks at the roles of the family and intergenerational relationships supporting our aging society.

For example, how will the smaller workforce cope with providing for a larger retired community? What is the role of the family in caring for more than one generation of elders? How will modern families decide to distribute and share resources with aging parents and stepparents?

THE ROLE OF THE FAMILY

Most of us live our entire lives in the context of a family. Our family provides us with the important resources we need to help us learn independence as children and remain independent as older adults.

Throughout our lives we exchange help and support within the family. These exchanges can involve providing emotional and physical care, as well as financial support.

The family becomes more and more important for the elderly as the need for support increases. Yet we must remember that the aging person and the family are all part of a larger society. Society impacts the resources and services available to older adults and their families.

Two terms, **generation** and **cohort**, are frequently used when discussing aging. These terms help explain family and societal aspects of aging.

We use the term **generation** to better understand the impact of aging on the family. A **generation** is a group of people at the same step in the line of the family. In a family, children, parents, grandparents, and great-grandparents reflect different generations.

People in the same generation often have common roles, responsibilities, and expectations. For example, those in the "parent generation" are responsible for raising their children, caring for their parents and/or grandparents, and taking care of their own personal responsibilities. This is why they have been called the "sandwich generation." Family members from different generations often have different ideas about life in the family and what it should be like.

We use the term **cohort** when we are talking about society instead of the family. A **cohort** defines a group of people who were born during the same time in history.

People in the same cohort were born around the same time, which means they have lived through time and history together. They may share common experiences and often common beliefs. For example, the "baby boomers" (born between 1946 and 1964) are a cohort. They experienced the years of the "traditional family" (e.g., mom, dad, and children), and the Vietnam era. The cohort born in the early part of the 19th century shared two World Wars as well as the Great Depression.

Having these common experiences molds a cohort's expectations of aging. Clashes between cohorts occur when people from different cohorts fail to recognize the differences in their experiences.

CHANGES IN THE STRUCTURE OF THE FAMILY

In the 1900s, families in the United States commonly had many children. Also, grandparents usually died before their grandchildren reached adulthood. This meant the family structure looked like a pyramid with a large number of children and parents and very few grandparents.

In the 2000s, however, the family model is more like a lopsided rectangle. More generations are alive at the same point in time than in past eras. Families have fewer children, but grandparents and great-grandparents are living longer.

By 2030 the boomers will be grandparents and greatgrandparents. This means the top of the pyramid will be quite broad, and there will be fewer parents and children.

Understanding the impact of these changes is important for families and society. More members in the older generation may help families raise children. But older members may require care and support. Policy makers must consider these changes as they plan for schools and health care.

INTERGENERATIONAL RELATIONS

We have all seen the ideal image of the family often portrayed by the media. On television, family members rarely argue.

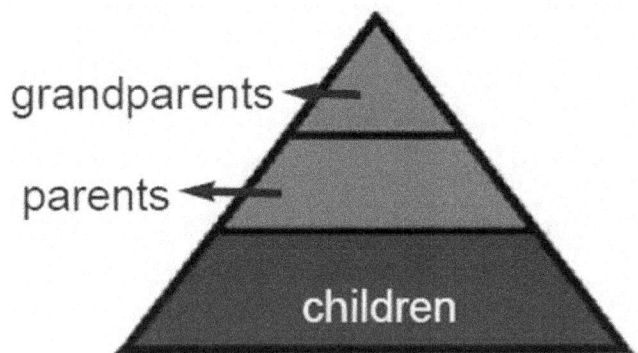
Family Structure 1900

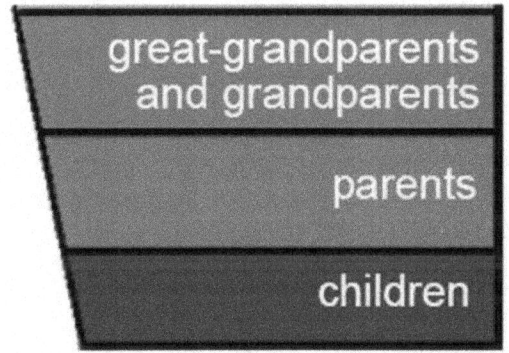
Family Structure 2000

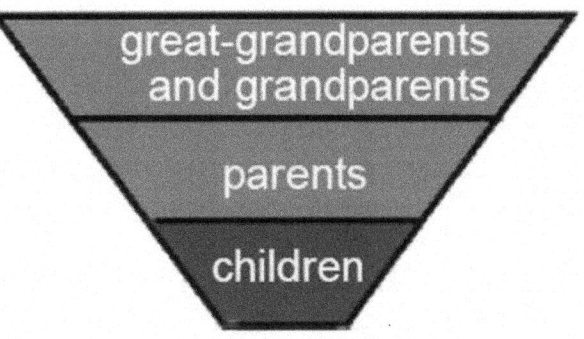
Family Structure 2030

And, when they do, the problems are solved before the program ends. In real life, family members often disagree. Sometimes they may decide to leave the family entirely. Frequently, the disagreements are between people from different generations.

Relationships between children and their parents, parents and grandparents, or children and their grandparents are called intergenerational relationships.

Generations interact differently in different families. Some are emotionally close, while others are emotionally distant. Some families spend a great deal of time together, while others rarely see one another.

Researchers look at three dimensions of intergenerational interactions to better understand families: 1) emotional closeness, 2) frequency of contact, and 3) social support.

Using these three dimensions we see five types of intergenerational relations in families:

- **Tight-Knit:** Families are emotionally close and have frequent contact with one another. If they live close together, they see each other often. If they live farther apart, they remain close emotionally with frequent phone calls, emails, or letters. These families take care of one another across generations.
- **Sociable:** Families are emotionally close across generations and have frequent contact with one another. They are less likely to provide care for one another.
- **Intimate:** Families describe themselves as emotionally close but don't visit frequently and may live far away from one another. They rely on others to provide care for family members.
- **Obligatory:** Families see one another frequently and provide support across generations. These families don't feel especially close emotionally but provide care and support if necessary.
- **Detached:** Families are not close emotionally, don't see one another often, and do not provide support or care for one another.

Did You Know?

1. Adult children are more likely to have a tight-knit relationship with their mothers than their fathers.
2. Adult children are also more likely to have a detached relationship with divorced parents.

SOCIAL SUPPORT

Older people often rely on family members for help. They may need help with the demands of everyday life because of a chronic illness or during a crisis. Adult children may have a strong sense of responsibility and commitment toward their aging parents. Many adult children provide caregiving in spite of time, distance, or competing responsibilities. The help provided to older adults is called **social support**. Family members provide four basic types of social support:

- **Instrumental:** Housework, transportation, shopping and personal care.
- **Emotional:** Confiding, comforting, reassuring, and listening to problems.
- **Informational:** Advice in seeking medical treatment, referrals to agencies, sharing family news.
- **Financial and Housing:** Help paying bills, sharing a home.

We know that families provide most of the help for frail and disabled elderly who live in the community. Family members and the elderly often prefer it that way.

There are two ways of understanding how older adults get help:

1. **Principle of Substitution**
2. **Task-Specific Model**

The **Principle of Substitution** describes the order in which older adults choose their care providers. Married older adults prefer to receive help from their spouses. If a spouse is not available or unable to help, they turn next to their children and other relatives. Friends and neighbors help by driving, picking up groceries and medicines, and checking on the older person. Older adults turn to professionals as a last resort.

The **Task-Specific Model** states that different tasks require the help of different people. For example, spouses and close family members provide the kind of help that requires a great deal of time and energy. They also perform personal tasks such as bathing. Friends and neighbors help with errands, provide transportation, and offer leisure activities. Professionals are called only when the tasks of social support become too time-consuming, too technical, or too difficult.

If the time comes when continued professional help is needed, the family may have to consider institutionalization, such as a nursing home. That choice is only made when the people identified in the **Principle of Substitution** are no longer able to continue managing in-home care.

For more information on *Aging in the 21st Century* please refer to the following publications and/or contact your local Extension office.

FURTHER READINGS

Blieszner, Rosemary, and Victoria Hilkevitch Bedford, eds. *Handbook of Aging and the Family*. 2nd ed. Westport, CT: Praeger, 2012.

Blieszner, Rosemary H., and Victoria Hilkevitch Bedford. *Aging and the Family: Theory and Research*. Westport, CT: Praeger, 1996.

Hareven, Tamara K. "Aging and Generational Relations: A Historical and Life Course Perspective." *Annual Review of Sociology* 20 (1994): 437–61.

Mancini, Jay A., and Rosemary Blieszner. "Aging Parents and Adult Children: Research Themes in Intergenerational Relations." *Journal of Marriage and Family* 51, no. 2 (1989): 275–90.

Waite, Linda J. "The Changing Family and Aging Populations." *Population and Development Review* 35, no. 2 (2009): 341–46.

Printed in the USA
CPSIA information can be obtained
at www.ICGtesting.com
LVHW080151130724
785372LV00021B/94